EUROPEAN *REVIEW* OF PHILOSOPHY

The Nature of Logic

4

edited by
ACHILLE C. VARZI

CSLI Publications
Center for the Study of Language and Information
Stanford, California

Copyright © 1999
CSLI Publications
Center for the Study of Language and Information
Leland Stanford Junior University

02 01 00 99   4 3 2 1
ISBN: 1-57586-179-8
ISBN: 1-57586-178-X (pbk.)

CSLI Publications reports new developments in the study of language, information, and computation. In addition to lecture notes, our publications include monographs, working papers, revised dissertations, and conference proceedings. Our aim is to make new results, ideas, and approaches available as quickly as possible. Please visit our website at
                      http://csli-www.stanford.edu/publications/
for comments on this and other titles, as well as for changes and corrections by the author and publisher.

The text in this book was set by CSLI Publications in Minion, a typeface designed by Robert Slimbach. The display type is set in Stone Sans, designed by Sumner Stone. The book was printed and bound in the United States of America.

EUROPEAN *REVIEW* OF PHILOSOPHY

Editorial Board
Manuel Garcia Carpintero
Roberto Casati
Eros Corazza
Jérôme Dokic
Petr Kotátko
Martin Rechenauer
Gianfranco Soldati
Tom Stoneham
Christine Tappolet

Contents

Introduction / 1
    ACHILLE C. VARZI

What Is Logic About? / 5
    ERMANNO BENCIVENGA

Wider Still and Wider...Resetting the Bounds of Logic / 21
    JOHAN VAN BENTHEM

The Intuitionistic Conception of Logic / 45
    DIRK VAN DALEN

Logic and Analyticity / 79
    A. P. HAZEN

The Implicational Nature of Logic: A Structuralist Account / 111
    ARNOLD KOSLOW

The Ontological Commitments of Logical Theories / 157
    MANUEL PÉREZ OTERO AND MANUEL GARCÍA-CARPINTERO

Validity / 183
    GRAHAM PRIEST

Is Logic a Theory of the Obvious? / 207
    GILA SHER

ACHILLE C. VARZI
Introduction

       Peirce once complained about the existence of nearly a hundred different definitions of logic. That was 1901—before the publication of the *Principia* and all that followed; before the tremendous growth of non-classical logics in the second half of this century and before the impressive development of logical calculi in various areas of computer science. If there were a hundred definitions then, today there are a hundred different theories, each of which stems from a different way of answering the question: What is logic?

       The existence of a variety of logical theories raises deep philosophical issues that go far beyond a simple pragmatic dispute. For what higher tribunal (as Quine once put it) could be invoked to settle the issue? If the discrepancy between two competing theories is not merely a matter of notational or phonetic conventions (if the two theories are not shown to be equivalent upon translating one into the other), what criteria could be invoked to adjudge the competition? Are the two theories about the same subject? If they disagree on the laws governing certain logical words or operations, are they still agreeing on what those logical words or operations are? Such matters are not easily settled by relativizing the choice of logic to this or that domain of application. Perhaps the opposition between, say, classical logic and quantum logic is one of a familiar kind: just as different physical theories apply to microscopic and to mesoscopic phenomena, so may different logics. The very notion of an "orthodox" logic would then dissolve under the pressure of different pictures of what the world is or could be. (Or perhaps it is the integration of different logics that *together* would yield the one and true logic.) But how do things get settled with respect to each domain? What tribunal could be invoked to settle the local issues?

The philosophical map is more intricate than that, too. You and I may both agree on the same logical theory—we may both be classical logicians, say—and yet disagree deeply with regard to the nature or distinctive character of logic. One may take logic to be concerned with truth, hence with a semantic property, a characteristic of sentences (statements, propositions); the other may take logic to be concerned with deduction, an eminently syntactic property, a characteristic of arguments expressing transitions from sentences to sentences (statements, propositions). The two approaches need not disagree on what counts as a valid sentence or argument, and one may indeed view a completeness theorem as establishing precisely the equivalence between a semantic and a syntactic approach. Yet they certainly express a different way of answering the question: What is logic? From this point of view, Peirce's concern was deeper than any concern we may have about the proliferation of logics available today. If we have a different conception of the nature of logic, then the interesting questions concern these different conceptions, whether or not we agree on treating the same class of statements as logically true, the same class of arguments as logically valid.

Nor is the semantic/syntactic opposition the only way we may dissent on the nature of logic while agreeing on its content. We may, for instance, agree on each and every bit of the classical quantification theory with identity, and yet disagree on the logical status of identity. One may insist that identity theory is part of logic on account of its universality and topic neutrality; the other may subscribe to identity theory and yet insist on the kinship between identity and other relations, such as parthood or membership, treating all as extralogical. We may, in fact, have a different view on what does and what does not belong to logic proper even if we then agree on everything else *as a matter of fact*. We may disagree on what makes logic a subject of its own, separate from (and in the background of) the concerns of other disciplines. We may even disagree on whether there are any objective grounds at all for a distinction between the logical and the extralogical.

And even if we agree on all that—even if we draw exactly the same boundaries and settle on the same laws—we may still dissent on the reasons. We may dissent on *what it is* for an expression to be a logical constant. We may dissent on *why* identity is to be ranked with the logical or with the extralogical apparatus, as the case may be. We may, so to speak, agree on the extension of all logical notions, but not on their intension.

This long list of worries is barely indicative of the importance of serious philosophical reflection on logic. It may indeed be surprising—if one looks at the recent philosophical literature—that the wealth of technical developments in all areas of logic has been accompanied by relatively few systematic attempts to analyze the underlying assumptions and philosophical motivations. Compared to the first half of the century, or even to the 70's and early 80's, there is a growing gap between the logician's work and the philosopher's need to understand the nature of that work. The aim of this collection is to fill in—albeit very partially—that gap. All the essays seek to provide material toward answering the above questions, as well as to raise new issues and pose new challenges. Some essays have a speculative, programmatic flavor; others put forward or defend articulated views; others still concern themselves with the link between technical aspects and philosophical issues. But all the essays share a common concern for the heart of the problem and stem from a common desire to clarify the nature of the logician's enterprise. The resulting collection is by no means representative of all current views on the nature of logic. (How could that be?) Together, however, the present essays offer a vivid, up-to-date, and I believe most exciting indication of where the debate on the nature of logic is—and of some directions along which it is likely to yield fruitful developments.

I am very grateful to all the contributors for the enthusiasm with which they joined the project that led to this collection and for the kindness and generosity with which they acceded to a number of editorial requests. I am also thankful to Robert Armstrong, Chris Dixon, Ihsan Dogramaci, Friederike Oursin, and Gurpreet Rattan for their help at various stages of this project.

Department of Philosophy
Columbia University
New York (NY), USA

ERMANNO BENCIVENGA
What Is Logic About?

1. Introduction

I am going to tell you a story here. But a few things must be clear from the beginning. First, this is an *imaginary* story. It doesn't even try to describe things that happened; if read that way, it would be grossly inaccurate. One might read it as describing what would have happened if indeed it were the case that "what is actual is rational";[1] or as an account of how someone, starting with certain basic intuitions about logic, *could* have come up with the kind of picture we have today of this discipline and with some of the problems we find ourselves facing. Second, it is a *biased* story. You may not share some of my basic intuitions about logic, and if you don't much of what I say won't make sense to you. But I am not worried about this outcome: for me, it is an indication that my story is more theory than chronicle. And undoubtedly there might be different theories, but in this field I often have the impression that it is not even clear what the theories are. My story tries to make one of them clearer; if it provoked you to write your own different story, it would have achieved one of its main purposes. Last, but not least, it is not *just* a story. It is more of an apologue, and I won't even try to hide its moral behind a figurative language. I will give it to you flat: I will point out that there are in this area of inquiry many confusions to be gotten rid of, many pseudoproblems to be avoided, many false subtleties to be explained away. Of course, not all the verses of my homily will be new with me, and occasionally I will make an effort to refer them back to their Founding Fathers, but the important thing is: it is time to put some of these pieces

---

1. This claim can be found in Hegel's *Elements of the Philosophy of Right* (1991, p. 20), though its interpretation is controversial—and will not be considered here.

together and suggest an overall picture that others can confront and criticize (I hope) in a constructive way.

2. Sentences

In the beginning, logic was about arguments. Arguments in everyday discourse, I mean: things like

(1) I should have expected rain. It always rains when I don't have my umbrella, and today in fact I don't.

or

(2) You will certainly pass this course. For you study hard, and no one passes unless they study hard.

There was a stable feeling that some of these arguments were good and others bad, that in some cases the premisses supported the conclusion and in others they didn't; logic was supposed to codify, and possibly explain, this feeling.

To codify it, nothing more than a catalogue, or a canon, was required; but to explain it, one needed a lot more. One needed a theory of what it is for an argument to be good—or for its premisses to "support" its conclusion. Some basic articulation of this notion of support was easily available: people were prepared to gloss it by saying, more or less, that "no matter what is the case, if the premisses are true then the conclusion is true." And some were even willing to carry part of the *explanans* from the metalanguage to the object-language and rephrase it as "no matter what is the case, the conditional sentence whose antecedent is the conjunction of the premisses and whose consequent is the conclusion is true."[2] But at this point the easy part of the task was over. For even assuming that we all know what it is for sentences to be true (or false), what exactly is it for them to be true (or false) *no matter what is the case*?

As usual in philosophy, initial answers came in the form of metaphors, later to be cashed out in theoretical terms. The first one was the *locked room*

---

2. Many would prefer to talk about a *proposition*, rather than a sentence. I would not agree, but I don't want (or need) to get involved in this discussion here. Those who like proposition-talk better are invited to rephrase what I say in terms of propositions—and then think that my criteria for the individuation of propositions are very strict.

metaphor. Suppose a logician is locked in a dark, windowless room, and knows everything about her language but nothing about the world outside. A sentence is presented to her, and she must try to evaluate it on the basis of her linguistic competence only. If she can do that, and specifically establish that the sentence is true, then the sentence is *logically* true, and if the sentence is a conditional then the corresponding argument is (logically) *valid*. Logical truth and validity are based on how our language is defined—independently of what extralinguistic reality might look like.[3]

So far so good. But this was not the end of it. For it would seem that logical truth is some kind of *truth*, hence that a logically true sentence is indeed true in the world out there. And if one sees it that way, one is ready for a new description of what the logician is doing, or trying to do, in her locked room. One may think of her, that is, as assuming that there is a world *w* beyond the windowless walls, but as making no assumptions concerning the structure of *w*—or, more precisely, assuming that *w* has some *arbitrary* structure. If she can prove on such limited assumptions that the sentence is true in *w* then she is entitled to generalize upon her result and conclude that, no matter what the structure of *w* is, the sentence is true. Which seems to be the same as saying that no factual, but only linguistic, considerations are relevant to the truth of the sentence, hence that the sentence is logically true. Thus the stage is set for a new metaphor, which will materialize as soon as one asks what it is that the logician is generalizing upon. "Structures the world might have," the natural answer goes, and "possible worlds" is a nice compact way of referring to such "entities."

Whereas the locked room metaphor was grounded on the linguistic character of logical truth, the new *possible worlds metaphor* insisted more on its semantical character, and in so doing modified the very notion of truth. A hidden variable was discovered in this notion, and old unqualified truth became a special case of the new relative notion of *truth-in-a-world*.[4] Of course, there was a risk involved in this move: that of taking the metaphor too seriously and forgetting the other (that is, the linguistic) side of the coin.

---

3. See Carnap's notion of *L-truth* in 1947, pp. 8, 10. And note how, in cashing out that notion, Carnap is "naturally" led from the present metaphor to the next one.
4. See the distinction between (absolute) truth and "correctness in an individual domain" in Tarski 1936.

To avoid the risk one had to constantly remind oneself of the ultimately linguistic nature of possible worlds—of the fact that the set of possible worlds is just the set of structures our language can describe.[5] Or, to play the game of reciprocity, one could "discover" the variable hidden in the notion of a possible world, thus moving from unqualified possible worlds to possible worlds-for-a-language. Which would make the possible worlds of the Eskimos quite different from those of the Mexicans, say, at least as far as snow is concerned.

But the relativization process did not stop there. For possible worlds have a structure, and the amount of structure one exposes is a function of one's analysis: the deeper the analysis, the richer the structure. In most cases, one can get a final verdict of logical truth (or validity) without analyzing all that there is to analyze. For example, in the case of

(3)   Either it rains or it doesn't

one need only analyze the language down to the level of atomic sentences, and the world(s) down to the level of atomic facts: any further development of the analysis or enrichment of the structure seems to be irrelevant. One can establish the logical truth of (3) without even considering the interpretation of such words as "rains"; indeed, one can abbreviate the whole sentence "It rains" by something that clearly displays an absence of meaningful components—something like "p"—and consequently abbreviate (3) by

(4) p or not-p.[6]

---

5. As I point out in Bencivenga 1989, this is not the only way one can conceive the relation between language and world(s). So here surfaces a clear sense in which my story is biased—specifically, in a *transcendentally idealist* direction. And, I would argue, a transcendentally realist story would cause us precisely to take the metaphor too seriously—and ultimately to be fooled by it.
6. To call expressions like (4) "abbreviations" might be regarded as excessively (and unfairly) deflationary of their significance and value. So let me emphasize that, according to my story, what is going on here is, to begin with, exactly the same as when we abbreviate, say, "United States" by "U.S.": if the *unity* of the *states* is irrelevant to our purposes, and all we want is to distinguish one country from another, we might as well use an expression that brings out exactly what we are interested in. Later in the story, these small economies of breath (or ink) will acquire a much more dignified status.

Then the logical truth of (4) (and of (3)) will follow from general considerations on the interpretation of negations and disjunctions—summarized in the general semantical statement

(5)   For every sentence p and every world w, "p or not-p" is true in w.

3. Schemata

Cases like the above came handy. For remember: logic was supposed to provide (among other things) a codification or catalogue, and such general statements as (5) made this task a lot easier. Once and for all, they established the logical truth not only of (3), but also of

(6)   Either it snows or it doesn't

(7)   Either the Earth is round or it isn't

(8)   Either I am Italian or I am not

and so on—that is, of all the sentences that *could* be abbreviated by (4). So one didn't have to list all those infinitely many sentences in one's canon: one could just write down (4) and consider it an (ambiguous) abbreviation for all of them.

Logicians exploited this fortunate circumstance, and looked for more of the same kind. Soon they realized that if they limited their analysis within a certain scope, they were able to infer the logical truth of all the sentences whose logical truth was discovered (or discoverable) by such limited means from general semantical statements like (5), hence to express the whole logical canon (within that scope) by abbreviations like (4). And then, unexpectedly, something began to go astray.

Logicians (with a few notable exceptions[7]) were not touched by the suspicion that this neat result was just a consequence of the rudimentary level of their analysis, and might disappear as the analysis got deeper. Instead, they were fascinated by the strange new look of their canon. All those abbreviations did not look like English sentences any more, but rather like pieces of a new mathematical symbolism, which in turn suggested the intriguing possibility that logic could finally be put on firmer grounds than linguistic competence

---

7.   See the illuminating remarks made by Lewis and Langford in 1932 (pp. 179ff) about the impossibility of doing a "good" logic exclusively in terms of universal statements like the one implicit in (4)—and explicit in (5).

or educated intuition—that it could become a part of mathematics and share with it its absolute certainty. It was some indication of the increasing success of this new attitude that abbreviations like (4) were now being referred to as "schemata," which made them sound more important; but such change of terminology was the least of the surprises waiting behind the corner.

Even in the early phases of this development, logicians used to call abbreviations (or schemata) logically true. It was only a derivative and secondary notion of logical truth, for expressions like (4) cannot themselves be logically true (or even true, for that matter). What was meant was that all the sentences that could be abbreviated that way (or whose structure was exposed by that schema) were logically true. As time went on, however, a curious reversal occurred, and logicians talked with increasing regularity of sentences being logically true *because* they *instantiated* (as the new jargon had it) a logically true schema.

The new talk was not, strictly speaking, inconsistent with the old; after all, an equivalence (such as that between a schema and all of its instances being logically true) can be used in either direction. But the *emphasis* of the new talk was different: it now sounded as if it was a schema that was logically true (and perhaps true) in the primary sense, and a sentence instantiating it was only (logically) true in a derivative and secondary one. Which was only a tiny little step away from conceiving logic as being primarily about schemata, and only derivatively about (English) sentences (or arguments).

This shift in emphasis had two major consequences. First, the schemata acquired a life of their own, and so did the artificial languages created to express them; soon indeed they began to have a backward action on the sentences (and the natural language(s)) that ultimately justified their existence—an action which largely took the form of a constellation of new "problems" about those sentences that only made sense via the reference to the artificial languages and the relevant Copernican revolution (hence probably made no sense at all). Second, and more important, a serious difficulty was generated (and paid little attention to) concerning the connection between the new and the old senses in which an English sentence is logically true. Were these two senses consistent with one another? Was the shift in emphasis, that is, *just* a shift in emphasis? I will briefly consider the "problems," and then turn to the difficulty.

One "problem" was this. Most schemata contain expressions that behave like variables and others that behave like constants. The reason is obvious: a schema represents only a partial logical analysis of any sentence that instantiates it (which is precisely what makes it possible for *several* sentences to instantiate it), and the variables represent the part of the sentence that has not been analyzed.[8] The constants, on the other hand, are the expressions for which there is in that context a logical analysis available, hence it is not inappropriate to refer to them *in that context*—that is, in the context of an artificial language expressing a *partial* (but, for some purposes, useful) logical analysis of (English) sentences—as "logical expressions."

When seen in this light, the notion of a logical expression reveals its relative character: its dependence on the level of logical analysis one has reached, so that at different levels there will be different sets of logical expressions. But if logic is conceived not as the study of English sentences, possibly *by means of* schemata and artificial languages, but as the study *of these very schemata and languages*, and if only a limited number of artificial languages are yet in view, it is tempting to regard the notion of a logical expression as an absolute one, and then perhaps pose the "problem" of what *English* expressions fall in this category. And once that "problem" is solved, usually by an essential and gratuitous limitation to some specific level of analysis,[9] the way is paved for a new "definition" of logical truth: a sentence (in English) is logically true if it is true for every (uniform) substitution of non-logical expressions for the non-logical expressions occurring in it.[10]

---

8. There are "degenerate" schemata containing no variables (for example, $\forall x(x=x)$—where the bound "variable" x is no indication of any lack of analysis: it is just an artifice used in analyzing the pronoun "everything"). That they even exist is a clear indication of the shift in emphasis I am discussing: why would anyone want to translate an English sentence into some abstruse symbolism without any gain in generality unless he were already convinced of the primacy of these formulations? But from now on, I will disregard such degenerate cases.
9. In this regard, it is instructive to consider Tarski's 'What are Logical Notions?' (1986). This text proceeds auspiciously to define logical notions as those which are invariant under all possible one–one transformations of the universe of discourse onto itself. But by the end, this neat definition has been exploded by the observation that set-theoretical membership is or is not a logical notion depending on whether we decide to treat it *as membership* or as just another binary relation. So, though it is indeed the case (as Tarski claims) that all notions of *Principia Mathematica* are logical in his sense, this fact does not single them out in any special way.
10. This definition is very popular in logic textbooks (and very difficult to justify to freshmen), and is often associated with the names of Bolzano and Quine.

Second "problem": It is obvious from what I said so far that a schema expresses (a certain amount of) the structure of the sentences that instantiate it. Another way to say this would be to say that the schema gives the *logical form* of those sentences to the extent that can be captured by the artificial language to which the schema belongs (or by the level of logical analysis the language represents). From this point of view, the relation between schemata and logical form is at best one of approximation, but if the emphasis is on schemata and artificial languages rather than sentences in natural language, and if some artificial language acquires for some reason a privileged role, one might be naturally inclined to conceive the schemata formulated in that language as exposing *the* logical form of the (English) sentences instantiating them, not just an approximation to it. And it might be just as natural to regard all the sentential structure that does not fit this Procrustean bed as irrelevant to logical considerations—as part of the sentences' "grammatical form."[11] Then, if people disagree on which artificial language is to be assigned such an exalted foundational role, the serious "problem" is going to emerge of how to choose among the competitors.

So much for the "problems," and now for the (related) difficulty. If the shift in emphasis we are discussing had been just that, and not, instead, a substantial modification of the notion of logical truth, then the same English sentences would have been logically true within both approaches (that is, independently of whether schemata or sentences had definitional priority). But this was not going to work out as everyone hoped. To see why, suppose that the logically true schema A gives (in terms of some artificial language L—that is, at some level of logical analysis) the logical form of some English sentence B. A also gives the logical form of infinitely many other sentences, infinitely many of which will contain more structure than A exposes and hence will also instantiate other (more complex) schemata. Suppose that one such sentence C instantiates *the negation D of* a logically true schema D'; then both a sentence and its negation will turn out to be logically true, which is unacceptable. Faced by this conclusion, we will have to deny the logical truth of either A or D'. We might be inclined to favor D', because it represents a deeper level of logical analysis, but what if B is *fully* analyzed by A—that is, if all the English expressions occurring in B and not corresponding to logical constants in A are, in an absolute sense, *non-logical*

---

11. One of the main culprits here is, of course, Bertrand Russell.

(English) expressions? For those who subscribe to this absolute distinction, denying the logical truth of *A* would entail irremediably losing the logical truth of *B*, which no further analysis could bring any closer to us.[12]

The assumption (call it "the consistency hypothesis") that nothing like the above ever happens—that no further analysis of instances of a logically true schema is ever going to issue in the negation of a logically true schema—might thus seem essential for the credibility of the new approach to logical truth. And, in fact, many logicians seemed to assume something even stronger, from which the consistency hypothesis would follow: a *preservation hypothesis* according to which any further analysis of a sentence once declared an instance of a logically true schema is always going to result in the sentence instantiating a logically true schema. The preservation hypothesis rang true to them—or at least it sounded as if it *should* be true. But intuitions are often misleading, the more so when they are not carefully analyzed. It was time then to subject both hypotheses to careful scrutiny.

4. The Breakdown

Consider the sentence

(9)   It is possible that it rains.

Whether you favor the locked room metaphor or the possible worlds metaphor, it is difficult to question the logical truth of (9)—if "possible" is given a sufficiently general reading (sufficiently similar to "logically possible"). If you know how "it rains" is used, you know that it can possibly rain, and no matter what world is out there, there certainly is some structure describable by our language in which it rains.[13] Given the usual abbreviation of "it is possible that" and the fact that "it rains" is for most authors a paradigmatic case of a non-logical expression, the schema

(10) $\Diamond p$

---

12. I don't think that this (absolute) distinction makes sense: for me, a logical expression is simply one of which we are studying the logic. Those who agree with me have (as I indicate below) an additional strategy available for handling this difficulty.
13. Note that there is no reason to take this existential statement too seriously: the sense of "there being" mobilized here adds nothing to our metaphysical warehouse—just as "there certainly is some impossible thing that I desire" does not.

would seem to provide a full analysis of (9); therefore, one would expect that (10) be logically true. But if that were the case then the sentence

(11) It is possible that both it rains and it doesn't,

which *also* instantiates (10), would be logically true as well, and the negation of (11) is a logically true sentence, as can be seen by consulting either the schema

(12) $\Diamond(q \& \sim q)$

or our elementary common sense. So either (10) or the negation

(13) $\sim\Diamond(q \& \sim q)$

of (12) should be denied the status of a logically true schema, and the judgment is likely to come down in favor of (13)—which means that within this framework the logical truth of (9) will never be established.[14]

Or consider the sentence

(14) The red thing is red.

Again, one might be strongly inclined to consider (14) logically true—though this case is less clear, since it depends on one's intuitions about the logical behavior of non-denoting singular terms. For reasons analogous to the above, the schema

(15) $P(\iota x P x)$

would seem to give a full analysis of (14), but again one could not consider (15) logically true, in view of instances like

(16) The thing which is red and not red is red and not red.

And, whatever one's attitude toward non-denoting singular terms, it certainly sounds odd that (14) cannot be logically true because *some other* sentence is not.[15]

The moral to be drawn from these examples was clear: neither the preservation nor the consistency hypothesis will hold if we want to save within the new framework the logical truth of all the sentences that were (or could

---

14. On this theme, see Cocchiarella 1975 and Bencivenga 1981.
15. See Bencivenga 1978, 1980.

be) logically true according to the old one. If the hypotheses are to hold, there seems to be no alternative to discriminating in a substantial way between the two approaches, and transforming the "shift in emphasis" into a whole new conception of logic.

Of course, *there was* an alternative, though not a palatable one for most authors working within the new framework (which brings up a connection with the first "problem" discussed earlier). One could deny the logical truth of (10) but recover the logical truth of (9) by way of a logical analysis of the expression "it rains"; in other words, one could block the process considered above by refusing to consider (10) a *full* logical analysis of (9). This solution would have made the non-logical status of "it rains" highly questionable, and if generalized would have ultimately destroyed the very distinction between logical and non-logical expressions, but the fact that the alternative was available is very important, for it shows that most of the developments we have been considering were *not* necessary consequences of the previous ones. They were rather "natural" results of a new way of looking at things, of a new fashion as it were, and shared with fashions apparent inevitability as well as lack of theoretical justification. No matter how "naturally" the distinction between logical and non-logical expressions follows from the new approach to logical truth and the resulting increased emphasis on schemata and artificial languages, it is not a necessary consequence of it.

Be it as it may with such consequence relations, this is the point where our story takes a precipitous course toward its abrupt end. Faced by the necessity of choosing between the two approaches, between a logic of sentences and a logic of schemata, most logicians favored the second one. This choice created complications for the technical development of their discipline: "secondary" semantics had to be devised to exclude schemata like (10) from the set of logical truths. And the serious philosophical problem remained of what to do about sentences like (9), which could be proven true on purely linguistic grounds but were missing the necessary status symbol of a validating schema.

To be sure, the new attitude brought some good news. The logics thus generated could often be axiomatized. But this was hardly a justification for the attitude itself—whatever its practical value. Indeed, it got to be very suspicious when it turned out that occasionally artificial languages were defined *in such a way that they could be axiomatized.*

5. Conclusions

We should go back to thinking about the foundations of logic in a major way. The amount of philosophical reflection on logic today, if compared with the number of new logical systems being generated, is totally inadequate—both in general and with respect to particular issues.[16] Completeness theorems are a dime a dozen, but there is hardly any discussion of what exactly it means to prove such a theorem.[17] And despite all talk about the "metaphysical commitments" of this or that logical system, the closest thing to a contemporary theory of the relations between logic and metaphysics—which is needed if the relevant debates are to rise to a theoretically respectable level—is still old (and often deprecated) logical positivism.

This lack of philosophical reflection may be due, at least in part, to the current philosophical obsession with arguments. Philosophical papers are not supposed to present (attractive or revealing) theses, but to argue for them. And one cannot argue for the principles of one's philosophical position; so one is best advised to sneak them in implicitly, and then build fantastic arguments on them.

My story is an attempt to go in a different direction—which explains its polemical characterization as a story. I use it to present the bare bones of a general view of logic, but I do not argue for that view. All I can say in its favor is that it seems to handle a number of problems successfully, and to eliminate a few others; but this feat could of course be accomplished in many other ways. I wish it *was* accomplished in many other ways.

Briefly, the view is as follows. Logic is a theory about language—more precisely, a theory about what it takes for an argument in language to be valid or invalid. Since the notion of the validity of an argument can be

---

16. Authoritative evidence of the enormous number of logical systems generated in the last half century or so is provided by the many recent (large) surveys that are (being) published. Gabbay and Guenthner's four-volume *Handbook of Philosophical Logic* (1983–89) is already in need of a revised (and much enlarged) edition; and in the 90s we have also witnessed the publication of a *Handbook of Logic in Artificial Intelligence and Logic Programming*, a *Handbook of Logic in Computer Science*, and a *Handbook of Logic and Language*. Whereas a simple look at one of the very few collections devoted to philosophical reflections on logic (say, Hughes 1993) will reveal how little has been done recently in this field.
17. Such a discussion was promised by Dana Scott in 1976. But I have never seen it appear.

reduced—within a framework that includes alternative states of affairs, and mine does—to the notion of the truth or falsity of a sentence in a state of affairs, logic can also be characterized (in such a framework) as a theory about what it takes for a sentence to be true in a state of affairs. Being this a theory, we cannot expect its principles to be themselves logically true. At best, they will be justified inductively, as those of any other theory, with one additional complication: that the data on which to operate inductively are much easier to manipulate than in most other cases. It is much more difficult to explain away a careful physical observation than to dismiss someone's logical behavior as just *wrong*. Normativity has a way of rearing its head here.

A world (or state of affairs) is a complicated matter, but often full-fledged worlds will not be needed to establish the validity of arguments or the logical truth of sentences: simple mathematical models of worlds (or, less pretentiously, rudimentary sketches of them) will do. In a parallel manner, often we won't have to consider full-fledged sentences or arguments: it will be enough to consider schemata of them, which bring out their most general structural features. But it is important to realize that (a) the relevance of the schemata may well be local (a schema that provides a useful summary for a class of logical truths in one context may have absurd instances in another), and (b) schemata will not be available in all cases—sometimes, it will be necessary to focus *on the exact words a sentence contains*, as in the case of

(17) Everything that is round is not square

or

(18) If something is red-all-over, it is not green-all-over.[18]

The reasons why sentences like (17) and (18) are true are not dissimilar from the reasons for which, say, (3) is true: given the way our language works, they couldn't but be true—or: our language is not in a position to describe a situation in which they are not true. Too much emphasis on schemata and mathematical models, however, is likely to obliterate this similar-

---

18. For a good example of how far one can get by refusing to do justice to the logic of words like "round" and "square," see Terence Parsons's "rehabilitation" of Meinong in his 1980.

ity, and favor instead unmotivated and dangerous dichotomies. To avoid such risks, logicians should be better aware of the "geographical" location of their discipline. Mathematical tools are useful in logic, as they are virtually anywhere else; but this instrumental role is all the role mathematics can (and should) play in logic.[19] Logic is not about sets or Boolean algebras: it is about language, this language, the one you and I speak.[20]

References

Abramsky S., D. Gabbay, and T. Maibaum (eds.), 1991, *Handbook of Logic in Computer Science*, Oxford: Oxford University Press.

Bencivenga E., 1978, 'Free Semantics for Indefinite Descriptions', *Journal of Philosophical Logic* 7, 389-405.

Bencivenga E., 1980, 'Free Semantics for Definite Descriptions', *Logique et Analyse* 23, 393-405.

Bencivenga E., 1981, 'On Secondary Semantics for Logical Modalities', *Pacific Philosophical Quarterly* 62, 88-94.

Bencivenga E., 1989, 'Free From What?', in *Looser Ends*, Minneapolis: University of Minnesota Press, pp. 120-29.

van Benthem J. and A. Ter Meulen (eds.), 1997, *Handbook of Logic and Language*, Amsterdam: Elsevier Science Publishers.

Carnap R., 1947, *Meaning and Necessity*, Chicago: University of Chicago Press.

Cocchiarella N., 1975, 'On the Primary and Secondary Semantics of Logical Necessity', *Journal of Philosophical Logic* 4, 13-27.

Gabbay D. and F. Guenthner (eds.), 1983–1989, *Handbook of Philosophical Logic*, Dordrecht, Reidel.

Gabbay D., C. Hogger, and J. Robinson (eds.), 1991–1995, *Handbook of Logic in Artificial Intelligence and Logic Programming*, New York: Oxford University Press.

---

19. An additional wrinkle in the *real* history of the relations between logic and mathematics is that not only has mathematics been fruitfully applied to logic but also some of the deepest and most illuminating applications of logic have occurred within mathematical discourse. This is an interesting and important fact, but also one that (unfortunately) has contributed to the widespread delusion that logical analysis is only respectable when it is couched in mathematical terms and in a mathematical context.
20. I thank Achille Varzi for his comments on a previous draft of this paper.

Hegel G. W. F., 1991, *Elements of the Philosophy of Right*, edited by A. Wood, Cambridge: Cambridge University Press.

Hughes R. (ed.), 1993, *A Philosophical Companion to First-Order Logic*, Indianapolis: Hackett.

Lewis C. I. and C. H. Langford, 1932, *Symbolic Logic*, New York: Dover; reprinted 1959.

Parsons T., 1980, *Nonexistent Objects*, New Haven: Yale University Press.

Scott D., 1976, 'Background to Formalization', in H. Leblanc (ed.), *Truth, Syntax and Modality*, Amsterdam: North-Holland, pp. 244–73.

Tarski A., 1936, 'Der Warheitsbegriff in den formalisierten Sprachen', *Studia Philosophica* 1, 261–405.

Tarski A., 1986, 'What Are Logical Notions?', edited by J. Corcoran, *History and Philosophy of Logic* 7, 143–54.

Department of Philosophy
University of California
Irvine, CA
USA

JOHAN VAN BENTHEM
Wider Still and Wider...
Resetting the Bounds of Logic

1. The Agenda of Logic

The original attraction of logic for many people is the discovery that, in the fast stream of unreflected talking, thinking and planning that we all do, there are stable recurring patterns, which can be brought out and studied as such. This is the same Platonic insight of an unchanging true reality behind the chaotic world of appearances, that underlies all of science and philosophy. Another attraction nowadays to some people might be a more manipulative element. Using logical patterns, we can design machines, or teach humans, to perform these, as well as extrapolated skills, with higher speed and accuracy.

But what precisely is the subject matter of logic? Looking at most textbooks, the implicit answer seems to be that logic is a science of formal systems. This is the usual textbook sequence: propositional logic, predicate logic, modal logic, higher-order logic, etc. These systems include a formal language, a semantics, and a proof calculus, as one package. Of course, the professional picture is more diverse. Developing these systems, other dimensions of classification arise. For instance, one could also see logic as a bunch of recurrent techniques: compactness arguments, semantic tableaux, recursive functions. And finally, some of the highlights of the field are theorems, like Gödel's completeness and incompleteness theorems, sometimes formulated for one formal system, sometimes with a much wider scope. Even so, all this is all about formal tools, most of them recent. One might expect logic rather to have natural chapters like "negation", "recursion", and other major ubiquitous structures in reasoning—not tied to any specific formal system. But no professional consensus seems to exist on what such a division would be.

Does logic have a more specific subject matter, and should it? I see two kinds of answer. One is methodological, saying roughly that logic is about ubiquitous patterns in information representation and reasoning, which arise in any subject matter whatsoever. The other is more content-oriented, saying that logic is some kind of cognitive science, be it with a somewhat peculiar relationship to its empirical domain. (When people do not reason the logical way, we can always switch to a normative stance and say they *should*. Or nowadays, we can threaten to design an intelligent machine which *does* behave...) The literature on this issue is diverse. Amongst others, logic has been viewed as a science studying "the laws of thought", the "universal grammar" of language and meaning, the Platonic universe of all possible ontologies, the foundations of human cognition, or the abstract structure of information processing by humans or machines. All these answers lead to border crossings with neighbouring disciplines like mathematics, linguistics, computer science, or cognitive psychology. I cannot offer a definite criterion of demarcation here, valid for all times. I am inclined to say that logic is most properly viewed as a methodological stance which applies to most domains of rational enquiry. But if a more specific "proper province" were requested, I would opt for logic as a foundational science of *information*, both its structures and its transformation processes. This makes it well-suited as an intermediary between the above-mentioned disciplines, which all represent aspects of an emerging "information science". Incidentally, a search for definitions is often a sign of an identity crisis, which spells ill for a field. By contrast, the temperament of this essay is optimistic. Logic in the 20th century has achieved much impressive and undeniable progress. But the art is to see *in which direction*.

Given this broader background, here is what I hope to achieve at the least. This essay concerns the architecture of logic. The agenda of our field is the outcome of historical choices that could have been, and can be, made differently. No science escapes from this flux. There is constant renegotiation of what is important, and reinterpretation of the value of major contributions. My aim is to shake up some "received views" on the business of logic, proposing some constructive alternative views and challenges.

2. Accidents of Formulation

2.1 *Language and System Imprisonment*

Classical logic has been immensely successful. But this very success has enshrined certain formats and procedures, that also have drawbacks. For instance, many themes suffer from what may be called "system imprisonment". We have to discuss the behaviour of negation inside specific formal systems, such as propositional or predicate logic—even though these systems do not correspond to meaningful distinctions in the "open space" of actual reasoning. Many inference patterns formulated in predicate logic are completely general, and have nothing to do with tool-related issues like "first-order" versus "higher-order", or axiomatizable versus non-axiomatizable. A good example is the ubiquitous inference rule called Monotonicity: "positive occurrence sanctions upward predicate replacement", which has no preferred linguistic home (van Benthem 1987). Note the tentative formulation. We even seem to lack a suitable vocabulary for formulating these principles in their true generality. Thus, users of logic must buy into specific formal languages, which spell out much more than may be needed for their needs. Contrast this with mathematics, where a user of the calculus need not buy a fully specified formal language and proof system at all. Thus, we have a problem of achieving the appropriate generality. Another drawback of the formal systems approach is that we are forced to spell out complete formal languages and deductive calculi to their full mathematical extent, including convoluted forms of statement and argument which have no counterparts in natural reasoning. This may generate theoretical issues that are non-starters from the point of view of capturing essences of reasoning.[1]

One might think that system imprisonment is really a severe case of a more general "language imprisonment". Logicians always introduce "formal languages", a habit which surprises (and vexes) many of its potential users. Why bother with the details of syntax, when we are after contents? But this is a mode of proceeding which I think is inevitable—provided that we see it in

---

1. "Full specification" does seem necessary for doing natural language processing, or programming of other kinds—but it is not the way in which people experience and structure reasoning. And even computationally, it may be an overly costly architecture, closing our eyes to alternatives. Language understanding and real-time reasoning might consist in massive parallel repetition of simple patterns, rather than elaborate recursive hierarchies.

its proper light. It is not important that we are dealing with "languages" in any received sense of that word, let alone any specific formal notation. But what is essential is that logic must bring out the interplay between cognitive content and its *representations* in order to get a handle on the relevant phenomena.

2.2 From Proper Names to Common Nouns: Getting at the Logical Phenomena

Lifting specific results to broader contexts occurs all the time in logic. Consider Gödel's Completeness Theorem: originally a specific statement about first-order predicate logic, now a type of theorem. Proper names become common nouns. In logic, losing one's capital is an honour. This is standard generalisation, found in any science. But one can take this trend much further, and seek general phenomena behind even standard logical items. For instance, "logical constants" are usually taken to be members of a conventional list of Boolean connectives, first-order quantifiers, and perhaps the identity predicate. But the real issue is the general *phenomenon of logicality*, and the degree to which it can occur in arbitrary expressions. Why is the business of logic with just these distinguished items, rather than with "logical behaviour"—broadly understood—which may be found to some degree in all linguistic categories? For so-called "generalised quantifiers", this point is becoming acknowledged nowadays—but it holds equally well for prepositions ("in", "with", "to"), or discourse particles ("if", "but", "although"). The same consideration applies to the other traditional focus of the field, namely the "laws of logic". Defining features of the field should not be sought in specific rules like Modus Ponens, or other boundary stones of some privileged domain of logical reasoning. In particular, no fixed set of core laws demarcates "logical" from non-logical reasoning. It is the spirit, not the letter of these laws that defines the field. What logic should be about is rather capturing the *phenomenon of inference* in general, as it occurs in the various connections (deductive, inductive, etc.) that humans use to drive the flow of information.

2.3 The Architecture of Diversity

Existing logical systems can hide presuppositions, which we do not see just because they are so successful. First-order predicate logic is a good example. It has done amazingly well as a focus for making modern logic more rigorous, and as a "laboratory" where the most important metatheorems of the field were developed. But as a paradigm for reasoning, it also has some features which one might question. In particular, stepping back a little, its very uniformity seems suspect. It would really be most surprising if one single linguistic formula representation could efficiently serve the purposes of such different activities as interpretation and deduction. Cognitive psychology suggests that memory and performance of humans over time require an interplay of different successive representations for the same information. Therefore, no such uniformity need be assumed for actual cognition, and a much more complex modular architecture might be needed, where semantics and deduction do not work on the same representations, and where information is passed between modules. And the same moral applies elsewhere. With information processing by machines, modularity is at the heart of performance. And to mention one further source, issues of architecture become unavoidable when we ponder the logical meso- and macro-structures of discourse and argumentation.

2.4 From Products to Activities

The previous concerns still follow traditional logic in the following important respect, which again hides a prevalent presupposition concerning the focus of logical research. They show an emphasis on static *products* of logical activities, such as statements or proofs, instead of those activities *themselves*. But interestingly, in natural language, the words "statement" and "proof" are both ambiguous between a reading as a product and as an activity. And rightly so. Indeed, in much current literature there is a "Dynamic Turn" putting (both physical and cognitive) activities at centre stage as a primary target of research. This move is highly relevant to our conception of the logical agenda. Reasoning is a logical activity, and its process structure is a legitimate research topic. Moreover, so are related intelligent activities like understanding the information in what is said, formulating intelligent questions, more general many-person communication, or playing other cognitive games. What we want to convey to students are the logical patterns that drive these skills. Thus, one alternative way of thinking about the architecture of the discipline is in terms of the cognitive skills that it contains. Its impact lies in this "know-how", rather than "know-that": the capital of accumulated truths.

3. The Major Parts of Logic

In order to introduce some alternative viewpoints, we need a brief sketch of established achievements of modern logic. These have been recorded in a number of well-known Handbooks, including volumes on Mathematical Logic (Barwise 1977), Philosophical Logic (Gabbay & Guenthner 1983–1989), Logic in Computer Science (Abramsky, Gabbay & Maibaum 1992–1999), Logic and Artifical Intelligence (Gabbay, Hogger & Robinson 1991–1995), and Logic and Language (van Benthem & Ter Meulen 1997). Our business here is not at all to belittle these accumulated achievements, but rather to change our perspective on what has been, and still can be, achieved.

Expressive Power. Logic studies formal languages, as well as types of ontology for them, and "logical semantics" studies connections between the two realms, dealing with expressive power of languages. This dual aspect makes logic so strange to working scientists—who tend to consider linguistic formulation as a necessary, but trivial evil. The logical stance reveals subtleties of interaction between linguistic form and structural behaviour, which one simply would not be aware of otherwise. Thus, logic has become a paradigm of meaning in the semantics of natural languages in linguistics, and that of computer languages in computer science. The "strong arm" of logical semantics is *model theory*, which also has purely mathematical applications. One of the most striking benefits of this dual perspective is the creation of *new* unintended models for existing deductive practices. Examples are the infinitesimals used in non-standard analysis.

Deductive Power. Logic studies proof calculi for various species of valid reasoning and their combinatorial properties, as well as the proof-structure of deductively organised theories. *Proof theory* started as a typical tool in the foundations of mathematics, studying proof structures and their effective transformations—but its patterns also occur in computer science, artificial intelligence, and also linguistics and even law. It is this aspect of logic which has most permeated general culture, as an ideal of precision and intellectual organisation. Despite the connotations of the term "proof", logic is not necessarily on the side of authority here. Proof need not always mean knockdown argumentation, ending in cognitive surrender of one's opponent. It is also a model for setting forth one's reasons and assumptions, putting them up for public scrutiny.

Computational Power. Logic has provided the first, and still most successful general analysis of computation, and its associated notion of complexity. Moreover, it contains precise theorems about the limits of effective computability, when Gödel discovered essentially "undecidable" problems. On the positive side, computer science has realised old ideals of "mechanising" logical tasks in automated deduction and logic programming. The scope of computational concerns covers both deduction and semantics. One can provide algorithms for valid inferences, but also for semantic queries. Finally, computational models have again led to new interpretations for old phenomena. An example is the treatment of randomness and learning in Kolmogorov complexity.

With many of these themes, boundaries are fuzzy with surrounding disciplines. For instance, some exciting recent advances in the study of reasoning go under the heading of Artificial Intelligence. This short enumeration shows that modern logic has developed a large body of insights and techniques in a relatively short historical period. These results have set patterns of rigour and coverage that have changed the traditional field beyond recognition, and irreversibly. Every subsequent critical turn in the field must eventually live up to these quality standards. Our coming discussion therefore falls under the above three headings. In each case, we discuss one trend within current research, and one which seems to require a more drastic shift.

4. Expressive Power

4.1 *Logicality and Invariance*

There is an asymmetry in logical theory, in that most results take some vocabulary for granted, and then develop various deductive and other systems on this basis. Most major results are about semantic consequence and computability given some language. The question how we chose its vocabulary in the first place does not arise. Modern logic has much more to say on derivability than on definability. And yet, we do have intuitions concerning the choice of logical operators. These form the "glue" of discourse, which does not itself carry any specific information about individuals or issues. Logical notions are "topic-neutral", as is sometimes said. One well-known way of making this idea precise is through *semantic invariances*. Consider any permutation of a domain of individuals: that is, a function shaking up their identity, leaving only their "patterns". Any such permutation induces permuted forms of sets of individuals, and likewise all the way up to objects in higher types. Now call a logical operator O of any arity and type *permutation-invariant* if it commutes with such permutations:

$$\pi[O(X, Y, ...)] = O(\pi[X], \pi[Y], ...)$$

A useful reformulation recasts this identity as invariance under isomorphisms:

$$(x, ...) \in O(R, S, ...) \text{ iff } (\pi(x), ...) \in O(\pi[R], \pi[S], ...)$$

Permutation invariance has been proposed as a general criterion for logicality by many authors independently (including Tarski 1986), gradually covering the algebra of sets and relations, generalised quantifiers, and eventually the whole range of possible categorial operators (van Benthem 1989a). In general, any operation defined in a logical language that does not refer to specific objects will be permutation-invariant. This is actually a very old perspective. Dual view-points on definability and invariance under suitable transformations date back far into the 19th century. For instance, in the ground-breaking work by Helmholtz and Heymans on perception, invariants of movement provided natural primitives for geometrical theories. Klein made this viewpoint the foundation of his Erlanger Program for the set-up of any mathematical theory. Similar ideas have been proposed by Weyl in this century for analysing the primitives of physical space-time (classical and relativistic), and they have also surfaced in so-called "ecological psychology".

Semantic invariances have two virtues. First, they provide a *general* formulation of logicality, which applies to operators in different syntactic categories. Thus, we see how Boolean operations really are logical in the same way as quantifiers, or less obviously "logical" items, such as the reflexivizer "self". Second, semantic invariance naturally admits of *gradations*. This makes pure logicality one extreme on a spectrum. The standard mathematical examples do not consider all permutations of their base individuals, but only special transformation groups preserving the relevant structure (geometric, topological, etc.). Thus, logicality is not an all-or-nothing matter—since arbitrary expressions can be classified for the amount of invariance that they support. (Logic is very robust, mathematics a bit less, while ordinary expressions will only show invariance under transformations respecting a lot of further structure.) Interestingly, similar views have been proposed for linguistic expressions. For instance, prepositions seem to lie in between logical operations with a completely fixed meaning, and lexical items whose interpretation is completely free, like adjectives or verbs. They are somewhat constrained, by being items that are stable under those shifts in orientation that tend to occur in our ordinary spatial movements.

Do semantic invariances "justify" types of expression, or do types of expression generate the appropriate structure-preserving transformations? Our analysis does not say, and indeed, one can look in either direction. Given the vocabulary, there are corresponding automorphisms, and one can show that further defined expressions will be invariant. One can also ask, conversely, for definability of invariant items (this question dates back to Weyl, who thought it was unsolvable). There are many "functional completeness theorems" classifying logical invariants of various kinds (van Benthem 1986a, 1991b). An interesting recent interpretation of the invariance approach is more computational (cf. Section 6.1 below). One can think of logical constants as defining simple evaluation processes (conjunction composes subroutines, disjunctions prompt a choice, etcetera). But then logicality is no longer an absolute notion. It depends on one's choice of process. A semantic equivalence gives us a notion of "simulation" between instances of the same procedure, running on different models. Invariance expresses the latter fact. Thus, "logical constants" reflect an implicit procedural notion of semantic evaluation.

4.2 Generality and Linguistic Form

Our second example merely elaborates a limitation that was already pointed out earlier. Sensitivity to syntax is a hall-mark of logical analysis. In particular, the fine-structure of formal languages contains a lot of semantic and computational information. For instance, when comparing truth of statements across different (or changing) situations, one may observe that certain statements remain true whenever the universe of discourse contracts. The Los-Tarski Theorem then tells us that (in first-order logic), these are precisely the statements that can be defined employing only *universal* quantifiers over objects. Likewise, we mentioned the inference rule of monotonicity (the "Dictum de Omni" of traditional logic) whose range of applicability depends on *positive* occurrence of its key predicate. As an algorithmic example, in proof search, one finds that some statements have a natural procedural interpretation as simple search instructions—and identifies *Horn clauses* as a vehicle for efficient logic programming. Nevertheless, there is also a problem here. Many of these observations seem to have a much wider scope than any given formal language, and they crop up all the time. Then, what is their true generality? Traditional logicians wrestled with the Dictum de Omni, and never managed to find a satisfactory general formulation (Sanchez 1991). As a result, we cannot even say what the true range of the classical syllogistic was. But a similar problem afflicts its modern successors... Thus, attention to linguistic form is both a very typical, and powerful source of logical insights, and a not always desirable constraint on their formulation.

5. Deductive Power

Deduction is connected to meaning, but it is also sui generis. Before broaching more specific issues illustrating this point, let us illustrate the "dangers of success". Consider the standard completeness theorem for predicate logic, one of the central results of the field. It is taken to say that formal deduction in Frege's or Hilbert's style indeed captures valid logical consequence. The latter semantic notion (due to Bolzano and Tarski) says that, whenever the premises of an inference are true in a model, so is its conclusion. Thus, proving completeness theorems has become something of an industry. Now, this result and this interpretation hide as many questions as they solve. For one thing, *why* should deductive systems be complete in this sense? (As Kreisel once observed, soundness says that the proof system will tell us nothing new, and completeness that the semantics will tell us nothing new...) And even if they are, completeness is only an "extensional" statement, saying that the sequents "premises-conclusion" forming the output by the deductive machinery are precisely those that satisfy some abstract semantic criterion for validity. But the most important features of a proof system are clearly its "intensional" ones, having to do with its account of inference, and with the deductive organisation of information which it supports or suggests. A completeness theorem tells us nothing about these intrinsic deductive virtues. Finally, more insidiously, the completeness theorem suggests various things ex silentio. One is that there is one unique notion of logical validity that forms the intuitive norm—something which is not obvious. The other suggestion, still more hidden, is that the comparison between the semantic and the deductive approach to logical validity is the crucial one, and that these two perspectives are the only players. But historically, neither of these two may be the original intuition of logical validity—which seems closer to having *winning strategies* in debate and discussion. The latter, more pragmatic account can be stated in more computational game-theoretical terms, which are close to actual argumentation. Thus, the agenda of standard textbooks (which tend to ignore or marginalise these other viewpoints) can be highly misleading—which again engenders a certain poverty in philosophical studies of logical consequence that do not question their presuppositions.

5.1 *Styles of Reasoning*

Is there just one notion of logical validity, to which all deduction must aspire? In the history of logic, other views have existed. Notably, "Bolzano's Program" in the early 19th century rather viewed logic as the science of styles of reasoning. Bolzano 1837 observed that human reasoning comes in varieties, with stricter or looser criteria for validity, ranging from domestic deliberation, through scientific reasoning, to what he considered the acme of thought: philosophical strict entailment. Bolzano's agenda for logic requires the identification of major styles of reasoning (deductive, inductive, and others), and the determination of their logical properties. (Similar broad agendas are still found with C.S. Peirce, towards the end of the 19th century.) Interestingly, logical constants play less of a central role here. On Bolzano's view, the basic distinction in inference is between those parts of speech whose meaning we keep constant (these will form the "logical skeleton") and those whose denotation is variable. These distinctions can be made in different ways, depending on context, and hence the main emphasis is on proof rules that do not involve the behaviour of special expressions like "not", "and" or "all". Rules of the latter kind are nowadays called *structural rules* of inference. And indeed, in logic and AI, various packages of structural rules have been used to identify major types of inference (van Benthem 1989b, Makinson 1994). Classical reasoning is characterised by structural rules that allow us to treat the premises as a "sufficient set". We can permute them, copy them, contract copies, and add things, without losing a conclusion once established. By contrast, for instance, default logics are non-monotonic. If we allow conclusions from ignorance, then further premises may invalidate the grounds on which an earlier conclusion rested. Thus, practical reasoning is deeply tied up with withdrawing conclusions, and *revision* of our theories. Yet another example is probabilistic reasoning, which need not be transitive: a chain of probable inferences may lose force along the way, and yield implausible conclusions. Finally, dynamic inference pays close attention to the sequential presentation of premises, and hence its conclusions may even be sensitive to permutations or contractions of premises.

Although this perspective on inference is not generally accepted, it falls within standard logic in the following sense. Varieties of non-standard inference can be developed using standard techniques, including formal semantics, representation and completeness theorems. Indeed, many combinatorial techniques of classical proof theory have been found to apply to logics with structural bases different from the classical one (cf. Schröeder-Heister & Dosen 1993). And yet, this abstract idea of "inference" seems alien to many logicians. Part of the reason is again the earlier-mentioned emphasis on products. Alternative inference systems often violate classical "laws of logic", and this seems like a deep loss if the latter are the heart of logic. A better view of this plurality is that these systems are not competitors in any sense. They just describe various "connections" between statements that humans find it useful to observe and develop. Also, the "yield" of these systems in terms of their valid sequents is in some sense a secondary output, which should not be at the focus of evaluation. What matters are the underlying ideas, such as the view of default logic where *"ignorance"* supplies conclusions, or the qualitative form of probabilistic reasoning where one considers only those models of the premises that best fit with one's *preferences*.

There is more to be said here. Radicalism usually only goes so far. Proponents of alternative reasoning styles have often stuck to standard methods for developing their systems, either model-theoretically or proof-theoretically. But of course, some other format might be much more appropriate, say, game-theoretic or yet different. Also, in line with our preceding section, these authors have usually taken the classical logical *vocabulary* for granted. But of course, expressive power and deductive power are not independent. If one sets up an alternative logic, then the question should come up what is its most appropriate logical vocabulary. Exceptions to this neglect are relevant logic and linear logic, where new proof systems have come with new views of logical constants. And indeed, Bolzano himself stated structural rules that involve explicit changes in the boundary between "fixed" and "variable" vocabulary.

5.2 Modular Architecture

Classical proof systems are uniform for one particular formal language, handling all its potential inferences. They do not contain further information about architecture. Now in natural language, this view is not quite plausible. For instance, many inferences seem to be shallow, involving only a few operators at a time. And more importantly, inferences seem to come in modules, small packages of rules for a special purpose (van Benthem 1986b). The clusters of this "natural logic" need not fit very well with the distinctions introduced in, say, first-order logic. For instance, nothing in natural reasoning corresponds to the standard emphasis on prenex forms. Examples of natural clusters are monotonicity reasoning, conservativity reasoning, and simple algebraic rules (by no means all of propositional logic). Again, the "phenomena" of reasoning do not fit the mathematics of formal syntax very well, and the latter may not be the most appropriate medium for bringing them out. What we need is a better account of logical architecture, which tells us what modules are, perhaps even based on different logics, and how they can efficiently interact and pass information.

The need for "logical architecture" becomes even clearer with other recent developments. For instance, current dynamic logics of reasoning suggest a natural distinction between short-term presentation-dependent and long-term memory-oriented inference, where the latter works on more abstract representations. Again, the architecture of such more complex reasoning systems is at present beyond the scope of logical theory. Putting this more generally, deductive logic so far has little to say about the meso- and macro-levels of reasoning, which is where most of our more strategic thinking takes place. This is not to say that no formal approach could work here. Philosophers of science, rather than logicians, have had many interesting things to say on these higher aggregation levels of both reasoning and theories, witness the influential works of Nagel, Sneed, or Lakatos. Likewise, the best formal accounts of modularity in the representation of information come from the theory of abstract data types in computer science, rather than logic itself. Nevertheless, "combination of logics" is becoming an acknowledged research area, facilitated by recent more flexible formats of "labeled deductive systems" (Gabbay 1996). Also relevant here are various newer approaches to "logical systems", collected in the anthology Gabbay 1994. The latter also illuminates other themes in this essay.

6. Computing Power

The theory of computability is a field in its own right, with concerns of its own that fall outside the scope of this discussion. We raise some issues here concerning interpretation and inference, viewed as cognitive activities that involve some sort of computation.

6.1 *Cognitive Dynamics*

As we observed before, classical logic is oriented towards the products of activities (mostly cognitive, but also more general ones), rather than the structure of those activities themselves. Logic is about reasoning, confirming, refuting, denying, etcetera. But it mainly talks about reasons, proofs, propositions, and other static traces of these activities. But contemporary dynamic logics are trying to put the latter on the map, thereby making the intuitions explicit that underlie much of classical theory.[2] In this way, logic becomes more of a general theory of information structures plus the processes that modify these. Prominent examples of this trend are the logics of update, contraction and revision in the theory of belief revision (cf. Gärdenfors & Rott 1995), as well as various logics of 'dynamic semantics' for natural and formal reasoning that are currently being developed in analogy with the semantics of imperative programming languages (cf. Muskens, van Benthem & Visser 1997). This "Dynamic Turn" makes traditional logical languages more like cognitive programming languages whose programs are instructions for modifying the information states of parties in communication.

Again, this is a broader research program for logic, pursued by classical means. Dynamic logics employ mathematical models of information states (both for factual information, and for epistemic information concerning other people's knowledge and ignorance), and their logical constants are much like program constructors of well-known kinds, familiar from rela-

---

2. For readers who have undergone the dynamic Gestalt Switch, implicit dynamic features are ubiquitous in even the most traditional textbook presentations of logic, clamouring for proper attention. For case studies in first-order and modal logics, cf. the chapter on "dynamification" in van Benthem 1996.

tional algebra and process algebra. This process view of logical constants fits very well with our invariance analysis of Section 4.1 (cf. van Benthem 1996). Of course, what are the appropriate logical constants will depend on one's view of the relevant cognitive processes. These need not be the same for all purposes: evaluation may indeed require different information states, and atomic moves transforming these, from the structures manipulated in inference.

Here is a concrete example. Think of propositions dynamically as transition relations on information states (standard propositional updates will even be deterministic functions, but propositional revisions may be indeterministic). In this move from Boolean set algebra to relational algebra, logical operators come to define algebraic combinations of binary relations. For instance, here are natural dynamic counterparts of the three classical Boolean operations • (and), + (or), ~ (not), respectively (for their motivation, cf. Groenendijk & Stokhof 1991, van Benthem 1996):

composition $R \circ S = \{(x, y) \mid \text{for some } z: Rxz \text{ and } Szy\}$

choice $R \cup S = \{(x, y) \mid Rxy \text{ or } Sxy\}$

impossibility $\sim R = \{(x, x) \mid \text{there is no } y \text{ with } Rxy\}$

One way of defining logical process operators employs the *permutation invariance* of Section 4.1. Notice that permutations of individual objects lift naturally to permutations of binary relations, taking them to relations having essentially the same abstract "arrow patterns". Now it is easy to show that the preceding relational operations of composition, choice and impossibility are invariant for permutations of their argument relations, whereas an operation referring to (say) the presence of a specific individual ("king Louis Napoleon I") or some specific relation ("being the founder of") would not be invariant. But the range of permutation-invariant relational operators is vast, and does not match known computational repertoires. So, we need a better approximation of processes. Here is one way of achieving that, which suggests a generalization of invariance to "safety".

In many theories of computation, a specific notion of process arises by first choosing some representation of states and transitions, and then imposing an equivalence relation. One common choice are *labeled transition systems* ("process graphs", "Kripke models") consisting of states with labeled arrows, identified under so-called *bisimulation* (cf. van Benthem 1996, Barwise & Moss 1997). Bisimulations are back-and-forth relations between states in two models which allow for running the same process with similar local states and similar available choices at each state.[3] Now, given this process model, we may require that natural operations O(R, S, ...) on binary relations "stay inside it". That is, if we have a bisimulation between two models that have atomic actions R, S, ... for the argument relations, then this *same* bisimulation should still bisimulate with respect to the newly defined relation O(R, S, ...). This new requirement is known as *safety for bisimulation*. (But safety also makes sense for other process equivalences.) It is easy to see that safety for bisimulation has permutation invariance as a special case. But it is much stronger. Van Benthem 1996 (chapter 5) shows that the only first-order definable relational operators which are safe for bisimulation are precisely those definable using the above dynamic propositional operators o , ∪ , ~. This is a functional completeness result for dynamified propositional logic, characterizing its operators in semantic terms. But it also demonstrates a more general analysis of dynamic "logicality".

Here as elsewhere, the outcome of the new program is not in conflict with the tenets of classical logic. There rather seems to be a "Correspondence Principle" at work, guiding the design of the newer systems. Passing to a suitable limit (disregarding sequential phenomena), the latter should "reduce" to the standard ones, in some reasonable sense. The same principle seems to work, incidentally, for varieties of inference. So far, all non-standard logics reduce to classical logic when one makes appropriate (consistent) additional assumptions. This observation explains a perhaps surprising empirical fact. Most alternative logics are weaker than classical logic, but they never *contradict* it.

---

3. More precisely, a bisimulation between two rooted Kripke models M, N is a binary relation Z connecting states in M to states in N subject to the following conditions. (1) ("Same Start") Z connects the two roots. (2) ("Local Harmony") Z only connects states which satisfy the same atomic propositions. (3) ("Back-and-Forth") For every atomic relation R, if sZt and sRu in M, then there exists some v in N such that tRv and uZv. And vice versa. This notion is well-known for matching the standard *modal* language: the same propositional modal formulas are true at M, x and N, y when xZy. Various converses are discussed in van Benthem 1996. Safety for bisimulation may be viewed as a natural extension of this invariance for Modal Logic to program operations in so-called Dynamic Logic.

6.2 Church's Thesis Revisited

It has sometimes been claimed that the basic notion of computation has been found by Turing in the 30s, bolstered by a bunch of equivalences with alternative frameworks. This then led to *Church's Thesis* stating that all reasonable models of computation amount to the same thing, namely the (general) recursive functions. But in the light of the preceding discussion, things are less clear-cut. Church's thesis is "extensional", in that it talks about the functions (the input-output graphs) of quite diverse algorithms and programming styles. The latter may differ considerably in their fine-structure. For instance, Turing machine programming is about the least perspicuous style of defining algorithms that has ever been invented. At a more intensional level, it is still unclear what a canonical notion of "algorithm" would be—so that the theory of computation still has its fundamental open questions. A strong version of Church's Thesis would give a uniform model for algorithmic structure. And what the latter would involve, presumably, is an account of natural "logical" or cognitive programming structure. In particular, what are the natural logical constants in the above dynamic setting? It seems safe to say that we do not know yet, even though a number of approaches exists.

Indeed, despite the success of Turing's model in AI as a paradigm for cognition, it is not even clear that machine models are the most appropriate mathematization of cognitive activities. One alternative which is gaining ground in the logical community is logical *game theory*. Cognition involves moves in a social setting, guided by higher-level strategies that we can follow to achieve our goals. Logical games exist for argumentation (Lorenzen dialogues), interpretation (Hintikka game semantics), model comparison (Ehrenfeucht-Fraïssé back-and-forth games), and for many other purposes.[4] Moreover, games provide genuinely novel perspectives on logical constants (e.g., negation becomes a "role switch", and disjunction a "choice") as well as valid inference (which becomes the existence of a winning strategy for the proponent of the conclusion against an opponent who has granted the premises). Games also seem to lend themselves more easily to analyses of the above-mentioned cognitive group behaviour, as well as the importation of non-deductive probabilistic considerations. But the jury is

---

4. A classical reference is Hintikka 1973. For a more recent survey and discussion of logical games, cf. van Benthem 1988, 1993.

still out on what should be the fundamental game model for logical activities, and thus, this intriguing alternative approach still awaits its Turing.

7. General Laws

The view of logic developed in the preceding sections takes existing logical notions to much broader formulations. But I feel that there is still something missing in our general conception of the field, which may be brought out through an analogy with the sciences. In physics, in addition to laws for specific domains of phenomena, or facts concerning particular applications, certain broad principles regulate our thinking about the world—which embody some of the most fundamental insights of the field. Examples are the principle of the Least Effort or Shortest Path, or the famous Conservation Laws of Energy or Momentum. Does logic have similar broad principles, that reveal something essential about information or cognition? Thinking about the issues in this essay so far, the following points come to mind, which I put up here, diffidently, for discussion only. I do not pretend to have any definite answers, but I do think we should try harder to crystallize some combined wisdom of the discipline at this general level.

Balance of Language and Ontology. Logical systems should have "the right" expressive power vis-a-vis their intended semantics. This balance can be measured by the existence of a characteristic semantic equivalence for the language, telling us when two models are indistinguishable. (Examples are back-and-forth relations like potential isomorphisms in first-order logic, or bisimulations in modal logic.) Some others have suggested that a measure for this balance is the existence of an Interpolation Theorem for the language.

Compositionality. This was the only constraint that Montague brought to light in his "Universal Semantics" unifying the semantics of natural and formal languages. Dummett has widely defended it as Frege's key insight that distinguishes modern from traditional logic. Logical syntax is given by recursive constructions, and our business is not just the lexical semantics of logical constants, but also the compositional semantics of these constructions. There is a law here: all good semantics can be made compositional, so that syntactic structure harmonises with semantic process structure.

Conservation of Complexity. The following reflects a pervasive experience in logical research. What one gains in expressive power, one loses in complexity of inference. In other words, the balance of expressive and algorithmic complexity seems constant. What is the appropriate measure of complexity for this conservation law? It might involve some suitably abstract notion of "information"—which we lack at present.[5]

The principles so far mainly concern the design of logical systems by themselves. But there are also general experiences concerning connections between different systems.

Translation Thesis. Church's Thesis tells us that all reasonable models of computation can be simulated on Turing machines. Many people feel that something similar holds for expressive power. Many major logics are equivalent under effective translation, provided that we take the latter term in a suitably liberal sense. For instance, intuitionistic logic is not faithfully embeddable into classical logic when we keep its language fixed—but it is embeddable when we transcribe its Kripke semantics with explicit quantification over information states. (This equivalence might even follow from Church's Thesis plus Conservation of Complexity.) So, is first-order logic a universal expressive medium?

Duality of Viewpoints. Related, though somewhat different in thrust, are certain broad dualities. In mathematics, there is a constant historical interplay between algebraic and geometrical viewpoints. Both seem to correspond to basic intuitions that we have, and there is constant re-encoding of one stance into the other. Likewise, logic has natural recurring stances. What can be said model-theoretically ("geometrically") has natural counterparts proof-theoretically ("algebraically"), and vice versa. Another instance of the same duality might be the above-mentioned relation (once articulated) between "algorithmic" and "semantic" information. And perhaps, when the time comes, this duality extends to a triangle affair with the game-theoretic stance.

Once again, these are musings, not definite outcomes. The more ambitious goal behind such principles, just as in the sciences, would be to find logical theories that *explain*, rather than merely *describe* the workings of information and cognition.

---

5. Indeed, we even lack a good bridge between well-developed more algorithmic notions of information (as found in Shannon's information theory; Ash 1965, or in Kolmogorov complexity; Ming Li & Vitanyi 1993) and the more qualitative notions of information that guide logical semantics (Barwise & Perry 1983, Barwise & Seligman 1996, Veltman 1996).

8. Summary

The main purpose of this paper has been to present a plea for a broader agenda of logic—partly inspired by the future, but partly also by the past of the field, before Frege gave the steering wheel a momentous push toward the foundations of mathematics. One part of our effort was an attempt to place known notions and results in proper generality. Varieties of "logical constants" and "deductive styles" were key examples. Another part was an openness to altogether new topics, such as the "logical architecture" of complex reasoning systems, or most conspicuously, the inclusion of dynamic "process structure" as a logical concern on a par with the traditional business of representational structure. These examples were driven by a grand purpose for the discipline. What best advances logic as a general science of information structures and processes, both in human cognition and artificial settings? This broad concern is not a threat to established logic. It rather adds to its impact, and refines some of its concerns (witness our discussion of Church's Thesis). Moreover, our broader canvas raises some, perhaps vague, but at least inspirational themes, like the above quest for fundamental laws of logic, far beyond specific rules of inference, or specific formal systems. These moves may have an intellectual interest. But our boundary discussions also hold a practical interest, at least for those logicians who are concerned with the academic position of their field.

9. Appendix: Actual Reasoning

A common reaction to deviations from the classical logical agenda classifies them as being concerned with "applications".[6] Application has not been the focus of our essay—and our more general view of logic does not automatically make it more "applicable". Indeed, there are many misconceptions about what it means to apply logic, or other methodological disciplines. These misconceptions form a rich subject which deserves a paper by itself. Here, we conclude by pointing out a number of ways in which actual reasoning differs from current logical systems. (This is why papers from non-logicians are often so much richer than ours when they dig into some specific reasoning task.)

---

6. This reflex makes quite theoretical fields like deontic logic "applied logic in philosophy", or generalized quantifier theory "applied logic in linguistics".

Real-Time Performance. Complexity awareness is a potential new item on the logical agenda. The known worst-case complexity of current logical systems does not come even close to the speed of human real-time performance on cognitive tasks. Here is one possible explanation for this mismatch. Humans may be fast, but not very sound or complete reasoners. Their procedures do not guarantee absolute certainty, but they are very good at revision when things go wrong. In this sense, our intelligence has to do, not with steady accumulation of eternal truths, but with quick rational response to challenges. Rationality is repair...This is a diagnosis outside of standard logical theory. Alternatively, one can also "internalize" the challenge of real-time performance, and redesign logical systems to achieve this effect. For instance, the undecidable systems of relational algebra and first-order logic have been remodelled in so-called Arrow Logic and Modal First-Order Logic (Venema 1996, van Benthem 1994, 1996). This program can be extended, towards lowering complexity of decidable (but still complex) to realistically feasible logics.

Heterogeneous Information. Information is certainly not all symbolic. Graphic information is important, too—and indeed about every physical sign can be a carrier of information that can be processed logically. Perhaps, one good thing about the (sometimes deplored) abstraction of logical systems is that they can handle this generality. Even so, good paradigms for integrating information from these various sources are as yet unavailable.

Packaging: Representation and Computation. Another take on human real-time performance might be this. It is the package which counts. Humans exploit advantageous representations that help keep complexity down, and try to perform minimal computation over these. This might reflect cognitive principles of "least effort", in line with the general principles of the preceding section, that explain something about human intelligent behaviour.

Architecture. This issue was raised before. Actual cognitive strategies seem ad hoc, calling many reasoning modules, and looking up information from all available sources. (For instance, even working logicians will often use a hodge-podge of semantic and proof-theoretic reasoning.) From this perspective, most logical systems are puristic: too clean and uniform. What is the architecture of opportunism, that allows us to get by so fast?

Mixing Deduction with Observation. No purism holds also for our information gathering. We deduce when we must, but we *observe*, or merely *ask* when we can, and this is shorter. Even scientists often prefer the outcome of an experiment to the result of laborious reasoning. (The happy mixture of a priori axioms and a posteriori experiments in Newton's work is a good example.) Conclusions are like queries, and we use whatever the situation offers.

The Genesis of Vocabulary. In practice, the formation of good vocabulary is essential to successful cognition. Some of this is local to discussion, or problem solving. Some of it is so generally useful that it gets encoded into our natural language. Many expressions then turn out to have a functional inferential role. For instance, it pays to reflect on the uses of a dispositional expression like "friendly", which encapsulates a whole default rule of inference. Moreover, again a conservation law seems at work here. We create new definitions to keep the complexity of interpreting our discourse, and reasoning, more or less constant.

Should the complexities noted in this Appendix become part of logical theory itself? There is a general danger lurking here, namely, that the true scientific account of anything in the world will turn out as complex as the reality it is intended to describe. Our preliminary answer is therefore: we do not know...

References

Abramsky S., D. Gabbay, and T. Maibaum (eds.), 1991–1999, *Handbook of Logic in Computer Science*, Oxford: Oxford University Press.

Ash R., 1965, *Information Theory*, New York, Interscience Publishers.

Barwise J. (ed.), 1977, *Handbook of Mathematical Logic*, Amsterdam: North-Holland.

Barwise J. and J. Etchemendy, 1995, 'Heterogeneous Logic', in J. Glasgow, N. Narayanan, and B. Chandrasekaran (eds.), *Diagrammatic Reasoning: Cognitive and Computational Perspectives*, Menlo Park: AAAI Press; Cambridge, MA: MIT Press, pp. 209–232.

Barwise J. and L. Moss, 1996, *Vicious Circles. On the Mathematics of Non-Well-Founded Phenomena*, Stanford: CSLI Publications.

Barwise J. and J. Perry, 1983, *Situations and Attitudes*, Cambridge, MA: MIT Press.

Barwise J. and J. Seligman, 1996, *Information Flow in Distributed Systems*, Cambridge: Cambridge University Press.

van Benthem J., 1986a, *Essays in Logical Semantics*, Dordrecht: Reidel.

van Benthem J., 1986b, 'The Ubiquity of Logic in Natural Language', in W. Leinfellner and F. Wuketits (eds.), 1986, *The Tasks of Contemporary Philosophy*, Schriftenreihe der Wittgenstein Gesellschaft, Vienna: Hölder-Pichler-Tempsky, 177–186.

van Benthem J., 1987, 'Meaning: Interpretation and Inference', *Synthese* 73:3, 451–470.

van Benthem J., 1988, 'Games in Logic', in J. Hoepelman (ed.), *Representation and Reasoning*, Tübingen: Niemeyer Verlag, pp. 3–15 and 165–168.

van Benthem J., 1989a, 'Logical Constants across Varying Types', *Notre Dame Journal of Formal Logic* 30:3, 315–342.

van Benthem J., 1989b, 'Semantic Parallels in Natural Language and Computation', in M. Garrido *et al.* (eds.), *Logic Colloquium. Granada 1987*, Amsterdam: North–Holland, pp. 331–375.

van Benthem J., 1991a, Editorial, *Journal of Logic and Computation* 1:3, 1–4.

van Benthem J., 1991b, *Language in Action: Categories, Lambdas and Dynamic Logic*, Amsterdam: North-Holland. [Paperback with Addenda, Cambridge, MA: MIT Press, 1995.]

van Benthem J., 1993, 'Modeling the Kinematics of Meaning', *Proceedings Aristotelean Society*, 93, 105–122.

van Benthem J., 1994, 'Dynamic Arrow Logic', in J. van Eyck and A. Visser (eds.), *Logic and Information Flow*, Cambridge, MA: MIT Press, pp. 15–29.

van Benthem J., 1996, *Exploring Logical Dynamics*, Stanford: CSLI Publications.

van Benthem J., 1997, 'Logic, Language and Information: The Makings of a New Science?', guest editorial, *Journal of Logic, Language and Information* 6:1, 1.

van Benthem J. and A. Ter Meulen (eds.), 1997, *Handbook of Logic and Language*, Amsterdam: Elsevier Science Publishers.

Bolzano B., 1837, *Wissenschaftslehre*, Sulzbach. (Translated by R. George as *Theory of Science*, Berkeley and Los Angeles: University of California Press, 1972.)

Gabbay D., 1996, *Labeled Deductive Systems*, New York: Oxford University Press.

Gabbay D. (ed.), 1994, *What is a Logical System?*, New York: Oxford University Press.

Gabbay D. and F. Guenthner (eds.), 1983–1989, *Handbook of Philosophical Logic*, Dordrecht: Reidel.

Gabbay D., C. Hogger, and J. Robinson (eds.), 1991–1995, *Handbook of Logic in Artificial Intelligence and Logic Programming*, New York: Oxford University Press.

Gärdenfors, P., 1988, *Knowledge in Flux. The Dynamics of Epistemic States*, Cambridge, MA: MIT Press.

Gärdenfors, P. and H. Rott, 1995, 'Belief Revision', a chapter in D. Gabbay, C. Hogger and J. Robinson (eds.), vol. IV, 35–132.

Groenendijk J. and M. Stokhof, 1991, 'Dynamic Predicate Logic', *Linguistics and Philosophy* 14, 39–100.

Hintikka J., 1973, *Logic, Language Games and Information*, Oxford: Clarendon Press.

Lakatos I., 1976, *Proofs and Refutations*, Cambridge: Cambridge University Press.

Ming Li and P. Vitanyi, 1993, *An Introduction to Kolmogorov Complexity and Its Applications*, New York: Springer-Verlag.

Makinson D., 1994, 'General Non-Monotonic Logic', a chapter in D. Gabbay, C. Hogger & J. Robinson (eds.), 1991.

Moschovakis Y., 1991, 'Sense and Reference as Algorithm and Value', Department of Mathematics, University of California, Los Angeles.

Muskens R., A. Visser, and J. van Benthem, 1997, 'Dynamics', a chapter in J. van Benthem and A. ter Meulen (eds.), 1997, pp. 587–648.

Nagel E., 1961, *The Structure of Science*, New York: Harcourt, Brace & World.

Sanchez Valencia V., 1991, *Studies on Natural Logic and Categorial Grammar*, Ph.D. thesis, Institute for Logic, Language and Information, University of Amsterdam.

Schröder-Heiser, P. and K. Dosen, (eds.), 1993, *Substructural Logics*, Oxford: Clarendon Press.

Sneed J., 1971, *The Logical Structure of Mathematical Physics*, Dordrecht: Reidel.

Tarski A., 1986, 'What are Logical Notions?', edited by J. Corcoran, *History and Philosophy of Logic* 7, 143–154.

Veltman F., 1996, 'Defaults in Update Semantics', *Journal of Philosophical Logic* 25, 221–261.

Venema Y., 1996, 'A Crash Course in Arrow Logic', in M. Marx, M. Masuch, and L. Pólos (eds.), *Arrow Logic and Multi-Modal Logic*, Stanford: CSLI Publications, pp. 3 34.

Institute for Logic, Language, and Computation
Universiteit van Amsterdam
Amsterdam, The Netherlands

☞ DIRK VAN DALEN
The Intuitionistic Conception of Logic

1. Introduction

If anything, the last decennia have brought the scientific world a proliferation of logics. Almost any calculus seems to be a logic. In order to remove possible confusion let us agree that by logic we mean the science or art of drawing correct conclusions. This definition leaves us enough room to incorporate most logics. The burden of this convention is carried by the adjective 'correct'. We might consider "correct according to the two-valued truth tables", or "correct according to the action of some machine". The latter is not as strange as it seems, the motivation of Girard's linear logic has certain features of the cigarette vending machine (Girard 1990).

In the present exposition we will look at 'correct' from the position of a constructivist, that is to say, we will require arguments to preserve 'constructive truth' or 'constructibility'. In the course of our discussion these expressions will be clarified.

The problem of constructive argument has been with us for over one-hundred years. It was Kronecker who insisted on effective constructions instead of abstract promises. One of his followers, Jules Molk, expressed the demands of the Kronecker school as follows: "definitions should be algebraic and not just logical. It is not sufficient to say: something is or is not". The central issue in the constructive tradition has always been 'existence', this notion was under pressure ever since Hilbert's miraculous proof of the existence of a finite basis for a class of invariants. It was the prototype of the so-called 'pure existence proofs'. Such proofs showed that something existed, without giving any indication how to find it. This technique had the advantage of simplicity, it provided short surveyable proofs; and it became the new standard in mathematics. Although the pure existence proofs caused some surprise, they were quickly incorporated in the arsenal of mathematical techniques. The event that caused the mathematical world to think twice about 'existence' was Zermelo's proof of the *well-ordering theorem*. Zermelo had shown that any set can be well-ordered; in the proof he relied on the *axiom of choice*. However, in the testcase of the continuum (the real line), nobody succeeded in defining the claimed well-ordering. Early constructivists, such as Borel, demanded that objects could only be granted an existence if they could be defined by finitely many words. None of them went, however, so far as to scrutinise the role of logic.

The first person to extend the criticism of abstract non-constructive practice in mathematics was L. E. J. Brouwer. In a revolutionary article, "The unreliability of the logical principles" (1908), he questioned the validity of the logical arguments. Already in his dissertation (1907) he had rejected the traditional place of logic in the context of mathematics. Whereas it was usually assumed that one needed logic in order to practice mathematics, Brouwer boldly reversed the order: 'Mathematics is independent of logic', but 'logic depends on mathematics'.

In constructive mathematics, one constructs the objects of mathematics and operates on large conglomerates of mathematical objects by means of constructive operations. A simple equation like $5 + 7 = 12$ is, for example, proved by first constructing 5, 7, and 12. Next the sum of 5 and 7 is constructed and the outcome is compared (by means of the comparison construction) with 12. The last-mentioned construction tells us that the left hand and right hand sides are equal.

For the *intuitionist* mathematical objects, such as numbers, triangles, functions, ..., are mental constructs. That is to say, we construct our own mathematical universe and hence we establish the properties of our mathematical objects also by means of constructions. Since the possibility of the constructions is on Brouwer's view anchored in the intuition of time, or mathematical ur-intuition (cf. Brouwer 1907, p. 8), he had coined the name 'intuitionism' for his particular philosophy and mathematics.[1]

Now we observe that the mathematical objects and its properties are described by language. In the use of the language of mathematics we observe

---

1. The term 'neo-intuitionism' has also been used for Brouwerian intuitionism.

certain regularities, which connect mathematical states of affairs. These regularities constitute logic, and the expressions of logic have a well-determined meaning in mathematics. It is a fact of experience that the language of mathematical logic is extremely modest; one needs a few connectives and quantifiers to describe almost all situations and procedures of mathematics. In fact it suffices to use '*and*' ($\wedge$), '*or*' ($\vee$), '*if ... then*' ($\rightarrow$), '*not*' ($\neg$), '*for all*' ($\forall$), and '*there exists*' ($\exists$).

2. Shaping Intuitionistic Mathematical Logic

Since logic leads in the hands of intuitionists to phenomena that markedly differ from that of classical two-valued logic, intuitionistic logic has to possess its own constructive interpretation. This interpretation, which is implicit in Brouwer's writings, was made explicit by Kolmogorov and Heyting. Heyting's interpretation is closest to Brouwer's (not surprisingly), Kolmogorov's interpretation is almost isomorphic to that of Heyting. To start with the *problem-interpretation* of Kolmogorov, we see that Kolmogorov considers mathematical statements as problems to be solved. A statement is true if it has a solution when considered as a problem. In terms of problems and solutions, one can give a meaning to the connectives: a solution of $A \wedge B$ is a pair (s_1, s_2) of solutions to A and to B; a solution of $\exists x A(x)$ is a pair (a, S) such that S is a solution of $A(a)$. Etc.

We will now consider Heyting's *proof-interpretation*. The basic idea is that a proof is a construction; this is in agreement with Brouwer's claim that the objects of mathematics are our own mental constructions. We have already met the construction that proves an atomic statement like '5 + 7 = 12'; it remains to explain the constructions that establish composite statements. The formulations are essentially parallel to those of Kolmogorov's problem-interpretation. E.g. a proof p of $A \rightarrow B$ is a construction that converts any proof q of A into a proof $p(q)$ of B; a proof of $\forall x A(x)$ is a construction that converts any element a of the domain under consideration into a proof of $A(a)$. The advantage of Heyting's formulation is that one needs only one kind of object, whereas Kolmogorov's interpretation requires two classes: solutions and operations.

We will introduce a suitable abbreviation in order to give a concise formulation of the proof-interpretation, also called the *Brouwer-Heyting-Kolmogorov (BHK) interpretation*. Let '$a : A$' stand for 'a is a proof for A'. Then the following table captures the interpretation of composite statements in terms of the interpretations of their parts. For convenience we use a few standard notations: (a_1, a_2) is the ordered pair of the objects a_1 and a_2, the particular codification is not important here. In the disjunction clause, the first component of (a_1, a_2) plays the role of case distinguisher: "if $a_1=0$ then ..., if $a_1=1$ then ...".

$a : A$	condition
$a : A \wedge B$	$a = (a_1, a_2)$, where $a_1 : A$ and $a_2 : B$
$a : A \vee B$	$a = (a_1, a_2)$, where $a_1 = 0$ and $a_2 : A$ or $a_1 = 1$ and $a_2 : B$
$a : A \rightarrow B$	for all p with $p : A$, $a(p) : B$
$a : \exists xA(x)$	$a = (a_1, a_2)$ and $a_2 : A(a_1)$
$a : \forall xA(x)$	for all $d \in D$, $a(d) : A(d)$, where D is a given domain
$a : \neg A$	for all $p : A$, $a(p): \bot$

For an intuitionist "A is true" means "A has a proof", i.e. "there is an a such that $a : A$". 'Constructive truth' thus means 'provability', albeit not formal provability. In order to interpret the negation of a statement A, we have to consider "the false statement". This rather elusive statement is not as exotic as one might think, it simply is a patently false statement, such as '0 = 1'. Let us use $\bot$ as a symbol for 'falsity'. Now intuitionists consider negation as an impossibility—as a 'negative' item. Thus 'not-A' is taken to stand for "from A a contradiction (i.e. $\bot$) can be derived." In symbols: $\neg A := A \rightarrow \bot$. Hence $a : \neg A$ if a is a construction that turns every proof p of A into a proof $a(p)$ of $\bot$. Now, $\bot$ has no proof—e.g., there is no construction that shows 0 = 1—so $a: \neg A$ stands for "if $p : A$ then $a(p): \bot$", hence A has no proof.

The reader should note that '$a : A$' can also be read as "a is a solution to A"; the clauses remain intact for the problem-interpretation. The clause for the disjunction indeed has the constructive character that one should expect: $A \vee B$ means more than "one of the two, but I don't know which one"—which is the usual interpretation. It requires that we can determine which of the two disjuncts is true (has a proof); one has only to check whether A or B is true.

This is the main reason why the *Principle of the Excluded Third* (PEM) fails constructively. Suppose $a: A \vee \neg A$, then $a = (a_1, a_2)$ and if $a_1 = 0$ then

$a_2 : A$, if $a_1 = 1$ then $a_2 : \neg A$, i.e., A has no proof. Since the actual possession of a proof, or at least an algorithm to get it, is the main thing, it is clear that in general we have no evidence for $A \vee \neg A$. It has always been an act of faith that a statement is true or its negation is true, but if one asks for positive evidence, there is little to offer. As Brouwer put it, the belief in the validity of PEM is an unwarranted extrapolation of its validity in finite domains—it is a historical artefact. He illustrated the dubious character of PEM as follows: consider some problem which has not yet been settled, e.g., "there is a sequence of 30 digits 9 in the decimal expansion of π".[2] If we take the above statement for A in PEM, then a proof of $A \vee \neg A$ should (1) decide between A and $\neg A$, and (2) for the chosen case provide a proof. I.e., we should either have a proof of "there exists a sequence ...", which means we should now indicate an index n, such that the decimals a_n through a_{n+30} are 9, or we should exhibit a proof that no such sequence can occur. At the present stage of mathematical development neither case is known to be true. So we cannot produce the requested proof. Hence there is no evidence for PEM.

The difference between a constructive and a non-constructive proof can best be observed in the case of existence statements. The following example nicely demonstrates the issue.

Claim: there are irrational numbers a and b such that a^b is rational.

Classical proof: Suppose the contrary. Then a^b is irrational for all irrationals a and b. In particular $\sqrt{2}^{\sqrt{2}}$ is irrational and therefore also $(\sqrt{2}^{\sqrt{2}})^{\sqrt{2}}$ is irrational. But $(\sqrt{2}^{\sqrt{2}})^{\sqrt{2}}=2$. Contradiction. Hence $\exists a,b \in \mathbb{R}-\mathbb{Q}\ (a^b \in \mathbb{Q})$. This is a proof by contradiction, it gives no clue as to the values of a and b, hence it cannot be accepted by an intuitionist. The claim happens to be intuitionistically correct, but it requires a good deal of number theory.

The actual development of intuitionistic logic took some time. Although Brouwer established the first theorem in intuitionistic propositional logic: $\neg\neg\neg A \rightarrow \neg A$ (1923),[3] he was not interested in the development of logic. A

---

2. Properties of the decimal expansion of π were for the first time considered by Brouwer in 1908. In the literature various "sequences in π" have been considered. The popular sequence 0123... 9 can no longer be used, see Brouwer 1908c, Borwein 1998.
3. In his terminology "Absurdity of absurdity of absurdity is equivalent to absurdity".

systematic development had to wait for Heyting's prize winning essay in 1928. The formalization was published in 1930 (Heyting 1930a, 1930b).

Heyting's formalization was not the first one; Kolmogorov had already in 1925 formalized a fragment of intuitionistic predicate logic with only $\to$, $\neg$, $\forall$, and $\exists$. In 1929 Glivenko had given an adequate formalization of propositional logic, moreover he established a striking connection between classical propositional logic and intuitionistic logic: $\vdash^c A \Leftrightarrow \vdash^i \neg\neg A$, where $\vdash^c$, $\vdash^i$ stand for "derivable in classical, resp. intuitionistic propositional logic".[4]

Heyting's formalization opened the way for metamathematical research of intuitionistic logic. The two major achievements of Heyting were his meticulous formalization and the formulation of the proof interpretation.[5] Progress, after Heyting, was made by Gentzen and Gödel. Both found structural properties of intuitionistic logic that made clear the rich possibilities of this particular logic.

By adding to Heyting's axioms a suitable non-intuitionistic principle, such as PEM or the *Double Negation Principle* (DNP), one obtains an axiom system for classical logic. Hence **IQC** (Intuitionistic Quantifier (Predicate) Calculus) is a sub-system of **CQC** (Classical Quantifier Calculus), similarly for the propositional versions **IPC** and **CPC**. Although Brouwer's informal arguments had shown that one could not expect PEM to be true intuitionistically, more was needed to show **IPC** $\nvdash A \vee \neg A$ in general. Heyting accomplished this in his 1930a, by means of a suitable three-valued truth table.

Heyting's goal at the time was a modest one: to give a systematic account of the logical formulas which are true under the intended proof interpretation. No completeness in the modern sense with respect to a particular semantics was intended. On the contrary, Heyting rejected the idea.

Intuitionistic mathematics, being a constructional activity, was not like axiomatic (or formal) mathematics in need of a consistency proof. Since the intuitionist deals directly with constructed or generated objects he never gets into the situation where $0 = 1$ (or a similar disaster) is the case, whereas the mathematician who plays a game with symbols, may by some inherent

---

4. Glivenko 1928, 1929. At the time of writing the latter paper Glivenko had seen Heyting's formalization, cf. Troelstra 1978.
5. Heyting 1930a, 1934. Heyting told me that he obtained his formalization by checking the axioms of the *Principia Mathematica*, and eliminating those that did not fit the intended (proof) interpretation.

fault stumble into 0 = 1. Hence intuitionistic mathematics was considered as the more dependable way of doing mathematics. The same held for intuitionistic logic, it was consistent by its nature. This extended to intuitionistic formalized arithmetic, as the axioms of arithmetic were justified by Heyting's interpretation. So the consistency of intuitionistic arithmetic was, rightly or wrongly, not in doubt, whereas the full force of Hilbert's program was directed at a consistency proof for classical arithmetic. This somewhat mysterious situation was clarified by Gödel, who provided translations of classical logic into intuitionistic logic. As Gödel's translation has become best known, we will spell out his translation. To each formula A of predicate logic we assign another formula A^o, its *Gödel translation*. The inductive definition runs as follows:

$\bot^o := \bot$

$A^o := \neg\neg A$ for atomic A distinct from $\bot$

$(A \wedge B)^o := A^o \wedge B^o$

$(A \vee B)^o := \neg(\neg A^o \wedge \neg B^o)$

$(A \to B)^o := A^o \to B^o$

$\forall x A(x) := \forall x A^o(x)$

$\exists x A(x) := \neg \forall x \neg A^o(x)$

In fact, if we erase the superscript the lefthand and righthand formulas are classically equivalent, but for an intuitionist the right hand formulas are weaker than the left hand formulas. For instance, for the atoms $\neg\neg A$ says that is impossible that A is not the case, or *it is impossible that we will never find* a proof, but that is not the same thing as *having* a proof. Similarly $\neg \forall x \neg A(x)$ says that it is impossible that $A(a)$ is false for all a, but that does not give us the a we were looking for. Hermann Weyl expressed something like this, which we roughly paraphrase as follows: a classical existence statement announces the presence of a treasure, without giving the precise location, thus it is of limited—mostly heuristic—value. An intuitionistic existence statement, on the other hand, really produces the treasure.

Gödel's translation takes a classically true statement and weakens it, so that it becomes intuitionistically correct. In symbols: $\vdash^c A \Leftrightarrow \vdash^i A^o$. In particular: $\mathbf{PA} \vdash^c \bot \Leftrightarrow \mathbf{HA} \vdash^i \bot$, but this is exactly the consistency property.[6] Hence Peano arithmetic, **PA**, is consistent if and only if intuitionistic arithmetic, **HA**, is consistent. It shows that as far as consistency is concerned intuitionistic formal systems are in general no better than their classical counterparts.

Gödel furthermore cleared up a point that in the thirties caused some confusion, namely, if one drops the principle of the excluded third, does one therefore accept an "excluded fourth"? To put it in another way, if one gives up the 0–1 truth tables, does one just move on to 3-valued (or possibly n-valued, for some n) logic? Gödel (1932) showed by a simple but clever argument that this is not the case: there are no n-valued truth tables that produce just the intuitionistically provable propositions.

3. Gentzen Systems and Proof Terms

So far the axiom-systems for logic had been modelled on the example of Euclid and Hilbert, that is to say, lots of axiom and few derivation rules. However, in logic one has to specify not only the axioms—the principles that one accepts—but also the means of getting new theorems from previously acquired ones. These means are laid down in so-called derivation rules. The principal example is *Modus Ponens*: from A and $A \to B$ derive B. In symbols: $A \to B, A \vdash B$ or $A \to B, A / B$.

In the so-called *Hilbert-type systems* one has few derivation rules (usually *Modus Ponens* and *Generalization*). Somehow these systems are not quite convenient for making actual derivations; some fairly simple propositions have long derivations. It was an ingenious move of Gerhardt Gentzen to introduce a radically different system, in which there were few axioms and lots of derivation rules. He formulated two systems: the *System of Natural Deduction* and the *Sequent Calculus*. Each system has its virtues; for our purpose the Natural Deduction system is best suited. It is a system with *no* axioms at all and for each connective two derivation rules, an introduction rule and an elimination rule. These rules are simple, they involve *only* the connective under consideration, and they specify (i) what one needs to know to infer the composite formula, (ii) what one may immediately infer from the

---

6. **PA** is obtained from **HA** by adding PEM.

composite formula. An example may serve better than an abstract description:

$$\wedge\text{-introduction} \quad \frac{A \quad B}{A \wedge B}$$

$$\wedge\text{-elimination} \quad \frac{A \wedge B}{A} \quad\quad \frac{A \wedge B}{B}$$

One has to know A and B in order to infer $A \wedge B$ (alternatively, A and B have to be given to justify $A \wedge B$, or one has to derive A and B in order to derive $A \wedge B$). The elimination rule tells us that if we know $A \wedge B$, we also know the conjuncts. Observe that there is a precise balance between the introduction and elimination rules. Nothing is lost, nothing is gained. The rules determine in an operational sense the meaning of the connectives (cf. Prawitz 1977).

One might wonder how the system succeeds in deriving theorems if there are no axioms. The redeeming feature of Natural Deduction is its capacity to cancel hypotheses. In order to facilitate the notation we will write $A_1, \ldots, A_n \vdash B$ for "there is a derivation of B from the hypotheses $A_1, \ldots, A_n$". The $\wedge$-introduction rule tells us in this notation $A, B \vdash A \wedge B$ and the elimination rule tells us $A \wedge B \vdash A$; $A \wedge B \vdash B$.

Let us now consider the most crucial propositional connective, $\rightarrow$. The elimination rule is none but our old Modus Ponens $A \rightarrow B, A \vdash B$. The introduction rule, however, presents us with a new feature: If $\Gamma, A \vdash B$, then $\Gamma \vdash A \rightarrow B$, where Γ is a finite set of formulas. In words: if from the hypotheses Γ and A the formula B is derivable, then from Γ alone $A \rightarrow B$ is derivable. Strange as it may seem, this is exactly our daily practice. Consider, for example, the well-known theorem of Euclid: if in a triangle two sides are equal, then the opposite angles are equal. In symbols $AC = BC \rightarrow A = B$. How do we prove this implication? By assuming that in the triangle ABC the sides AC and BC are equal, and then proceeding via a specific argument to show $A = B$. I.e. we show $\Gamma, AC = BC \vdash A = B$ and we abbreviate the result as $\Gamma \vdash AC = BC \rightarrow A = B$ (Γ is the set of Euclid's axioms). Thus Gentzen's systems cleverly exploits (or lays down, if you like) the meaning of the implication. We say that in the $\rightarrow$-introduction rule the hypothesis A is *cancelled*.

A gratifying aspect of Gentzen's Natural Deduction system is that it exactly fits the proof interpretation. Consider the ∧-rule. Let $a : A, b : B$; then $(a,b) : A \wedge B$, where (a,b) is some suitable pairing of the proofs a and b. So we can incorporate the proofs into the Gentzen notation:

$a : A, b : B \vdash (a, b) : A \wedge B$ and
$(a, b): A \wedge B \vdash a : A$
$(a, b): A \wedge B \vdash b : B$

In fact, a bit of extra notation may further simplify the exposition. We introduce in addition to the pairing operation (a, b), two projection operations π_1 and π_2, such that $\pi_1(a, b) = a$, $\pi_2(a, b) = b$, and $a = (\pi_1 a, \pi_2 a)$. Then the elimination rules look like:

$p : A \wedge B \vdash \pi_1(p) : A;\ p : A \wedge B \vdash \pi_2(p): B.$

Similarly we introduce an extra operation in order to handle the implication. Consider for example a term $x + y$, as used in ordinary algebra. We may consider this as a function in the variable x, this function is denoted by $\lambda x(x + y)$, say $f = \lambda x(x + y)$. We now evaluate f at (say) 5 by plugging in 5: $f(5) = 5 + y$. We see that f is a function that accepts numbers as inputs and yields (for each choice of y) numbers as outputs. We can make another step by applying λy (this is called λ-abstraction—it makes a function out of a term): $\lambda y(\lambda x(x + y))$. This new function takes numbers as inputs and yields functions as outputs. In general all kinds of input-output combinations are possible. There is a specific rule for the behaviour of λ-abstraction terms:

$\lambda x.t(x)(a) = t(a)$

This is called the rule of *lambda-conversion*. We will now show the connection between λ-conversion and implication:

If $\Gamma, x : A \vdash t(x) : B$ then $\Gamma \vdash \lambda x.t(x) : A \rightarrow B$.

This is the perfect analogue of the proof interpretation of the implication: the left hand says if x is an arbitrary proof of A (that is why we use a variable in $x : A$), then $t(x)$ is a proof of B. Hence $\lambda x.t(x)$ is an operation on proofs of A which yields a proof of B. This is exactly what we wanted for a proof of $A \rightarrow B$.

One can carry out a systematic correspondence between the rules of Natural Deduction and the clauses of the proof interpretation (cf. Troelstra and Dalen 1988, Girard *et al.* 1989). This correspondence was first observed

The Intuitionistic Conception of Logic 55

by Curry, and later systematically extended by Howard. It is called the "*propositions-as-types*", or Curry–Howard, interpretation.[7] The operations that are introduced above have, in fact, types: this prevents the danger of self-application—and all disastrous consequences. The typing of the operations can be read off for the simple case of implicational fragment of propositional logic, from the table below on the right-hand side. The name, propositions-as-types, may seem a bit strange, but there is a natural explanation. We have to return to the beginning of this century, at the time when mathematics was threatened by the paradoxes. Bertrand Russell looked for a solution to the Russell paradox by introducing a mathematical universe consisting of types. That is to say, he considered an immediately given collection of objects (e.g. the natural numbers), and next introduced the collection of all subsets. This step was iterated arbitrarily often, each time introducing objects of a higher type. One may do the same thing for functions: start with (say) the collection N of natural numbers, and continue by considering the class of all functions from $\mathbb{N}$ to $\mathbb{N}$. Now carry out this function-space formation for arbitrary function spaces already obtained. These function spaces are called types (or, one could say, 'have types'). A convenient, and suggestive notation for these types is borrowed from logic: the function space, or type, of functions from class A to a class B is denoted by $A \to B$. Alternative notations are B^A and $(B)A$. So $\mathbb{N} \to \mathbb{N}$ is the type of functions from $\mathbb{N}$ to $\mathbb{N}$, $\mathbb{N} \to (\mathbb{N} \to \mathbb{N})$ is the type of functions from $\mathbb{N}$ to $(\mathbb{N} \to \mathbb{N})$, etc.

Now there happens to be a perfect parallel between the pairs (proof, proposition) and (element, type) at least for implication. For full logic one has to add some more technical devices. Here is the parallel:

$a : A$	$a \in A$
a is a proof of A	a is an element of A
$a : A$	$a \in A$
$a : A, p : A \to B$ then $p(a) : B$	$a \in A, p \in A \to B$ then $p(a) \in B$
if $x : A \Rightarrow t(x) : B$ then $\lambda x.t(x) : A \to B$	if $x \in A \Rightarrow t(x) \in B$ then $\lambda x.t(x) \in A \to B$

---

7. Cf. Howard 1980, Bruijn 1995, Gallier 1995, de Groote (ed.) 1995.

By adding a pairing operation one can handle the other propositions in a similar, parallel way. Nowadays, the analogy between intuitionistic logic and type theory is satisfactorily worked out by a number of logicians, e.g. Martin-Löf, Girard, Coquand, Barendregt.[8]

There is a general feeling that logic influences mathematics, but that mathematics influences logic hardly, if not at all. This happens to be an artefact from classical mathematics. Classical predicate logic being complete for the standard two-valued truth tables leaves little opportunity for mathematics to make itself felt. In intuitionistic mathematics there are lots of examples of the influence of mathematics. Here are two:

1. The full axiom of choice implies PEM (Diaconescu).

    Since there is a very simple proof, let us have a look at it. Consider a proposition P. Define two sets A and B:
    $$A = \{n \in \mathbb{N} \mid n = 0 \vee (n = 1 \wedge P)\}$$
    $$B = \{n \in \mathbb{N} \mid n = 1 \vee (n = 0 \wedge P)\}$$

    Clearly $\forall X \in \{A, B\} \exists x \in \mathbb{N}(x \in X)$. If $\{A, B\}$ has a choice function f, then $f(A) \in A$, $f(B) \in B$ and $f(A) = f(B) \vee f(A) \neq f(B)$, because f takes natural numbers as values and for those equality is decidable. $f(A) = f(B)$ implies P and $f(A) - f(B)$ implies $A \neq B$ (extensionality), and hence $\neg P$. This shows $P \vee \neg P$.

2. Apartness and inequality on the reals are equivalent iff Markov's Principle holds. Here Markov's Principles is formulated for decidable predicates (Cf. Troelstra and van Dalen 1988, p. 205):
    $$\forall x(A(x) \vee \neg A(x) \wedge \neg \neg \exists x A(x) \rightarrow \exists x A(x).$$

In intuitionistic logic there is a specific phenomenon that has been the cause of some surprise, the closure under derivation rules. We have seen that $\vdash \exists x A(x) \rightarrow \vdash A(t)$ for a suitable term (cf. van Dalen 1997a, §6.3). However, $\exists x A(x) \vdash A(t)$ may fail for all t. We express the above by saying that **IQC** is closed under the rule $\exists x A(x) \vdash A(t)$.

---

8. Barendregt 1992, Martin-Löf 1984, Coquand and Huet 1988, Girard et al. 1989, Howard 1980, Troelstra and van Dalen 1988.

Closure under rules is particularly interesting for realistic theories, such as intuitionistic arithmetic, **HA**. Here are some examples.

1. Closure under Church's rule:
   HA ⊢ ∀x∃yA(x, y) ⇒ **HA** ⊢ ∀xA(x, {e}x) for a suitable e.
   I.e. if **HA** proves a ∀∃ statement, then there is a recursive function that picks the right y values.

2. Closure under Markov's rule:
   HA ⊢ ∀x(A(x) ∨ ¬A(x)) ∧ ¬¬∃xA(x) ⇒ **HA** ⊢ ∃xA(x).
   Markov's principle is a general formulation of the idea that if it is impossible that a Turing machine on a certain input never halts, then it halts.

3. Closure under the rule of Independence of Premiss Principle:
   HA ⊢ ∀x(A(x) ∨ ¬A(x)) ∧ ∀xA(x) → ∃yB(y) ⇒ **HA** ⊢ ∃y(∀xA → B(y))

   (cf. Smorynski 1973, pp. 366, 369; Troelstra and van Dalen 1988, p. 507).

4. Choice Aspects

So far we have dealt with the effective aspects of the intuitionistic universe. There is, however, one particular feature that makes intuitionism different from most versions of constructivism. It was introduced by Brouwer in 1918. Since intuitionistic mathematics is a more or less freely developing mental activity of the individual, it makes sense to allow for infinite sequences that are chosen (more or less) freely. Indeed, the notion is an almost inescapable consequence of Brouwer's philosophical construction of the universe. In his early writings, and again in the Vienna Lectures he points out that the subject experiences sequences of sensations;[9] there is a certain identification of 'similar' sequences, and the more stable ones (i.e. the ones that are not or little depending on free will) play the role of objects. The sequences modulo the above mentioned identification go by the name of *causal sequences*. Since there is no reason whatsoever that these causal sequences are ruled by laws—on the contrary they are partly the product of actions of the free will—the notion of infinite sequence is from the begin-

---

9. Cf. Brouwer 1907, pp. 81 ff.; Brouwer 1929, p. 153; Brouwer 1949, p. 1235. See also van Dalen 1999 for motivation and background material.

ning open-ended. From the causal sequences to mathematical choice sequences is but one step. It is of the greatest importance to note that here there is a clear-cut break with tradition. So far all foundational considerations had led to the conclusion that the infinity of a sequence $a_0, a_1, a_2, a_3, \ldots, a_n, \ldots$ would only be guaranteed by a law (Borel, Hölder, Weyl): Brouwer placed the burden of the responsibility for infinity at the individual's doorstep. It is the individual who guarantees or promises that he will go on producing new members of the sequence.

The basic question is how to exploit choice sequences mathematically. Some uses are unproblematic, e.g. consider two sequences (a_n) and (b_n) of rational numbers which determine two real numbers a and b (so-called Cauchy sequences). The sum of a and b is determined by the sequence $(a_n + b_n)$. Such uses are, however, too specific to bring out the characteristic feature of choice sequences. Brouwer discovered in 1916 how to make use of the choice-feature of infinite sequences (say of natural numbers). Suppose one has a function F operating on choice sequences and yielding natural numbers as outputs. Then for each choice sequence α the value $F(\alpha)$ is a natural number n that can be computed in finitely many steps. Now, since in general a limited amount of information about α is added at each next choice step (not the total infinite behaviour, unless you are very lucky), the output is determined when only an initial segment of α has been produced, and the value $F(\alpha)$ is determined by this initial segment. Hence two choice sequences α and β which share this particular initial segment yield the same output. In order to formulate this idea in mathematical logic, let us introduce some notation: $\overline{\alpha}(k)$ denotes the sequence $(\alpha(0), \alpha(1), \ldots \alpha(k-1))$ (the initial segment of length k). The above considerations tell us that F is determined by another function, say f, which operates on initial segments as follows:

$$\forall \alpha \exists k (F(\alpha) = f(\overline{\alpha}(k)))$$

and hence

$$\forall \alpha \exists k \forall \beta (\overline{\alpha}(k) = \overline{\beta}(k) \rightarrow F(\alpha) = F(\beta))$$

This is Brouwer's *continuity principle for functions*. A similar argument yields the general continuity principle:

$$\forall \alpha \exists x A(\alpha, x) \rightarrow \forall \alpha \exists x \exists k \, \forall \beta (\overline{\alpha}(k) = \overline{\beta}(k) \rightarrow A(\beta, x))$$

That is to say, if for all choice sequences α there is a number x such that $A(\alpha, x)$ holds, then there is an x that only depends on an initial segment of α.

The continuity principle for functions is introduced in Brouwer 1918, p. 13, in just four lines without any comment, even without a name! Brouwer used the principle to show that the set of choice sequences is not denumerable. The argument is simple: let F be a function from the set if choice sequences ($\mathbb{N}^{\mathbb{N}}$) to the natural numbers ($\mathbb{N}$), then for each $\alpha \in \mathbb{N}^{\mathbb{N}}$ there is a k such that all β's which have the same initial segment $\bar{\alpha}(k)$ yield the same value $F(\alpha)$. Hence F cannot be a bijection (is not one-one). This proof replaced the traditional diagonal argument of Cantor.

In 1924 Brouwer further analyzed the behaviour of functions on choice sequences, and, by implication, real functions. On the basis of a conceptual argument he obtained a form of transfinite induction, called *bar-induction*. Only after the formalization of intuitionistic logic by Kleene and Kreisel, the principle got its perspicuous form. We will just consider one particular variant here, the *Principle of Monotone Bar Induction* (BIM):

$$\left. \begin{array}{ll} \forall \alpha \exists x\, A(\alpha(x)) & \text{(bar)} \\ \forall n \forall m (A(n) \to A(n * m)) & \text{(mon)} \\ \forall n (\forall x A(n * (x)) \to A(n)) & \text{(prog)} \end{array} \right\} \Rightarrow \forall n A(n)$$

In the above formulation m and n stand for (coded) finite sequences, $m * n$ stands for the concatenation of two finite sequences m and n, (x) stands for the sequence consisting of the single element x.

In order to get a feeling for the principle, it is convenient to use a geometric metaphor: finite sequences of natural numbers are partially ordered by the relation 'initial segment of', thus the set of all finite sequences of natural numbers forms a partially ordered set, more specifically a tree. That is, there is a top node (element), the empty sequence, and from each node one can get in a finite number of (immediate predecessor-) steps to the top. This particular tree is called the universal tree. We will think of the tree as going downwards.

A choice sequence gives us an infinite path through the tree.[10] A bar in the tree is a set of nodes that 'bar' all the paths, that is, each infinite path

---

10. The set of infinite paths through the universal tree in fact is a topological space with basic open sets "all paths through a given node". This topological space goes by the name of Baire space. It certainly is no coincidence that Brouwer's basic principles for choice sequences are topological in nature.

passes through a node of the bar, think of a set that somehow runs from left to right, intersecting all paths. Imagine that $A(n)$ is the predicate 'red'. Then the bar condition tells us that every choice sequence will eventually pass through a red node of the tree. The monotonicity condition says that all nodes below a red node are red. The progressive-condition inverts this: if all nodes immediately below n are red, then n is red. The three conditions together imply that the whole tree is red. Kleene, Kreisel and Troelstra considered a number of variants of the principle of bar induction. Kleene showed how delicate the formulations are, one wrong move and one gets a contradiction (Kleene and Vesley 1965, p. 112; Troelstra and van Dalen 1988, p. 220).

There is an intimate and obvious connection between bar induction and transfinite induction (cf. Howard and Kreisel 1966), indeed the condition *bar* says that the non-red nodes form a well-founded tree within the big tree. The connection between well-founded trees and ordinals is familiar (cf. Shoenfield 1967); it was already observed by Brouwer in his early papers (Brouwer 1918b).

The principle of bar induction yielded a simple proof of the *fan theorem*:

Consider a finitely branching tree (a finitary tree, or *fan*), then:

$$\forall \alpha \exists x (A(\overline{\alpha}(x))) \rightarrow \exists z \forall \alpha \exists y \leq z \, A(\overline{\alpha}(y))$$

In words: if in a fan each infinite path α hits a red node, then there is a finite depth such that there is a red bar above it. Or, alternatively, if $A(\overline{\alpha}(x))$ is read as "the sequence α is cut at moment x", then the fan theorem says that if all paths α are eventually cut, at a certain depth all paths have been cut.

In topological terms, the fan theorem simply says that the natural topology on a fan is compact. Observe that the contraposition of the fan theorem is *König's infinity lemma*: in an infinite fan there is an infinite path. König's lemma is intuitionistically not correct, neither is its counterpart in analysis, the Bolzano-Weierstrass theorem. Brouwer showed, using the fan theorem, that the continuum is locally compact, and that every real-valued function on a compact subset of $\mathbb{R}$ is uniformly continuous. This is the famous locally uniform continuity theorem (Brouwer 1924). For the details the reader is referred to Troelstra and van Dalen 1988, vol. 1.

The moral of the above is that formalized intuitionistic mathematics was at the first-order level a subsystem of the classical system (in particular in arithmetic), but at the second-order level major departures from classical mathematics occurred. The notion of choice sequence forced certain principles on the theory, that contradicted classical mathematics. Here is a small example. In the classical system one has: $\forall \alpha(\exists x(\alpha(x) = 0) \vee \forall x(\alpha(x) \neq 0))$. One can reformulate this as: $\forall \alpha \exists! y[(y = 0 \wedge \exists x(\alpha(x) = 0)) \vee (y = 1 \wedge \forall x(\alpha(x) \neq 0))]$. So there is a function F with:

$$F(\alpha) = \begin{cases} 0 \text{ if } \alpha \text{ produces a } 0 \\ 1 \text{ else} \end{cases}$$

According to Brouwer's continuity theorem this F must be continuous, but that is impossible: consider $F(\lambda x.1) = 1$. Continuity of F tells us that there is an initial segment $(1,1, \ldots 1)$ such that all continuations β of the segment yield $F(\beta) = 1$, i.e. no extension of $(1, 1, \ldots, 1)$ can have a 0. Quod non. So here the classical and intuitionistic systems clearly diverge.

The continuity principle in combination with bar induction gave intuitionistic second-order arithmetic (this system with choice sequences is usually called *analysis*) considerable strength, which confused Brouwer's contemporaries who thought intuitionistic mathematics to be essentially a fragment of classical mathematics. There is significant distinction between second-order logic (arithmetic) with function variables and with set variables. The reason is that sets have little constructive content, they are basically as good or as bad as propositional logic. One may consider $S = \{x \in 0 | A\}$. If A holds $S = \{0\}$, if A is false $S = \emptyset$, but in general one can say just as little about S as about A. The subsets of $\{0\}$ (or any singleton set) correspond to the propositions modulo logical equivalence. So $\mathcal{P}(\{0\})$ can be considered as the set of truth values of intuitionistic propositional logic. For this reason sets, say of natural numbers, are considerably 'wilder' than functions. Hence it is no surprise that the familiar correspondence between functions and sets breaks down: also decidable sets have characteristic functions. For if $\forall x[(x \in S \leftrightarrow f(x) = 1) \wedge x \notin S \leftrightarrow f(x) = 0)]$, then the existence of such a characteristic function f implies, in view of the fact that equality on $\mathbb{N}$ is decidable (i.e. $\forall xy (x = y \vee x \neq y)$, $\forall x(f(x) = 0 \vee f(x) \neq 0)$ and hence $\forall x(x \in S \vee x \notin S)$. Indeed, the elusive character of the subsets of a given set is the motivation for *Troelstra's Uniformity Principle* for subsets of $\mathbb{N}$:

$\forall X \exists x A(A,x) \rightarrow \exists x \forall X A(X, x)$.

The traditional counterexample, $x = 0$ if $X = \emptyset$ and $x = 1$ if $X \neq \emptyset$, does not work here, because it is undecidable whether X is empty, hence the existence of the claimed x cannot be shown!

Beyond second-order arithmetic, there are the various theories of higher-types and of intuitionistic set theory. Arithmetic of all finite types is a direct descendant of Gödel's theory **T**, which, so to speak, is the logic-free part of higher-type arithmetic. Gödel introduced in (Gödel 1958) functionals of finite types as a tool for a constructive interpretation of arithmetic. He used a logical translation of **HA** into type theory, and by a final elimination of the quantifiers, he obtained equations in the higher-type calculus **T**. Given the intuitive constructive character of these functionals, a consistency proof was obtained. The particular interpretation is known as the Dialectica Interpretation. In Troelstra (1973) the proof theory of the functional interpretations is extensively elaborated.

5. Semantics

From a metamathematical viewpoint, intuitionistic logic is a subsystem of classical logic, hence it should have more models (interpretations). This presented a serious problem: the familiar Tarski semantics was so geared to classical logic, that it automatically validated PEM. So an extension of the notions of model became necessary. The earliest, and most obvious, approach to this problem was via truth tables. One such construction was provided by Jaskowski in 1936. Another semantics was introduced by Tarski in 1935 (see Tarski 1938). He generalized the Boolean-algebra semantics to the algebra of open sets of a topological space. The trick is to mimic the Boolean interpretation, taking care to stay within the collections of open sets by taking interiors of sets whenever necessary. Let us use $Int(U)$ for the interior of U, and U^c for the complement of U. The interpretation of propositional logic in a topological space X, with the collection $\mathcal{O}(X)$ of open sets is given by:

$$[\![\bot]\!] = \emptyset$$
$$[\![A \wedge B]\!] = [\![A]\!] \cap [\![B]\!]$$
$$[\![A \vee B]\!] = [\![A]\!] \cup [\![B]\!]$$
$$[\![A \to B]\!] = Int([\![A]\!]^c \cup [\![B]\!])$$
$$[\![\neg A]\!] = [\![A]\!]^c$$

The interpretation is extended to predicate calculus logic by putting

$$[\![\forall x A(x)]\!] = Int(\cap_{d \in D}[\![A(d)]\!])$$

$$[\![\exists x A(x)]\!] = \cup_{d \in D}[\![A(d)]\!]$$

where D is the given domain. A sentence A is true under the interpretation if $[\![A]\!] = X$.

The topological interpretation allows one to manufacture simple counterexamples to non-intuitionist, classical tautologies. Here are some examples. Consider $[\![A]\!] = \mathbb{R} - \{0\}$; then $[\![\neg A]\!] = Int(\{0\}) = \emptyset$ and $[\![\neg\neg A]\!] = \mathbb{R}$. Observe that $[\![B \to C]\!] = \mathbb{R}$ iff $Int([\![B]\!]^c \cup [\![C]\!]) = \mathbb{R}$, i.e. $[\![B]\!] \subseteq [\![C]\!]$. So we see that $\neg\neg A \to A$ is not true in this model. Similarly $[\![A \vee \neg A]\!] = \mathbb{R} - \{0\} \neq \mathbb{R}$.

The extension of Tarski's topological interpretation was given by Mostowski 1948. In view of the algebraic character of the topological interpretation, it comes as no surprise that, in analogy to Boolean algebras, algebras for intuitionistic logic turned up (see Stone 1937). Nowadays these algebras are called *Heyting algebras*. A thorough treatment of interpretations by means of Heyting algebras and topological spaces was given by Rasiowa and Sikorski 1963, see also (Johnston 1982).

In spite of their elegance, the above-mentioned interpretations could not match the 0–1 interpretation for classical logic, as a philosophically motivated technique. The first significant improvement in this respect was given by Beth in 1956. He considered trees (or partially ordered sets) with certain truth value assignments. This so-called *Beth-semantics* was more or less put in the shadow by a similar semantics formulated by Kripke in 1963. Since Kripke's semantics is somewhat simpler, we will consider it instead of Beth's original notion. The heuristics for Kripke's semantics is provided by Brouwer's notion of the *creating subject* (see below): represent the stages of constructive activity of the individual by nodes in a partially ordered set, where '<' stands for 'later'. The individual is carrying out two activities simultaneously, he constructs new objects and establishes new facts about his universe. There is a simple assumption: no objects are destroyed and no basic facts are forgotten.

In order to allow an efficient presentation, we need some notation: $(K, \leq)$ is a partially ordered set, the elements are denoted by $k, l, \ldots, k_0, k_1, \ldots, l_1, l_2,$ .... For each $k \in K$ there is a traditional structure, i.e. a domain with relations and total functions, denoted by $\mathfrak{U}_k$. It is understood that the similarity type (signature) is fixed

$$\mathfrak{U}_k = \langle |\mathfrak{U}_k|, R_{1k}, R_{2k}, ..., f_{1k}, f_{2k}, ..., c_{1k}, ... \rangle$$

The structures have the same constants. "The individual knows the sentence A at stage k" is denoted by '$k \Vdash A$'. The above mentioned monotonicity aspects of domains and basic facts is rendered by the following conditions:

for $k \leq l$ we have

i. $|\mathfrak{U}_k| \subseteq |\mathfrak{U}_l|$
ii. $R_{ik} \subseteq R_{il}$
iii. $f_{ik} \subseteq f_{il}$

This collection of structures, indexed by a partially ordered set and satisfying the monotonicity condition, is called a *Kripke model*. The structures $\mathfrak{U}_k$ are often called (possible) worlds.

It now remains to define "A holds in world k", in symbols '$k \Vdash A$', for all sentences A:

$k \Vdash A$	conditions
$k \Vdash A$, for atomic A	$A_k \vDash A$ (in the sense of Tarski)
$k \Vdash A \wedge B$	$k \Vdash A$ and $k \Vdash B$
$k \Vdash A \vee B$	$k \Vdash A$ or $k \Vdash B$
$k \Vdash A \rightarrow B$	for all $l \leq k$, $l \Vdash A \Rightarrow l \Vdash B$
$k \Vdash \exists x A(x)$	there exists an $a \in |\mathfrak{U}_k|$ such that $k \Vdash A(a)$
$k \Vdash \forall x A(x)$	for all $l \leq k$ and all $a \in |\mathfrak{U}_l|$, $l \Vdash A(a)$

By definition we put $k \Vdash \neg A \Leftrightarrow k \Vdash A \rightarrow \bot$, where, of course, for no k, $k \Vdash \bot$. The analogy with the proof interpretation is not exact, in the sense that the 'uniformity' in, for example, the clause for implication is hidden. The subject 'knows', so to speak, that if in the future evidence for A turns up, evidence for B will automatically follow.

Kripke models are very flexible, and convenient for metamathematical purposes. For a quick demonstration, let us give some counterexamples to classical tautologies. Observe that $k \Vdash \neg A$ means that at no later stage A will be established. So $k \Vdash \neg\neg A$ means that at no later stage l, we will have $l \Vdash \neg A$, therefore there must be a stage $m \geq l$, at which A holds. That is, $k \Vdash \neg\neg A \Leftrightarrow \geq \forall l \geq k \exists m \geq l (m \Vdash A)$. Now we can simply refute the double negation law: consider a model with two nodes k, l and $k < l$, assume that for an atom A, $k \nVdash A$ and $l \Vdash A$ (this is just part of the specification of the particular model). Then $k \Vdash \neg\neg A$, and hence $k \nVdash \neg\neg A \to A$. The same model shows that $k \nVdash A \vee \neg A$, for $k \nVdash A$ and $k \nVdash \neg A$.

It is a little bit more complicated to get a countermodel for the following instance of De Morgan's law: $\neg(A \wedge B) \to \neg A \vee \neg B$. Consider a model with three nodes, k, l, m, where $k < l$ and $k < m$, but l and m are incomparable. Now put $l \Vdash A$ and $m \Vdash B$, then for no node $A \wedge B$ holds, so $k \Vdash \neg(A \wedge B)$. But if $k \Vdash \neg A \vee \neg B$, we should have $k \Vdash \neg A$ or $k \Vdash \neg B$. Neither is the case, according to the definition. So $k \nVdash \neg(A \wedge B) \to (\neg A \vee \neg B)$.

For all of the above-mentioned semantics there are completeness theorems, in the sense that **IPC** $\vdash A$ iff A holds in all models of the specified class: cf. Rasiowa and Sikorski 1963, Kripke 1965, Fitting 1969, van Dalen 1997a, Troelstra and van Dalen 1988, Smorynski 1973. The semantic methods lend themselves to a large variety of metamathematical results (which often had been obtained previously by other methods).

The above semantics were further exploited to investigate second-order theories, e.g. arithmetic with set variables (**HAS**), arithmetic with choice-sequence variables (analysis), the theory of the reals, topology, etc. Dana Scott extended in 1968 the topological interpretation to a model for the intuitionistic continuum (cf. Scott 1968, 1970). Jan Moschovakis (1973) adopted Scott's methods to give a topological interpretation of intuitionistic analysis in Kleene's formalization, van Dalen 1974 did the same thing for **HAS**; a model for analysis in Beth semantics followed in van Dalen 1978. In a sense, these papers can be seen as predecessors of a more general sheaf semantics introduced by Scott in the seventies (Fourman and Scott 1979). The sheaf models introduced a novelty, that so far had been beyond existing formalizations and semantics: 0existence as a predicate and partial operations.

In order to understand the need for such novelties, one has to go back to ordinary arithmetic on the reals. Addition, subtraction, and multiplication present no problem, but the inverse asks for some caution. One of the methods mathematicians use to define real numbers from the rational numbers is that of the *Cauchy sequences*; a real number is defined by a 'converging sequence' of rationals, that is to say, one requires that for the sequence (a_i) the following holds: $\forall k \exists n \forall m > n (|a_n - a_m| < 2^{-k})$. In order to invert a real number a, given by a Cauchy sequence (a_n), one usually simply inverts all the a_n's (except those identical to 0). Classically that is good enough, because if $a \neq 0$, then from a certain n on all a_n's are distinct from 0. Intuitionistically, there is a problem; one can very well imagine a real number a, distinct from 0, without having any guarantee that (a_n^{-1}) is again a Cauchy sequence, that is to say, the convergence of (a_n^{-1}) is problematic. In fact it can only be established if from a certain index on all $(|a_n|)$ are greater than a fixed positive rational number. This notion of 'strongly distinct from 0' is traditionally called "apart from 0". The conditions for invertibility is formulated as $\exists x(a \cdot x = 1) \Leftrightarrow a\#0$. Hence, the inverse is essentially a partial operator, it is only defined for reals apart from zero. And $a\#0$ is not decidable. The classical trick of making the inverse total does therefore not work here.[11]

So, an existence predicate makes sense. Let us write $E(x)$ for "x exists", then $Ea^{-1} \Leftrightarrow a\#0$. Of course, the addition of an existence predicate to logic requires an overhaul of the system. One has to revise the theory of identity in order to respect the basic tenet that only existing objects can be identical. Hence one would require $x = y \to Ex \land Ey$. There are similar changes for quantification, $\exists x A(x)$ means that there has to be an *existing* object a such that $A(a)$. This suggests a modified existence introduction rule: $A(a) \land E(a) \vdash \exists x A(x)$. Similarly, one universally quantifies over existing objects: $\forall x A(x), E(a) \vdash A(a)$. For a complete exposition see Scott 1979, Troelstra and van Dalen 1988.

The sheaf semantics fits this approach to existence like a glove. Consider, for example, all continuous functions with open domain in $\mathbb{R}$. They can be considered as entities in their own right, and they can be put into relation with each other, they can be pointwise added, multiplied etc. In short, they behave as the reals themselves. Now, obviously, such a partial function 'exists only on its domain', therefore it is plausible to put $Ea = \{t \in \mathbb{R} | a(t)$ is defined$\}$. Now if we put $[\![a\#0]\!] = \{t \subset \mathbb{R} | a(t) \neq 0\}$ (which is an open set!), then a simple calculation shows us that $[\![Ea^{-1} \leftrightarrow a\#0]\!] = \mathbb{R}$. The objects in these models, in general, exist only partially. This has consequences for the theory of identity. The connection between identity and existence can be formulated "objects are identical to themselves precisely in as far as they

---

11. Classically one may say "a^{-1} is the unique b such that $ab = 1$ if $a \neq 0$, and 0 else".

exist": ⊨ $a = a \leftrightarrow Ea$ (cf. Scott 1979, Troelstra and van Dalen 1988, pp. 50ff., 709ff.).

The sheaf semantics has brought out a number of characteristic features of intuitionistic systems. There is, for example, a quite simple demonstration that the real numbers defined via Cauchy sequences, are different from those defined by Dedekind cuts (cf. Fourman and Hyland 1979, Grayson 1981); as a consequence the axiom of countable choice fails in sheaf models over suitable connected topological spaces. Similarly, it is quite straightforward to show the failure of the fundamental theorem of algebra in the model over $\mathbb{R}^2$ (Fourman and Hyland 1979). Thus there are polynomials that do not have zeros in the complex numbers, this seems in conflict with Brouwer's earlier proof of that theorem, but Brouwer made tacitly use of the countable axiom of choice.

Sheaves, however, are not the end point of our tour of the world of semantics. It turns out that the collection of sheaves on a topological space carries a natural higher-order structure: one can define power sheaves, function space sheaves, etc. In technical terms: sheaves on a space form a topos. That is to say, it is a special kind of category with convenient closure properties. To be precise, a topos is a category with all finite limits and a subobject classifier. Since we will not go into the categorical side of intuitionistic logic, we refer the reader for a comprehensive treatment to Lambek and Scott 1986, MacLane and Moerdijk 1992.

An important feature of topos theory and its categorical interpretation of intuitionistic logic, is that it offers a unifying approach to all semantics that have been formulated before. The topological interpretation, the sheaf semantics, the Beth and Kripke semantics, all represent specific topos constructions. There is even a particular interpretation that has not been discussed so far, and that more or less to the surprise of earlier researchers, fits nicely into the categorical framework. A topos can be viewed as an example of the (or 'a') intuitionistic universe, and the categorical properties are closely tied to the logical properties.

The flexibility of the general sheaf-semantics was demonstrated by Moerdijk, who constructed a specific model in which the so-called lawless sequence found a natural interpretation (Hoeven and Moerdijk 1984). The first semantic interpretation of lawless sequences was given by Van Dalen in a Beth semantics (which happens to be eminently suited for analysis interpretations). (See van Dalen 1978).

Lawless sequence go back a long way. Brouwer mentioned the idea (without the name) in a letter to Heyting (26.4.1924, Troelstra 1982). Kreisel 1962 introduced the notion in the literature. A sequence is lawless if at any stage of the generation only the given initial segment is known; there are and will be no restrictions on future choices. Depending on one's view, the connection between various lawless sequences may or may not be allowed. The simplest version does not allow for an interplay between lawless sequences. So when a certain sequence α is lawless, the sequence β with $\beta(2n) = \alpha(2n + 1)$, $\beta(2n + 1) = \alpha(2n)$, cannot be considered as lawless, since it is not completely free with respect to the context.

Lawless sequences were used to give intuitionistic versions of the logical completeness theorem (Kreisel 1962, Troelstra and van Dalen 1988, Ch. 13). Furthermore, because of their simple nature, they lent themselves perfectly for the investigation (refutation) of classical tautologies. The consistency of the theory was established proof theoretically long before the first semantics was found. Kreisel discovered that in a sufficiently strong theory of analysis one could eliminate lawless sequences by means of a translation. The technique was later extended to wider families of choice sequences (Kreisel and Troelstra 1970).

One should not get the impression that all semantics of intuitionistic theories take place under artificial circumstances. Indeed, one can use a Tarski-style semantics, giving the connectives their intended constructive interpretation. Some results show that a worthwhile model theory can be developed. E.g. van Dalen 1992 showed that $\mathbb{R}$, $\mathbb{Q}^c$, $\mathbb{Q}^{cc}$ (the negative irrationals and the not-not rationals) are elementarily equivalent with respect to <, #, =.

The topological sheaf semantics has many, if not all, characteristics of a universe with choice sequences. There happens also to be a specific topos that reflects the algorithmic aspects of constructive mathematics.

6. Recursive functions and Intuitionistic Logic

In 1945 Kleene presented a specific interpretation of intuitionistic arithmetic, called *(Recursive) realizability*. The underlying idea was that the "truth" of a statement should be established by algorithms. For example, if one had an algorithm that 'established' A and another one that 'established' B, the pair would establish $A \wedge B$. Since one would need algorithms operating on algorithms, it was natural to consider partial recursive func-

The Intuitionistic Conception of Logic 69

tions (or Turing machines), for each such function f has a description which can be coded as a natural number, usually called the index of f, and instead of having an algorithm operate on an algorithm, one can simulate this effect by letting a partial recursive function operate on the index of another such function.

Following the tradition we will denote "the function with index e applied to the number n" as $\{e\}(n)$. Observe that $\{e\}(n)$ may be undefined (think of a Turing machine getting into a loop), so some care is required—for example by calling in the help of the existence predicate. Instead of 'n establishes A' we will say 'n realizes A'. Now here is a way to handle implication: e realizes $A \to B$ iff for any a which realizes A, $\{e\}(a)$ realizes B. In spite of the similarity of this clause to the proof-interpretation, Kleene took his cue from Hilbert-Bernays, rather than from Heyting, cf. Kleene 1973. The notion 'n realizes A' is inductively defined below.

Note that in arithmetic closed atoms are decidable (just compute the left and right hand side of the equation), so the initial clause is offered for free. $(n)_0$ and $(n)_1$ are the two projections of the standard pairing function $\langle p, q \rangle$ (i.e., $(\langle p, q \rangle)_0 = p$, $(\langle p, q \rangle)_1 = q$, $\langle (n)_0, (n)_1 \rangle = n$).

$n\mathbf{r}A$	condition
$n\mathbf{r}A$, A atomic	a is true
$n\mathbf{r}A \wedge B$	$(n)_0\mathbf{r}A$ and $(n)_1\mathbf{r}B$
$n\mathbf{r}A \vee B$	$(n)_0 = 0 \Rightarrow (n)_1\mathbf{r}A$ and $(n)_0 \neq 0 \Rightarrow (n)_1 B$
$n\mathbf{r}A \to B$	for all m, $m\mathbf{r}A \Rightarrow \{n\}m\mathbf{r}B$
$n\mathbf{r}\exists xA(x)$	$(n)_1\mathbf{r}A((n_0))$
$n\mathbf{r}\forall xA(x)$	for all m, $\{n\}(m)\mathbf{r}A(m)$

Surprising as it may seem, the idea worked: $\mathbf{HA} \vdash A \Rightarrow n\mathbf{r}A$ for some n. There is no total success in the sense that the interpretation is complete: there are realizable statements which are not provable in $\mathbf{HA}$. One particularly important such statement is *Church's Thesis*. In computability theory the thesis of Church claims that every numerical algorithm can be simulated by a Turing machine, or a recursive function. It is truly a thesis in the sense that it connects an informal concept—computability—with a precise mathematical notion—recursivity (or Turing computability). One can either reject the thesis by presenting an acknowledged algorithm, which cannot be simulated by a Turing machine, or one can give conceptual arguments in favour of the thesis. The latter was done by Alan Turing in his 1937. Nonetheless, the thesis can never get the status of a theorem. The precise extent of the realizable statements of arithmetic was established by Troelstra in his axiomatization (1973).

In constructive mathematics one can do a little bit better by reflecting on the meaning of the "$\forall x \in \mathbb{N} \exists y \in \mathbb{N}$"-combination. According to the proof interpretation $a : \forall x \exists y A(x, y)$ mean that for all $n, a(n) : \exists y A(n, y)$, and thus $\pi_1(a(n)): A(n\ \pi_2(a(n)))$, hence $\lambda x.\pi_1(a(n)) : \forall x A(x, \pi_2(a(x)))$. Therefore there is a choice function selecting the required y, and more, if the A contains only lawlike parameters (in particular no set- or choice parameters) the choice function is itself lawlike. So Church's Thesis would decree that the choice function is Turing computable. We can formalize this result:

$$\text{CT} \quad \forall x \exists y A(x, y) \to \exists e \forall x A(x, \{e\}(x))$$

Here it is tacitly assumed that $\{e\}$ is total.

We see that in **HA** Church's Thesis can be formulated as an arithmetical schema. Hence it is open to meta-mathematical treatment. Here the realizability technique offers some help: CT turns out to be realizable, so it is consistent with **HA** (observe that it certainly is not derivable!). In other words, there is no objection to carry out arithmetic under the assumption of Church's Thesis, as long as one avoids PEM. Hyland 1982 extended this result by constructing a topos in which CT holds, the *effective topos*.

CT has far reaching consequences for the daily practice of mathematics. Specker 1949 had already pointed out that certain classical theorems of real analysis were no longer true if one required recursive results. For example: a recursive continuous real function f with $f(0) < 0$ and $f(1) > 0$ need not have a recursive zero. In the setting of the effective topos one can drop the adjective 'recursive', and simply say that there are continuous real functions with positive and negative values without zeros. In such a computable universe, indeed many traditional theorems lose their validity. More examples: [0,1] is not compact; a bounded continuous function on [0, 1] need not have a supremum (let alone a maximum); there are functions, positive on [0, 1], without a positive lower bound, etc. Here also the work of Pour El and Richards 1979 on the solutions of differential equations becomes relevant. These facts are on the negative side. On the positive side there is the result that (assuming Markov's Principle) every real function is continuous. So, although the recursive universe and the choice universe are on opposite sides of the spectrum, they share certain features.

Another, rather unexpected, fact about CT is that it allows no non-standard models for arithmetic (McCarty 1988). In view of the rich variety of non-standard models for Peano's arithmetic, this certainly indicates that life with CT is an exciting experience.

7. The Creating Subject

A sketch of intuitionistic logic would not be complete without the mentioning of Brouwer's later extension of his theory of choice sequences. In the earlier papers, Brouwer used the technique of *Brouwerian counterexamples* to show that certain classical mathematical facts could not be considered to be intuitionistically true. The technique consisted of a reduction of some theorem to a patently unsolved problem. The drawback of this method was that it only allowed weak statements, like "there is no evidence that ...". In the twenties, Brouwer himself progressed beyond these 'doubtful' statements by showing that it is not the case that each real number is rational or irrational: this was an immediate consequence of the continuity theorem. He wanted, however, an extension of the Brouwerian counter-example method. In his Berlin Lectures (Brouwer 1992), Brouwer formulated such an extension. It appeared in print only after the Second World War (Brouwer 1948). The method is that of the *creating subject*.[12] The basic idea is that with respect to a certain statement A the subject may, by hook or by crook, try to establish its truth. If A is true, then the creating subject will experience this in due course, so he can create a function that keeps track of the situation by writing down zeros, as long as A has not been established, and as soon as he sees that A is true, he writes down a one. This was formalized by Kripke's Schema:

$$K\ S \exists \alpha (\exists x \alpha(x) = 0 \leftrightarrow A)$$

Myhill 1966 showed that under Kripke's Schema the extended continuity

---

12. Erroneously called 'creative subject' in the literature.

principle, "∀α∃β-continuity", fails. Quite recently van Dalen 1997b used the idea to extend Brouwer's undecomposibility of the continuum to the irrationals and similar sets. This makes it clear that the method is not just a tool for refutations of certain principles, but it has structural consequences as well.

8. Intuitionistic Completeness

A final remark on the intuitionistic status of metamathematics: the usual techniques for establishing e.g. completeness results heavily rely on non-intuitionistic procedures, such as proof by contradiction. The question, therefore, is how far can one prove, say, completeness for Kripke models using exclusively intuitionistic means.

Early investigations of Gödel and Kreisel (see Kreisel 1962), had shown that the completeness proof could be constructivised up to a point: Markov's principle was required. This principle asserts that for primitive recursive predicates the impossibility of the non-existence of an element yielded the existence of an element:

$$MP : \neg\neg \exists x A(x) \to \exists x A(x)$$

or in general, replacing the primitive recursiveness by decidability:

$$\forall x (A(x) \vee \neg A(x)) \wedge \neg\neg \exists x A(x) \to \exists x A(x)$$

Since Markov's principle could not be given a convincing intuitionistic justification (it can be paraphrased as "if it is impossible that a Turing machine with a given input tape never stops, then it stops"), this seemed to block the development of a truly intuitionistic completeness theorem. Veldman broke this stalemate in 1974 by presenting an extension of the standard notion of Kripke model (Veldman 1976). In this new semantics one can indeed give an intuitionistically acceptable completeness proof. For a systematic survey see Dummett 1977 and Troelstra and van Dalen 1988.

References

Barendregt H. P., 1993, 'Typed Lambda Calculi', in S. Abramsky, D. Gabbay, and T. Maibaum (eds.), *Handbook of Logic in Computer Science, vol.2*, Oxford: Oxford University Press, pp. 118–414.

Beth E. W., 1956, 'Semantic Construction of Intuitionistic Logic', *Kon. Nederlandse Ac. Wetenschappen afd. Letteren: Mededelingen* 19/11, 357–88.

Borwein J. M., 1998, 'Brouwer–Heyting Sequences Converge', *Math. Intelligencer* 20, 14–15.

Brouwer L. E. J., 1907, *Over de grondslagen der wiskunde*, PhD thesis, Amsterdam.

Brouwer L. E. J., 1908, 'De onbetrouwbaarheid der logische principes', *Tijdsch Wijsbegeerte* 2, 152–58.

Brouwer L. E. J., 1918, 'Begründung der Mengenlehre unabhängig vom logischen Satz von ausgeschlossenen Dritten. Erster Teil, Allgemeine Mengenlehre', *Kon Ned Ak Wet Verhandelingen* 5, 1–43.

Brouwer L. E. J., 1924, 'Beweis dass jede volle Funktion gleichmässig stetig ist', *Nederl Ak Wetensch Proc* 27, 189–93.

Brouwer L. E. J., 1929, 'Mathematik, Wissenschaft und Sprache', *Monats Math-Phys* 36, 153–64.

Brouwer L. E. J., 1948, 'Essentially negative properties', *Ind Math* 10, 963.

Brouwer L. E. J., 1949, 'Consciousness, Philosophy and Mathematics', *Proceedings of the 10th International Congress of Philosophy, Amsterdam 1948*, Amsterdam, vol. 3, 1235–49.

Brouwer L. E. J., 1992, *Intuitionismus* (ed. D. van Dalen), Mannheim: Bibliographisches Institut, Wissenschaftsverlag.

de Bruijn N. G., 1995, 'On the Role of Types in Mathematics', in P. de Groote (ed.), *The Curry-Howard isomorphism*, Louvain-la-Neuve: Academia, pp. 27–54.

Coquand T. and Huet G., 1988, 'The Calculus of Constructions', *Information and Control* 76, 95–120.

Dalen D. van, 1974, 'A Model for HAS. A Topological Interpretation of Second-Order Intuitionistic Arithmetic with Species Variables', *Fund. Math.* 82, 167–74.

Dalen D. van, 1978, 'An Interpretation of Intuitionistic Analysis', *Ann Math Log* 13, 1–43.

Dalen D. van, 1992, 'The Continuum and First-Order Intuitionistic Logic', *J Symb Logic* 57, 1417–24.

Dalen D. van, 1997a, *Logic and Structure* (3rd ed.), Berlin: Springer Verlag.

Dalen D. van, 1997b, 'How Connected Is the Intuitionistic Continuum?', *J Symb Logic* 62, 11.

Dalen D. van, 1999, *Mystic, Geometer and Intuitionist. The Life of L.E.J. Brouwer. Vol. 1: The Dawning Revolution.* Oxford: Oxford University Press.

de Groote P. (ed.), 1995, *The Curry-Howard isomorphism*, Louvain-la-Neuve: Academia.

Dummett M., 1977, *Elements of Intuitionism*, Oxford: Oxford University Press.

Fitting M., 1969, *Intuitionistic Model Theory and Forcing*, Amsterdam: North-Holland.

Fourman M. P. and Hyland J. M. E., 1979, 'Sheaf Models for Analysis', in M. P. Fourman, C. J. Mulvey, and D. S. Scott (eds.), *Applications of Sheaves* (LNM 753) Berlin: Springer Verlag, 280–301.

Fourman M. P. and D. S. Scott, 1979, 'Sheaves and Logic', in M. P. Fourman, C. J. Mulvey and D. S. Scott (eds.), *Applications of Sheaves* (LNM 753), Berlin: Springer Verlag, 302–401.

Gallier J., 1995, 'On the Correspondence Between Proofs and λ-terms', in P. de Groote (ed.), *The Curry-Howard isomorphism*, Louvain-la-Neuve: Academia, 55–138.

Girard J.-Y., 1990, 'La logique linéaire', *Pour la Science* 150, 74–85.

Taylor P., Girard J.-Y., and Lafont Y., 1989, *Proofs and Types*, Cambridge: Cambridge University Press.

Glivenko V. I., 1928, 'Sur la logique de M. Brouwer', *Acad. Royale des Sciences de Belgique. Bull Sc.* 14, 225–28.

Glivenko V. I., 1929, 'Sur quelques points de la logique de M. Brouwer', *Acad. Royale des Sciences de Belgique. Bull Sc.* 15, 183

Gödel, K. 1932, 'Zum intuitionistischen Aussagenkalkül', *Anzeiger der Akademie der Wissenschaften in Wien* 69, 65–66 (*Coll. Works I*, pp. 222–225).

Gödel, K., 1958, 'Über eine bisher noch nicht benützte Erweiterung des finiten Standpunktes', *Dialectica* 12, 280–87 (*Coll. Works II*, pp. 217–52).

Grayson R. J., 1981, 'Concepts of General Topology in Constructive Mathematics and in Sheaves', *Ann Math Log* 20, 1

Heyting A., 1930a, 'Die formalen Regeln der intuitionistischen Logik', *Die Preussische Akademie der Wissenschaften. Sitzungsberichte. Physikalische-Mathematische Klasse*, 42–56.

Heyting A., 1930b, 'Die formalen Regeln der intuitionistischen Mathematik II, III', *Die Preussische Akademie der Wissenschaften. Sitzungsberichte. Physikalische-Mathematische Klasse*, 57–71, 158–69.

Heyting A., 1930c, 'Sur la logique intuitionniste', *Ac. Royale de Belgique. Bull.de la Classe des Sciences* 5, 957–63.

Heyting A., 1934, *Mathematische Grundlagenforschung. Intuitionismus, Beweistheorie*, Berlin: Springer Verlag.

Hoeven G. F. and Moerdijk I., 1984, 'Sheaf Models for Choice Sequences', *Ann Pure Appl Logic* 27, 63–107.

Howard W. A., 1980, 'The Formulas-as-Types Notion of Construction', in J. R. Hindley and J. P. Seldin (eds.), *To H. B. Curry: Essays on Combinatory Logic, Lambda calculus and Formalism.*, New York: Academic Press, 479–90.

Howard W. A. and Kreisel G., 1966, 'Transfinite Induction and Bar Induction of Types Zero and One, and the Role of Continuity in Intuitionistic Analysis', *J Symb Logic* 31, 325–58.

Hyland J. M. E., 1982, 'The Effective Topos', in D. van Dalen and A. S. Troelstra (eds.), *The L. E. L. Brouwer Centenary Symposium*, Amsterdam: Elsevier, pp. 165–216.

Jaskowski S., 1936, 'Recherches sur le système de la logique intuitionniste. *Congr. Int. Phil. des Sciences, 1935*, Paris: Hermann, pp. 58–61.

Kleene S. C., 1973, 'Realizability: A Retrospective Survey', in H. Rogers, jr., and A. Mathias (eds.), *Cambridge Summer School Mathematical Logic* (SLNM), Berlin: Springer Verlag, pp. 95–112.

Kleene S. C. and Vesley R. E., 1965, *The Foundations of Intuitionistic Mathematics especially in relation to Recursive Functions*, Amsterdam: North-Holland.

Kreisel G., 1962, 'On Weak Completeness of Intuitionistic Logic', *J Symb Logic* 27, 139–58.

Kreisel G. and Troelstra A. S., 1970, 'Formal Systems for Some Branches of Intuitionistic Analysis', *Ann Math Log* 1, 229–387.

Kripke S. A., 1965, 'Semantical Analysis of Intuitionistic Logic I', in J. N. Crossley and M. A. E. Dummett (eds.), *Formal Systems and Recursive Functions*, Amsterdam: North-Holland, pp. 92–130.

Lambek J. and Scott P. J., 1986, *Introduction to Higher Order Categorical Logic*, Cambridge: Cambridge University Press.

MacLane S. and Moerdijk I., 1992, *Sheaves in Geometry and Logic. A first Introduction to Topos Theory*, Berlin: Springer Verlag.

Martin-Löf, P., *Intuitionistic Type Theory*, Napoli: Bibliopolis.

McCarty C., 1988, 'Constructive Validity Is Nonarithmetic', *J Symb Logic* 53, 1036

Moschovakis J., 1973, 'A Topological Interpretation of Intuitionistic Analysis', *Comp Math* 26, 261

Mostowski A., 1948, 'Proofs of Non-deducibility in Intuitionistic Functional Systems', *J Symb Logic* 13, 204–7.

Myhill J., 1966, 'Notes Towards an Axiomatization of Intuitionistic Analysis', *Logique et Analyse* 9, 280–97.

Pour El M. B. and Richards I., 1979, 'A Computable Ordinary Differential Equation which Possesses No Computable Solution', *Ann Math Log* 17, 61–90.

Prawitz D., 1977, 'Meaning and Proofs: On the Conflict Between Classical and Intuitionistic Logic', *Theoria* 43, 2–40.

Rasiowa H. and Sikorski R., 1963, *The Mathematics of Metamathematics*, Warsaw: Panstowe Wydawnictwo Naukowe.

Scott D. S., 1968, 'Extending the Topological Interpretation to Intuitionistic Analysis', *Comp Math* 20, 194–210.

Scott D. S., 1970, 'Extending the Topological Interpretation to Intuitionistic Analysis II, in A. Kino, J. Myhill, and R. E. Vesley (eds.), *Intuitionism and Proof Theory (Proc. Conf. Buffalo 1968)*, Amsterdam, 235–55.

Scott D. S., 1979, 'Identity and Existence in Intuitionistic Logic', in M. P. Fourman, C. J. Mulvey, and D. S. Scott (eds.), *Applications of Sheaves* (LNM 753), Berlin: Springer Verlag, 660–96.

Shoenfield J., 1967, *Mathematical Logic*, Reading: Addison and Wesley.

Smorynski C. S., 1973, 'Applications of Applications of Kripke Models', in A. S. Troelstra (ed.)., *Metamathematical Investigation of Intuitionistic Arithmetic and Analysis*: Berlin: Springer Verlag, pp. 324

Specker E., 1949, 'Nicht konstruktiv beweisbare Sätze der Analysis', *J Symb Logic* 14, 145–58.

Stone H., 1937, 'Topological Representations of Distributive Lattices and Brouwerian Logics', *Can Pestovani Math. Ceskoslv Akad. Ved.* 67, 1–25.

Tarski A., 1938, 'Der Aussagenkalkül und die Topologie', *Fund. Math.* 31, 103–34.

Troelstra A. S., 1973, *Metamathematical Investigation of Intuitionistic Arithmetic and Analysis*, Berlin: Springer Verlag.

Troelstra A. S., 1978, 'Commentary' (on Heyting 1930a), in E. M. J. Bertin, H. J. M. Bos, and A. W. Grootendorst (eds.), *Two Decades of Mathematics in the Netherlands. 1920*, Amsterdam: Mathematical Centre, pp. 163–75.

Troelstra A. S., 1982, 'On the Origin and Development of Brouwer's Concept of Choice Sequence', in A. S. Troelstra and D. van Dalen (eds.), *The L. E. J. Brouwer Centenary Symposium*, Amsterdam: North–Holland, 465–86.

Troelstra A. S. and D. van Dalen, 1988, *Constructivism in Mathematics, I, II*, Amsterdam: North–Holland.

Turing A., 1937, 'On Computable Numbers, with an Application to the Entscheidungsproblem', *Proc. London math. Soc.* 42, 230–65.

Veldman W., 1976, 'An Intuitionistic Completeness Theorem for Intuitionistic Predicate Logic', *J Symb Logic* 41, 159–66.

Philosophy Department
University of Utrecht
Utrecht, The Netherlands

A. P. Hazen
Logic and Analyticity

1. Logic

There is a familiar ambiguity in English arising from the circumstance that the same word can sometimes be used to refer both to a scholarly discipline and to what it studies. History, in one sense, is the total mass of past events, and in the other is the effort to identify what events have happened and to understand them. The chemistry of a river, in one sense, may be what prevents certain species of aquatic organisms from living in it, and in the other it may be something underdeveloped because of a lack of funding for environmental studies. Logic, in the sense of a discipline, is the the study of valid inference (and related topics), but we also speak of "the logic of an argument," and this is not a discipline, but is rather what it is about the argument which might make it valid. We might, in a rough preliminary characterization, say that the logic of an argument is the collection of some of its structural properties: those of its properties which are of interest to logic in the disciplinary sense.

The ambiguity becomes more troublesome in speaking of "logical truths" or "truths of logic." In the disciplinary sense, a proposition is a truth of logic if it is a truth which it is the business of logicians *qua* logicians to discover. In the sense corresponding to past conquests and taxations, or to concentrations of dissolved oxygen and toxic wastes, a logical truth is a proposition having some property of propositions related to the property of arguments, validity. (The property of propositions in question is, in an elegantly simple and widely taught formulation, that of being such that any argument at all with the proposition in question as conclusion is valid: this formulation, however, would be rejected by, *e.g.*, relevance logicians such as

Anderson & Belnap 1975.) It is not at all obvious—indeed, it seems to me highly unlikely—that the two senses of logical truth are coextensive. One of the greatest logical discoveries of the Nineteenth (Twentieth) Century was the fact that an argument having as conclusion Euclid's Parallel Postulate (the Axiom of Choice) and as premisses the other Euclidean axioms (the other axioms of Zermelo-Fraenkel set theory) is not valid, a fact demonstrated by proving the existence of countermodels, the existence proof itself being a sophisticated and complex piece of geometrical (set-theoretic) reasoning. Clearly, then, it is the business of the logician *qua* logician to study, and prove theorems in, metric geometry (set theory), for this turns out to be an essential part of what went into important discoveries about validity. On the other hand, to say that all the theorems of geometry (higher set theory) are logical truths in the non-disciplinary sense would be to adopt a controversial thesis in the philosophy of mathematics: Logicism.

Just what counts as a truth of logic in the disciplinary sense is not a very interesting question: the universe is not the university, and there is no good reason to think that the boundaries between the areas studied by academic departments are lines that carve nature at the joints. The notion of a logical truth in the other sense is potentially more interesting: it seems that the logical truths, in this sense, might be the propositions with some distinctive semantical features, or of some epistemologically special class. We have clear and generally agreed paradigms of such truths: they are those propositions whose truth can be established by the use of any of the large number of familiar equivalent proof procedures for First-Order Logic. It is not, however, satisfactory simply to *define* a logical truth, stipulatively, as one which can be so demonstrated and leave it at that. For one thing, it is not obvious that First-Order Logic exhausts the logical. As it happens, I will not in this paper discuss any examples lying outside the class of First-Order validities, but one might (and on another occasion I would) argue that certain extensions of First-Order Logic are, in the honorific sense, *logical*: perhaps First-Order Logic with Identity, or with variable-binding term-forming operators, or with predicate modifiers, or perhaps, going a bit further afield, Russell's Ramified Theory of Types. Each of these (putative) logics has a proof procedure (in the case of Ramified Type Theory, whose semantic interpretation is contentious, is defined by reference to a proof procedure) with very much the same character or "feel" as the proof procedures for First-Order Logic. At least for the first three, mathematical techniques essentially the same as those used in proving Gödel's completeness theorem for First-Order Logic can be used to show these proof procedures complete relative to a well-understood and intuitively correct semantic interpretation. On the other hand, each of these allows us to prove "logical" truths in a formal language of greater expressive power than that of First-Order Logic: see the Appendix.

Whether or not, in the end, we decide that the province of logic is coextensive with that of First-Order Logic, however, the very possibility of asking the question presupposes that we have an at least notionally independent conception of what it is to be a logical truth: we could not meaningfully ask whether First-Order provability exhausted logical provability unless we conceived of the *logicality* of First-Order proofs as a feature distinguishable from their property of simply being First-Order proofs. Now, it is possible to take a sceptical view here, and deny that we have any clear concept of logicality which can be distinguished in this way. (The sceptic will doubtless explain the subjective impression some of us have that there is a separate concept of logicality as a result of mistaking the fuzzy, vague, confused, pre-analytic concept of logic—which differs from the concept of First-Order Logic precisely by its fuzziness—for a clear concept which we could, by further analysis and reflection, come to understand clearly.) Quine is the most prominent proponent of this view: he has, vehemently and repeatedly, urged the identification of logic with First-Order Logic, but has also characterized this identification as purely stipulative and, in the end, of no theoretical importance. Still, even Quine regards the stipulation as a natural one. First-Order Logic, in his view, has enough inner unity, and enough special properties distinguishing it from other, more or less similar, parts of mathematics, to merit a special name quite apart from the accidents of history: calling it "logic" is not like giving a body of doctrine a name simply because it is treated in what comes after physics in some editor's arrangement of Aristotle's works. The identification of logic with First-Order Logic is, for Quine, one that can be *defended*. In his 1969, he gives a sample of the kind of defense called for, in arguing that a certain extension of First-Order Logic (that obtained by adding the so-called "branching," or finite partially ordered, quantifiers) probably shouldn't be counted as logic. The key point is that the extension does not have a complete proof procedure.

I would like to propose the contrary hypothesis, that our sense that there is something special about logical truths betokens an imprecise, but improvable, grasp of a potentially clear concept, that logicality is a distinctive semantic or epistemological property possessed by the truths of First-Order Logic and perhaps by some others, and to enquire a bit more deeply into what this property is. The key fact guiding the investigation will be that logical truths are provable: to put it in semi-serious terms, I will take the emphasis on proof procedures in the argument of Quine 1969 as evidence of Quine's grasp of the concept he denies.[1] It seems to me that the phenomenology of proofs promises some insight into the nature of logicality.

There are, of course, many formal proof-procedures for First-Order Logic, with features making them useful in different ways. Some are easier to teach to beginning students, to give them a taste of what a formal proof-procedure is like, and others are more efficient for those who (in connection, say, with the formal verification of computer programs, or the formalization of significant mathematical theories) have occasion to write out many long formal derivations.[2] Some are easier to adapt for automated proof search, and others allow proofs that are more perspicuous or easier for human logicians to discover. In addition to all these, there are informal proofs: one can convince oneself, or an intelligent listener, of the truth (and validity) of a truth of First-Order Logic by informal argument, without appeal to any textbook formal system. In doing this one may use any of a wide variety of arguments, including some which, arguably, go beyond pure logic. (Boolos 1987 describes an example of what *I* think—Boolos himself took it as evidence that logic itself was more inclusive than I like to think—is a logical truth that we can only prove to be true by appeal to extra-logical, mathematical, principles.) Some of these arguments are of a clearly logical nature,

---

1. Perhaps there is more than one concept in the neighborhood. In taking proof to be central, I seem to be committed to holding that an extension of First-Order Logic can only be logical if it has a proof procedure, which means that I am drawing the lines more restrictively than Tarski 1986: cf. Sher 1991 for discussion.
2. As Carlo Cellucci has emphasized to me in correspondence, the demands of these applications can conflict. In teaching Beth-Smullyan tableaux to beginning students, I would not try to teach them the more efficient but more complicated variant rule described at the bottom of p. 54 of Smullyan 1968, but I would not want to do without it, or some similar rule of "Existential Instantiation" in a non-tableau deductive system, if I had to produce a formal derivation of many thousand lines.

and the formal proof procedures based on their patterns seem to me to deserve their name of systems of *natural deduction*. In what follows I will take for granted that the derivations of natural deduction systems, either in the arboriform version of Gentzen 1934 (followed by such textbooks as Van Dalen 1983) or the—logically almost exactly equivalent—paper-economizing linearized formulation of Fitch 1952 (followed by Thomason 1970 and many other American undergraduate logic texts), perspicuously represent important features of an important kind of intuitive proof, and won't bother always to distinguish the formal derivation from the intuitive pattern of reasoning it represents. (These systems are reasonably efficient for medium-length derivations, though the system of Cellucci 1988 produces smaller derivations for many—though not all—test problems. They are reasonably easy to teach, and the rules defining correct derivations in them are not much more complicated than those of Beth-Smullyan tableaux, though the tactics of *finding* derivations seem harder for many students to master than the use of tableaux.)

To summarize, then, one important fact about logical truths is that one important means by which we come to recognize their truth is that of mentally rehearsing or working through proofs of them, proofs which can be written out as derivations in natural deduction. In complicated cases, of course, human memory can do with assistance, and it may in practice be necessary to write out the proof if we are to check it. In such cases it might be said that we come to recognize the truth (and validity) of a logical truth (in part) by perceiving, and examining carefully, a physical object: a pattern of ink-marks on one or a series of sheets of paper. This, however, is the sort of consideration we are used to ignoring in an idealizing theoretical account. *In principle*, to use the familiar philosophical weasel-phrase, the written proof is irrelevant, in principle we could satisfy ourselves by thinking about the proof with our eyes closed. In principle, our knowledge of logical truths does not depend on empirical intuition. So I propose to look at the features of proofs of logical truths to see what they suggest about the nature of logicality. I will put off to the end a consideration of the ontological status of proofs, and of whether there is any helpful purpose served by analogizing our recognition, or "seeing," of a proof to standard sorts of perception, but the features of proofs that will most interest me are those that are clearly, and literally, visible when the proof is written out in the form of a derivation in a system of natural deduction.

2. Analyticity and Quantifiers

Provability is an epistemological property of logical truths, certainly related to their semantic properties, but not itself explicitly semantic. There is, however, a long tradition of attempts to characterize the logical in semantic terms. Logical truths are supposed to be analytic. Now, there is a sense in which this is surely true: there is something to the commonplace that they are true in virtue of their meaning. Given the structure of a logically valid proposition and the concepts involved in it, it cannot be false. (Ignore for the moment the ontological question of whether propositions are things that can be said to have structures, or to have concepts involved in them (as constituents?): we can take the relevant structure to be the grammatical structure of the sentence expressing the proposition, and the concepts involved to be the meanings of the words occurring in that sentence.) Unfortunately, so are many propositions which are not logical truths. Trivially, there are such boring analytic truths as that bachelors are unmarried and aunts female. (It is surely a significant fact about natural languages and the ways in which they are learned and understood that most of the clearest and most generally agreed upon analyticities involve kinship terms!) There is, however, a sketch of a response available to this objection. Logical truths, the respondent admits, are a special case of analytic truths, but the narrower class can itself be characterized in semantic terms. The analytic status of "All bachelors are unmarried" depends on the meanings of "bachelor" and "unmarried" as well as those of "all" and "are," whereas that of "If Socrates is mortal then Socrates is mortal" depends only on its structure and the meaning of "if...then.": the meanings of the particular name and predicate involved are irrelevant. Logical truths, the defender of the semantic characterization of logicality will say, are those which are analytic in virtue of (their structure and) the meanings of a small number logical constants. Of course, in making the definition of logical truth depend on the notion of a logical constant, there is a threat of circularity or triviality. Tarski 1986 seems happy to allow a variety of senses of logicality, corresponding to different, more or less arbitrary, choices of lists of logical constants. The alternative is to seek some principled way of demarcating the logical constants. One tempting approach is that they are those concepts which, in some sense or other, are fully determined by their associated inference patterns: this is the path taken in the Gentzen-Prawitz project of characterizing logical constants by inferential "definitions".

Unfortunately for the semantic characterization of logical truths, there is a more interesting family of (arguably) non-logical (arguable) analyticities. Kurt Gödel, in a number of his later essays, defended the view that all of logic—where he understood "logic" as referring to a much broader domain, the totality of a "theory of concepts," than I am considering—and set theory are analytic. There is certainly a sense in which this seems very plausible when we interpret analyticity as truth in virtue of meaning alone. Typical empirical truths are not analytic because, even when their structure and the concepts involved in them are determined, their truth value depends on contingent features of the world. Set theory (or mathematics in general), on the other hand, is precisely a theory of abstract structural possibilities: is it possible, for example, to have a collection of objects which can be put into one-one correspondence with an infinite subset of the real numbers but not into one-one correspondence either with the real numbers themselves or with the rationals? This subject matter does not depend on contingent facts: on the contrary, our notion of contingency is derivative from the facts of this subject matter. (When the sports commentators say, at a certain stage in the season, that it has become mathematically impossible for a certain team to win the league championship, the claim about possibility is based on a mathematical truth. Our judgment that 85 is more than half of 168 is not based on any antecedent facts about the possible outcomes of the baseball season.) Thus, once the structure of a set-theoretic proposition has been established and the particular set-theoretic concepts involved in it identified, there is no further contingency to its truth value: its truth or falsity is a necessary consequence of its structure and constituent concepts. (If one prefers to hear something about reference in a story about why a proposition is true, one might prefer this reformulation: set theoretic statements refer to non-contingent objects, and any purely mathematical description of such an object, since it is phrased in terms of the object's non-contingent properties, will be rigid. Thus in set theory the meaning of a description determines the denotation necessarily, with the result that, again, the truth value of a statement is a necessary consequence of its meaning.) The moral to be drawn here, it seems to me, is that if analyticity is to be used as a defining character of the truths of logic in some sense more restrictive than Gödel's, analyticity must not be interpreted in the broad sense of mere truth in virtue of meaning.

To analyze, etymologically, is to break up. Chemical analysis determines the constituents of a sample. Following this hint, one might try to define an analytic truth as one which can be ascertained by analysis, by breaking up the statement, or by examining what is contained in it. Now, it may not be obvious what the metaphors of breaking up and containment come to in semantics, but it is clear that, for our purposes, they must be interpreted quite strictly. The metaphor of containment is often used in logic simply for implication: one statement contains another if it entails it. If we were to interpret containment in this broad sense, however, we would immediately either be taken back to the broad sense of analyticity (if we interpreted entailment as strict implication) or to a trivially circular account of the logical (if we interpreted it as logically valid implication). Analysis, in the strict sense we want, then, must reveal only the concepts and conceptual structures actually involved in the proposition analyzed. Now we must ask whether logical truths are analytic in some sense related to this: is the truth of a logical truth revealed by analysis?

Hintikka has argued (1970) that various principles of quantificational logic are not analytic. The argument is perhaps most easily presented in terms of an example, a miniaturized toy version of the example from Boolos 1984. Consider the argument with premises

(i) $\forall x \forall y (Rxy \rightarrow \exists z \exists w (Sxz \,\&\, Szw \,\&\, Swy))$
(ii) $\forall x \forall y (Sxy \rightarrow \exists z \exists w (Txz \,\&\, Tzw \,\&\, Twy))$
(iii) $\forall x \forall y (Txy \rightarrow \exists z \exists w (Uxz \,\&\, Uzw \,\&\, Uwy))$
(iv) $\forall x \forall y ((Uxy \,\&\, Fx) \rightarrow Fy)$

and conclusion

$\forall x \forall y ((Rxy \,\&\, Fx) \rightarrow Fy)$.

(To make it an example of a logical truth, consider the conditional with the conclusion as consequent and a conjunction of the premises as antecedent.) Now, it is easy enough to see that this is valid. Intuitively: imagine (or draw, if you prefer, but I recommend imagining) a diagram of two spots, one to the left of the other, with a red arrow from the left one to the right one, symbolizing a typical pair of objects connected by the relation R (put the dots a fair way apart if you are drawing it). Premiss (i) tells us that, in any situation such as represented in the diagram, we may interpolate two more dots, with green arrows from the leftward of the original pair to the first interpolant, from the first interpolant to the second, and from the second interpolant to the rightward of the original pair: the diagram will now depict a chain of four S-related objects. Premiss (ii) licenses us in similarly interpolating two further dots between each neighboring pair of these four, and connecting adjoining dots left to right with blue arrows: a chain, now, of ten T-related things. Premiss (iii) licenses yet another stage of interpolation, using, say, black arrows: the diagram will depict a chain of 28 U-related objects. Highlight the leftmost dot in yellow marking pen to represent the assumption that the original lefthand object, the one R-related to the original righthand object, has the property F. Premiss (iv) tells us that yellow marker ink spreads along black arrows, so ... (27 steps later) ... the rightmost dot will get highlighted. But the original pair, as the saying goes, represented an *arbitrary* pair of R-related objects, so we may assert the general (that is, universally quantified) conclusion. The—what shall I call it? exercise? thought experiment?—just described is totally convincing. Hintikka suggests, plausibly, that it is an example (particularly when imagined?) of what Kant thought of as the essential dependence of mathematical reasoning on (pure) spatial intuition. Mathematics is not, according to Kant, analytic, because in reasoning mathematically we have to perform thought experiments of this sort, constructing at least imagined diagrams, and this is a use of intuition rather than a mere analysis of conceptual content. In fact we can show that something more than analysis is involved by a simple count: the four premisses and conclusion, as written, contain a total of 16 quantifiers between them, so in understanding the argument, or considering the corresponding conditional proposition, we are thinking a thought that involves only 16 conceptual representations-of-objects. The proof *had* to be constructive rather than analytic: it involved the creation of object-representations that were not contained in the proposition originally considered.

There are numerous points that need further consideration in the argument just given. For a start, the assumption that we may identify the quantifier count with a count of object-representations stands in need of further justification. It is, however, intuitively plausible enough. Think of how one would use diagrams to illustrate the meaning of a First-Order sentence, or explain it to someone uncomfortable with the notation. Suppose, for example, that you were asked to explain what premiss (i) in the example amounts to. Well, you might say, it is a universal quantification, so it makes a general statement about situations of a certain kind: since it starts with two universal quantifiers, situations involving a pair of objects: at this point you draw a pair of dots. Now, the scope of these quantifiers is a conditional, so the generalization made is in particular about situations involving two objects satisfying the antecedent of the conditional (here you draw the red arrow from left to right), which says that one is related to the other by R. The claim made about such situations is that given by the consequent of the conditional, namely that the situation involves two further objects (draw the additional dots), the four objects being related by S thusly (drawing in the green arrows on the word "thusly"). The content of the quantified statement, then, is to the effect that a certain picture is generally accurate with respect to situations of a certain kind, and the representations of individual objects in the picture correspond exactly to the nested quantifiers of the sentence. Far from being a far-fetched assumption, it seems that a large part of the semantic function of the sentence is to *be* a picture, a picture in which the quantifiers and their attached variables function as the representations of objects.

That sentences can be thought of as pictures, or, more accurately, that sentences and pictures are related forms of representation in which homologous features can be discerned, is by now a familiar theme in the philosophy of language. (Since similarity of function is at issue, "analogous" might seem a better word than "homologous," but if one imagines a quasi-evolutionary process transforming diagrammatic into sentential representations the stronger term seems justified.) The central idea of Wittgenstein's *Tractatus* was his picture theory of meaning, according to which (atomic) sentences were pictures, with the names in them representing objects.[3] A similar idea occurred somewhat earlier to Peirce, but whereas Wittgenstein developed it as a purely theoretical piece of semantics, Peirce attempted to embody the insight in a diagrammatic logical notation—his system of "existential graphs"—which would allow the process of inference to be represented as one of manipulating pictures. (In Peirce's diagrams, in contrast to that of our example, dots are the predicates of atomic formulas, and the lines connecting them—the "lines of identity" in his terminology—are the quantified variables. A trivial seeming difference, but, given our tendency to think of dots as fixed solids and lines as flexible, perhaps suggestive of a very different metaphysics....) Both recognized that propositional connectives destroy the purely pictorial character of sentences: Wittgenstein's theory was that sen-

---

3. The most insightful discussion of Wittgenstein's picture theory I know is in Sellars 1962.

tences in general were truth functions of pictorial elementary sentences, and Peirce supplemented his dot-and-line pictures with a less literally pictorial (though still perhaps in some sense "iconic") notation for Boolean structure: Wittgenstein basing his theoretical description and Peirce his notation and inference rules on a single generalized (variably polyadic) Sheffer connective. When it came to quantifiers, Wittgenstein somewhat unhelpfully analogized them to generalized conjunctions and disjunctions; Peirce devised an ingenious set of rules (involving the elongation and contraction of lines of identity) to embody the ways in which quantifiers specify pictures as applying generally or only in special cases.

Still, even standard logical notation, and conventional natural-deduction proof systems, for First-Order Logic display an affinity with the sort of diagrammatic construction described in our example, and in a way that reinforces the connection between quantified variables and the dots in the diagram. Suppose we try to construct a natural-deduction derivation of the conclusion, above, from the premises (i)-(iv). Since the conclusion is a (double) universal quantification, we will set up what Fitch calls a (pair of nested) *subordinate proof(s)* with *eigenvariables* (Gentzen's terminology this time), say a and b. If we can deduce

$((Rab\ \&\ Fa) \to Fb)$

in the (inner) subproof, the rule of Universal Quantifier Introduction will allow us to assert the conclusion. This, in turn, is a conditional, so we set up a third subordinate proof inside the ones we already have, with

$(Rab\ \&\ Fa)$

as a hypothesis: if we can derive

Fb

from this hypothesis the rule of Conditional Introduction will allow us to assert, as a line of the outer subordinate proofs though not of the third, the desired

$((Rab\ \&\ Fa) \to Fb)$.

But now compare this to the initial stage of the diagrammatic proof, where we had drawn our first two dots and connected them by a red arrow: at this stage of writing out the natural-deduction derivation we have a very similar "picture" drawn according to slightly different conventions. The predicate letter R takes the place of the arrow (and F that of the yellow highlighting), the *eigenvariables* a and b that of the dots: a picture, as Wittgenstein would put it, with a different mode of projection. Our task, in the rest of the derivation, is to construct a series of steps leading up to the writing of an F before ("highlighting") an occurrence of the second *eigenvariable*. (This picture is more abstract than our earlier diagram in one respect: there an object was represented by a single, concrete, dot, which could be highlighted and have many arrows to it or from it. Here, since each occurrence of a predicate letter has to have its own arguments, the representative of an object is an *eigenvariable type*, with perhaps many occurrences.) The next stage in the diagrammatic proof was to appeal to premiss (i),

$$\forall x \forall y (Rxy \rightarrow \exists z \exists w (Sxz \,\&\, Szw \,\&\, Swy)),$$

to justify drawing in two more dots connected by green arrows. The appeal, analyzed into single steps by the rules of natural deduction, may not seem quite as immediate as it did there, but it is still direct. We instantiate (Universal Quantifier Elimination) to

$$(Rab \rightarrow \exists z \exists w (Saz \,\&\, Szw \,\&\, Swb)),$$

after which a few propositional steps yield the (double) existential quantification

$$\exists z \exists w (Saz \,\&\, Szw \,\&\, Swb).$$

At this point we set up another (pair of nested) subordinate proof(s), with *eigenvariables* c, d, the innermost starting with the hypothesis

$$(Sac \,\&\, Scd \,\&\, Sdb);$$

the rule of Existential Quantifier Elimination telling us that an Fb derived in these subordinate proofs may be asserted in the proofs to which they are subordinate.

And so on. The derivation can mimic the diagrammatic construction almost exactly, and the 28 nested subordinate proofs for the quantifier rules, each with its own *eigenvariable*, each "generated" by a quantifer will correspond to the 28 dots as representatives of 28 imagined or conceived-of objects: the final oozing of the yellow highlighting along the black arrows being transformed into a large number of applications of *modus ponens*. The correspondence of these quantifier-associated elements of the proof with the dots of the diagram strengthens the case for taking the number of quantifiers in a First-Order sentence (containing no individual constants) as revealing the number of object-representations it contains, and so the argument that logical truths, like our example, established by proofs exhibiting more object-representations than there are quantifiers in the statement itself are not, in the strict sense, analytic. (It might be replied that the additional object-representations are somehow *implicit* in the original statement, but then some explication of the notion of a representation being implicit in a proposition would have to be given: an explication which, on pain of circularity, would have to amount to more than the fact that the representation is constructed in the course of a proof.)

I will finish this section with three more comments on Hintikka's argument. First, there are proof procedures for First-Order Logic of what seems like a clearly analytic character: they procede by, literally, breaking up the sentence to be proven into its subformulas, the proof being completed when the fragments fall into a certain pattern. (Beth-Smullyan tableaux—sometimes called "analytic tableaux"—are the most familiar example; the study of a somewhat similar scheme was central to much of Hintikka's early logical research.) Only in propositional logic, however, are the subformulas of a sentence literally parts of it: in quantification theory the result of chopping off a quantifier and replacing its bound variable with *any* term, including terms that have no occurrence in the original sentence, counts as a subformula. Hintikka's original formulation of his argument was in terms of such systems: the "analytic" proofs of examples like ours showed they were not analytic because the purported analysis led to the introduction of new terms beyond the number of quantifiers, just as the natural deduction proofs involve the introduction of large numbers of *eigenvariables*.

Second, the proof given above is not the only proof available for the logical truth of our example. In fact the natural deduction proof described has a very special property: it is *normal* in the sense of Prawitz 1965. This is the property of proofs that Gentzen 1934 characterized by saying that the proof "makes no detours" (*er macht keine Umwege*); it corresponds to the property of *cut-freeness* for derivations in the sequent calculi he introduced as a technically more tractable alternative to natural deduction. Now, notoriously, cut-free proofs are *conceptually* simple but the conceptual simplicity can lead us into a combinatorial explosion in overall proof size, and particularly in the number of *eigenvariables*. (Boolos 1984 presented the example inspiring ours precisely in order to show the importance of *not* restricting ourselves to cut-free methods of proof.) In our example, an alternate proof would start by deriving the "lemma"

(v)　$\forall x \forall y((Txy \,\&\, Fx) \rightarrow Fy)$

from premisses (iii) and (iv), then (by a completely parallel argument) the second lemma

(vi)　$\forall x \forall y((Sxy \,\&\, Fx) \rightarrow Fy)$

from (v) and premiss (ii), and finally the conclusion (by the same pattern of argument again) from (vi) and premiss (i). This alternative proof-strategy makes a significant (and, in Boolos's original example, astronomical) reduction in the number of nested subordinate proofs and *eigenvariables*, but from the standpoint of trying to show that logical truths are analytic is no help: the lemmas, (v) and (vi), are not subformulas of the statement under consideration, are not found by breaking it up into its constituent parts. (It might be replied that they are *implicitly* contained by the premisses, but containment here would merely be a metaphor for logical implication.) And there are examples (such as that of Boolos 1987) in which no such alternative proof strategy will reduce the number of object-representations in the proof enough to make it seem analytic.

The final comment is about Kant and Aristotle. To find examples of synthetic judgements in mathematics, Kant turned, not to First-Order Logic, but to arithmetic (and geometry). This would cast doubt on Hintikka's interpretation of Kant's notions of analyticity and syntheticity were it not for the fact that Kant had a terrifyingly narrow-minded, and mathematically trivial, conception of the province of logic: Kant identified logic with Aristotelian syllogistic.[4] And syllogistic *is* analytic in the respect in which full First-Order Logic, I have argued, is not, despite the obvious continuity of the forms of inference in the move from syllogistic to the more general system. It is easiest to describe the difference in terms of the natural deduction system, in which

---

4.　It is usual to make excuses for Kant on this point, and say that the real advances of logical theory beyond its Aristotelian state didn't come until the work of Frege and Peirce most of a century later, but in fact a relevant advance on Aristotle had been made in the medieval theory of "oblique syllogisms" developed by Ockham and others—cf. Thom 1977 for discussion and references.

the construction of new object-representations takes the form of setting up new subproofs, with new *eigenvariables*, in the course of applying the Existential Quantifier Elimination rule.

We may state this rule as follows:

> (∃ Elim) A formula, φ, may be asserted as an item of a proof after two other items, (i) an existentially quantified formula ∃ξψ(ξ) and (ii) a subordinate proof of φ (*i.e.*, a proof having having φ as one of its asserted lines) having ψ(a) (*i.e.*, a formula like ψ(ξ) except for containing occurrences of *a*, the *eigenvariable* of the subordinate proof, in just those places where ψ(ξ) contains free occurrences of ξ), *provided* that the *eigenvariable a* does not occur in φ.

Despite the prickly hedge of technical jargon, this is a familiar and intuitive form of reasoning, and one that Aristotle himself recognized, under the name *ecthesis*. Suppose one wanted (not having a copy of the *Prior Analytics* on hand to refer to) to prove the validity of an instance of the syllogistic mood Disamis: to deduce, say, the conclusion that some Urodeles are Neotenous from the premisses that all Ambystomids are Urodeles and that some Ambystomids are Neotenous. Arguing by ecthesis we say "Let Montezuma be one of the Ambystomids which are Neotenous; by the major premiss he is a Urodele, so some Urodele is Neotenous." (If one *had* had a copy of *Prior Analytics* 28b on hand, one would have noted that Aristotle appeals to ecthesis in arguing for the validity of Datisi but not that of Disamis, but this is an accident of his presentation: Aristotle, after all, took first figure syllogisms as axiomatic, whereas modern textbooks would derive even Barbara from more fundamental rules of First-Order Logic.) Formalized in First-Order Logic—showing the validity of a few categorical syllogisms is often the first exercise beginning students are set after being taught the rules for the quantifiers—this turns into an application of Existential Quantifier Elimination:

1	∀x(Ax → Ux)	Premiss
2	∃x(Ax & Nx)	Premiss
3	(Aa & Na)	Hypothesis
4	Aa	3, & Elim
5	(Aa → Ua)	1, ∀ Elim
6	Ua	5,4 → Elim
7	Na	3, & Elim
8	(Ua & Na)	6,7 & Introduction
9	∃x(Ux & Nx)	8, ∃ Introduction
10	∃x(Ux & Nx)	

where the final conclusion is derived from premiss 2 and the subordinate proof 3–9 by ∃ Elimination. (For those worried by the appeal, at line 5 *within* the subordinate proof to premiss 1 outside it: this is legitimate because the premiss does not contain any free occurrence of the *eigenvariable*, as would have been clear from a fuller statement of the conventions governing subordinate proofs.) But—and this is something not all undergraduate logic students master—this "ecthetic" use of ∃ Elimination has a special feature that suggests a far less general rule. The conclusion (ϕ in the statement of the rule) can be any formula not containing the *eigenvariable* of the subordinate proof (thus the various ∃ Eliminations in our earlier example all had F*b* as their conclusion), but in the syllogistic example it is in fact obtained by existentially quantifying (and so de-eigenvariabling) a formula containing the *eigenvariable* of the subordinate proof. And, in fact, some students end up thinking ∃ Elimination is the simpler, weaker, rule

("Ec") An existential quantification ∃ξψ(ξ) may be asserted as an item of a proof after two other items, (i) an existential quantification ∃ξϕ(ξ) and (ii) a subordinate proof, with *eigenvariable a*, in which ψ(*a*) is derived from the hypothesis ϕ(*a*).

First-Order Logic owes its strength, mathematical interest, and much of its non-analytic character to the fact that logicians have formulated the more general ∃ Elimination instead of resting content with the special case Ec that was familiar to Aristotle and Kant.

3. Analyticity and Propositional Logic

Although Hintikka has argued that (at least some) principles of quantificational logic are synthetic, he is happy to classify truth-functional *propositional* logic as analytic. Looked at from an abstract viewpoint, this seems like an obvious classification. The analytic proof procedures (such as Beth-Smullyan tableaux) provide proofs of propositional tautologies of a more definitely analytic character than their proofs of quantificational theorems: every formula occurring in the completed tableau for a propositional formula is (give or take minor exceptions due to the handling of defined connectives) literally obtainable from the starting formula by breaking it up into pieces, or at worst is the negation of a formula so obtainable: nothing new gets added the way new instantial terms get added in constructing a quantificational tableau. (In a sense one might say that this is what makes the propositional calculus decidable: barring repetitions, no branch in a closed tableau for a given propositional formula can contain more formulas than there are symbols in the starting formula itself, in contrast to the situation with full First-Order Logic, where no recursive function of the length of the starting formula can bound the length of branches in closed tableaux for theorems of that length.) Looked at more concretely, from the practical standpoint of a human—or even an electronic—reasoner, things are not as clear. The length of the branches in a propositional tableau may be strictly limited, but their number—and so the total number of formulas in the tableau—can, in the worst cases, grow explosively. A bound on the maximum size of tableaux for tautologies of a given length can be calculated, but it is exponential.[5] To put it perhaps a bit overdramatically, no being of limited lifespan and computational resources can be confident of being able to construct closed tableaux for all the propositional tautologies it encounters. From a *practical* standpoint, the sort of analysis represented by Beth-Smullyan tableaux is as inadequate for propositional logic as it is in *theory* for quantificational.

One way of arguing that truths of propositional logic are not analytic, or at least that our knowledge of them is not derived from any analytic character they may possess (that, in Kantspeak, our judgments of their validity are not analytic *judgments*), would start from a theorem showing that some non-analytic proof procedure, and in fact one like natural deduction with good claims to represent patterns of our intuitive reasoning, is better than the analytic procedures. Some delicacy is required here, however. If we could show that there is, for some proof procedure, a bound on the size of proofs of propositional tautologies which is polynomial in the length of those tautologies, we should have solved one of the outstanding, and apparently very difficult, open questions of contemporary mathematics: not, indeed, the famous P=NP problem, but the closely related NP=co-NP one.[6]

---

5. For references and a fairly recent review of what is known about the efficiencies of various proof procedures for propositional logic, see Urquhart 1995: the point made above is summarized by saying that Beth-Smullyan tableaux are below the dotted line on the map of page 429.
6. For a review of the relevant area—computational complexity theory—see Stockmeyer 1987; for a more leisurely, semi-popular, introduction to the basic concepts and problems, Garey & Johnson 1979. The basic definitions are in Urquhart 1995.

Although it has not been proven (and most investigators feel it is unlikely to be true) that any proof procedure can provide small proofs of *all* propositional tautologies, it *has* been shown that some, including familiar systems of natural deduction, do significantly better than the analytic procedures in special cases. It is possible to define a class of propositional formulas such that the tautologies in this class have natural deduction proofs of a size bounded by a polynomial function of their lengths but have smallest Beth-Smullyan tableau proofs of sizes exponentially greater than their lengths. The example of (the very clearly written) Urquhart 1987 is one such class: Urquhart proves that axiomatic systems ("Hilbert-style" systems to logicians, "Frege systems" to complexity theorists) are dramatically more efficient than resolution for formulas in this class, but since tableaux can be "translated" into resolution proofs, and axiomatic proofs into natural deduction, without exponential increase in size, our result follows as well. (The usual textbook algorithm[7] for translating natural deduction into axiomatic proofs seems to risk exponential size-increase, since the reduction of nested subproofs involves repeated multiplications of the number of lines in the proof; as a result it is difficult to carry out by hand in even moderate-sized examples without making mistakes. A reasonable exercise for intermediate-level logic students is to design a more efficient algorithm for which the size increase is *obviously* bounded by a low degree polynomial. Quadratic, I think.)

In coming to know the truths of logic—even of propositional logic—we make use of proofs, and, often at least, the styles of proof that convince us are more akin to formal systems of natural deduction than to such explicitly analytic proof procedures as Beth-Smullyan tableaux. The complexity-theoretic lore in the previous paragraph shows that this is not a mere historical accident or eccentricity on the part of the human species: there are logical truths which could not be established by means of tableaux, because of the size of the necessary tableaux, but which could be proven by natural deduction. (Often, when logicians speak of what could and could not be proven in various formal systems, "could" is just idiomatic shorthand for a mathematical existence claim: there exists a formal proof. This is one of the places where "could" means *could*.) I argued in the previous section that natural deduction proofs are not *in general* analytic, but it remains to argue that the

---

7. See Thomason 1970 or Anderson & Belnap 1962, for clear presentations.

particular proofs we are forced to make use of in recognizing truths of propositional logic are synthetic. It seems to me, however, that we can appeal here to another complexity-theoretic result. Recall the way in which our alternative proof of our quantificational example, working through lemmas (v) and (vi), failed of analyticity. The proof contained statements—the lemmas themselves—which were not contained in the principle to be proven in a straightforward and literal sense: though framed in the same vocabulary (without even the addition of instantial terms), they were not subformulas of it. Proofs of this character are essential in propositional logic. By the results of Ajtai 1988 and Buss 1987 (described in Urquhart 1995, p. 454) there is another class of propositional formulas whose tautologies have axiomatic proofs bounded by a polynomial function of their lengths, but which require exponentially long proofs if a bound is put on the logical complexity of the formulas occurring in the proofs. (The textbook algorithm for translating natural deduction into axiomatic proofs also produces excessively complex formulas, but a better one would not increase the relevant sort of complexity—Urquhart's *depth*—of the formulas in the natural deduction proof by more than the addition of a constant. Two, I think.) For the formulas of this class, then, small proofs will have to contain complex lemmas, lemmas that cannot be contained in the formula proven. Lemmas, to put it in Kantspeak, that we have to construct, put together, in a word *synthesize*. In principle, then, it seems that our knowledge of some truths of propositional logic must depend on proofs of a synthetic character rather than on analysis.

4. The Epistemology of Logic

I have not given a precise definition of the narrow sort of analyticity, and any definition I could give would be controversial. One way in which it might generate controversy would be over the question of whether it captured Kant's intentions (Kant's intension?), but this seems likely to be an academic issue in the derogatory sense of the term. Logical theory has advanced too much since Kant's day for his views to have any precise application to it: what he says may be suggestive, but he never conceived of the semantic and proof-theoretic structures he would have had to think about in order to formulate a clear concept of analyticity. As a result there are many possible concepts of analyticity, all with some claim to Kantian inspiration, and the interesting philosophical controversies will be over the relevant importance of these different concepts. It is easy, for example, to make a case for the analyticity of logical truths (in a sense of analyticity most easily grasped by considering the case itself!) starting from the very natural deduction proofs I have emphasized. After all, by Gentzen's *Hauptsatz* (I am counting Prawitz 1965's normalization theorem as a form of the *Hauptsatz*) any natural deduction proof can (in the mathematical existence sense of "can") be transformed into a closed Beth-Smullyan tableau, and tableaux in turn can be seen as developments, explicitations, of the semantic structure of First-Order sentences: hence their popular names of "semantic" or "analytic" tableaux. From this point of view one can say that the provability of a First-Order sentence is simply a combinatorial corollary of its semantic structure, or (the same thing from a different angle) that natural deduction proofs encode facts about the semantic structure of their conclusions: what more could one ask in the way of analyticity?

This sort of analyticity, however, is purely abstract: it is a property of the statements themselves, one they have independently of any real possibility of our coming to know them to be true: analyticity in this sense, one might say, *transcends* real provability. I have, in contrast, been emphasizing more epistemological issues. One might say that analyticity, in the sense I have been urging, is in the first instance a property of judgements rather than of propositions, though of course propositions can be classified as analytic in a derivative sense. (Just as, to cite a parallel case where Kripke 1972 makes a related distinction between metaphysical and epistemological notions, a proposition can be called *a priori* in derivative senses if it is or can be known *a priori*.) In claiming that logical truths are synthetic I want to highlight what seems to me an important feature of logical reasoning: it is, in a sense I will try to make clear, intuitive as well as inferential.

Sometimes our grasp of the fact that a conclusion is implied by a premiss is immediate: we are aware of it as soon as we entertain the two propositions, and, if in considering the premiss we feel confident of its truth, we immediately come to feel a similar confidence in that of the conclusion. Simple analytic connections give rise to pairs like this: no one reflecting on John's bachelorhood will hesitate in inferring that he is unmarried. There are also, perhaps, cases of single propositions whose truth is recognizable in a similar fashion: Descartes, famously, found that whenever he considered the question of his own existence, he clearly and distinctly perceived that he existed. Some of the inference rules of natural deduction (and other) systems license inferences of this sort. From the premiss that 2 is even *and* 2 is prime, the conclusion that 2 is even follows immediately (& Elimination); it seems equally immediate to infer that either 2 is prime or 5 is prime from the premiss that 2 is prime (∨ Introduction). Other rules specify a similar sort of inference of a conclusion from two premisses: & Introduction (A, B, therefore (A&B)) and *modus ponens* ((A→B), A, therefore B) are like this. Call a chain of argument in which each step follows from one or two previous ones in this way (or is itself perceived with Cartesian clarity and distinctness) *purely inferential*. Since the validity of each step in a purely inferential piece of reasoning is grasped by simple reflection on the propositions, the *meanings* of the statements serving as premiss(es) and conclusion, it seems fair to call this analytic reasoning.

What seems to me important, however, is that some of the rules of systems of natural deduction, those involving subordinate proofs, are not like this. The Universal Quantifier Introduction rule, typified by the use of the two outermost subordinate proofs in the example of section 2, is simple and typical:

> (∀ Int) A universally quantified formula $\forall \xi \phi(\xi)$ may be asserted as an item of a proof if an earlier item of the proof is a subordinate proof, with *eigenvariable a* and with no hypotheses, of the formula $\phi(a)$ which is like $\phi(\xi)$ except for containing free occurrences of a in exactly the places where $\phi(\xi)$ contains ξ.

Suppose one reasons in accordance with this rule (as pointed out earlier, at least some informal reasoning follows patterns that can be identified as those of, possibly abbreviated, natural deduction proofs) to a conclusion $\forall \xi \phi(\xi)$. What is this conclusion inferred *from*? Gentzen 1934 and other accounts influenced by Gentzen's presentation speak as if $\forall \xi \phi(\xi)$ was inferred from $\phi(a)$, the last line of the subordinate proof. (Thus, in formulating the notion of a normal derivation, Prawitz 1965 defines $\phi(a)$ as the major premiss of the inference.) This does no formal damage (you can make words mean whatever you want as long as you pay them overtime in the form of explicit definitions), but conceptually it conceals the structure of natural deduction proofs rather than revealing it. In ordinary rules, of the sort I have called purely inferential, the validity of the inference does not depend on how the *premiss* was established: the implication can be recognized by consideration of the premiss and conclusion alone, without regard to any prior justification of the premiss. Universal Quantifier Introduction, however, has provisos: $\phi(a)$ must be established in a way not depending on any premisses or (undischarged) hypotheses containing the *eigenvariable a*. Thus, in verifying the correctness of the inference to $\forall \xi \phi(\xi)$, not only $\phi(a)$ but the whole region of proof above it (in Gentzen's arboriform notation) must be examined. Fitch's presentation is, in this respect, more perspicuous: he speaks of the conclusions of purely inferential rules as *direct consequences* (technical term) of their premisses, but the conclusion of an instance of Unversal Quantifier Introduction is spoken of as a direct consequence of the entire $\forall$ Int subordinate proof, and not just of its last line. The subordinate proof as a whole is the item whose properties legitimate the assertion of $\forall \xi \phi(\xi)$, so Fitch's terminology and notation point us in the right direction, but the relation of "direct consequence" can't, in this case, be an *inferential* one.

This is a purely grammatical point: inference is a move from premiss (or premisses) to a conclusion, and premisses are propositions: a subordinate proof is not the sort of thing that *can* be a premiss. So just what is one doing in reasoning by $\forall$ Int? The puzzle gets, if anything, deeper when one considers semantic issues. The *eigenvariable* behaves, syntactically, like a proper name (individual constant), but it is not interpreted as one: it does not name any object in the domain. Fine 1985 has argued that the *eigenvariables* of Gentzen or Fitch-style quantificational arguments, as well as a range of other sorts of terms occurring in other deductive systems, should be interpreted as standing for abstract generic objects, and the technical results obtained (cf. also Fine 1983) speak for the theoretical fruitfulness of this idea, but other interpretations are possible. The common alternative term "dummy name" for the *eigenvariables* of quantificational rules suggests another: the formulas occurring in the subordinate proof are simply *not* fully interpreted, but are seen as forming a skeleton, or template, on which arguments can be fashioned by inserting a real name in the place of the dummy. On this interpretation, someone asserting a universal quantification after seeing that an appropriate subordinate proof has been provided is not inferring it from any proposition expressed by a formula in the proof, but rather is doing so in recognition of the fact that a form of argument—the dummy-containing subordinate proof—exists which could be applied to any object in the domain (after, if necessary, baptizing it) to produce a proof that the quantified statement holds in its case. If the universally quantified conclusion is inferred from any proposition, it is from the *metalinguistic* proposition, that an appropriate proof-template exists for proving the instances of the quantified statement. And this metalinguistic proposition is known, not by inference, but by... inspection!

I would like to make similar claims for the rules of propositional logic employing subordinate proofs, such as the familiar rule of conditional introduction, or conditionalization:

> (→ Int) A conditional formula (ϕ → ψ) may be asserted as an item of a proof if an earlier item is a subordinate proof of ψ having ϕ as hypothesis.

As with the quantificational rules, and for similar reasons, the Gentzen-Prawitz presentation (on which the formula ψ, which for Fitch is an item of the subordinate proof, is the premiss of the inference) is conceptually imperspicuous: the whole subordinate proof, and not just its last line, has to be examined in checking that the conditional is properly justified. Semantically things are less clearcut because of the absence of an *eigenvariable*, but the idea of the subordinate proof as a template which can be used for the production of many specific proofs is present in the Brouwer-Heyting account of the meaning of the conditional. In constructing the subordinate proof for an instance of → Int, one is making something which can be applied to (well, added to the end of) any proof of the antecedent to transform it into a proof of the consequent. (Even the *eigenvariable* reappears in the notation of Martin-Löf 1984, which is based on the "propositions as types" idea!) In the case of elementary, classical, logic, however, it must be admitted that there is no semantic motivation for thinking of the subordinate proofs of propositional logic as schematic templates, as there is for those of quantificational reasoning. Still, it is clear that the whole subordinate proof, rather than simply its last line, is relevant to the correctness of the "inference," so the premiss, if the conclusion of an instance of a rule like → Int is to be thought of as inferred from a premiss, must be some metalinguistic statement about the existence of an appropriate subordinate proof.

Logical reasoning, then, involves some steps that are, in the sense described above, inferential, and others that turn on the inspection or observation of a subordinate proof. Such inspection, however, in Kantian terminology is a matter of *intuition*. It will be, I suppose, a case of pure intuition if the subordinate proof is only imagined, and of empirical intuition if it is written out: complicated logical arguments, if they are to be rationally compelling, *require* empirical intuition (just as complicated mathematical proofs may require us to observe the behavior of computers if they are to yield mathematical knowledge). The distinction between pure and empirical intuition, however, seems to lose much of its importance once one frees oneself from preconceptions associated with a kind of Cartesian substance dualism. Simple proofs we can follow just by thinking about them, more complicated ones we have to write down, much more complicated ones we need computers for: to think that these differences mark fundamental epistemological boundaries is to overlook the fact that human intellect is essentially embodied and, for that matter, essentially social. The individual human brain, even when thought of as a mechanism for the recognition of purely logical proofs, is part of a larger system that includes the hands, the paper the hands write on, computing machinery, and the brains of colleagues, for, as working mathematicians know, it is foolish to place much confidence in a proof one hasn't discussed with colleagues who can spot the lacunae we might ourselves overlook.

There is, however, a sense in which the subordinate proof observed or inspected is not a physical object: how else can we explain the fact that in some cases *imagining* it—seeing "in one's mind's eye"—can be as good as actually seeing it? What is relevant to supporting a conclusion is not the perception of a particular physical web of inkmarks on paper, or even the perception of any such object at all. What matters is rather an abstraction, the form of the proof, the type of which one or another physically written proofs may be a token. We can, in some cases, be convinced of the existence of such a type without perceiving any token of it, and independently of the question of whether any physical token exists: this is what happens when an outline of a proof is shown us and we think "Yes, I know how to fill in the missing steps" (did you write out the full proof with 28 *eigenvariables* back while you were reading section 2?), or when a metamathematical argument is given that there is (mathematical existence again) a formal proof. On occasion this can be as compelling, and it seems to me as *rationally* compelling, as actually inspecting a written proof, and, at least when the inferred proof is a logical one by natural deduction, it seems to me that it is rationally compelling for much the same reason that seeing a proof written out for our inspection is. The metamathematical premiss, then, supporting the assertion of the conclusion of an instance of one of the rules involving subordinate proofs is to the effect that a proof *type* exists. The vulgar nominalists, I know, make much of the difference between abstract entities and concrete, and go on scholastically about how platonica are causally inert and so (a causal account of perception being presupposed) imperceptible. Perceivability, however, is a complex matter, perhaps a matter of degree, and the distinctions that matter to the epistemology of logic and mathematics are not located at the border between the abstract and the concrete. As Parsons 1980 has argued, such abstract entities as linguistic types (or, the simplest examples of these, Hilbertian stroke-numerals) are at least "quasi-perceivable": what it seems important to recognize is that, in the basic case where we come to know of the existence of a (subordinate) proof by actually constructing it, our logical reasoning incorporates and depends on what can analogously be called quasi-inspection and quasi-intuition.

It seems to me that the view of logical reasoning urged here has benefits beyond the basic one of being true. One is in broadening the perspective of logicians: if even the most rigorously formal reasoning in logic involves the intuitive observation of patterns, it seems foolish to restrict the discipline of logic to studying forms of reasoning that have purely linguistic expression, and to ignore sorts that employ pictures and diagrams.

Appendix on Expressive Power

The "expressive power" of a formal language can be measured in more than one way, and there is a need for conceptual clarification to sort out just which measures of expressive power are most important in various contexts. Particularly since Lindstrom's Theorem (cf. Hodges 1983 for an accessible treatment) is often loosely and informally characterized as saying that no language sharing certain abstract features of First-Order Logic can have greater expressive power, in one sense, than First-Order Logic itself, it is worth reviewing how and in what senses the examples mentioned in Section 1 are of greater expressive power. For First-Order Logic with identity, the point is elementary and familiar: there is no way in First-Order Logic, without using an identity predicate, to affirm or deny the existence of indistinguishable objects in a model. For Russell's Type Theory, Hazen 1992 shows that a certain mathematical structure—the rational numbers under their order relation—with a decidable First-Order theory has an undecidable ramified Second-Order theory. Thus there is no effective way of identifying the propositions about this structure expressed by sentences of its ramified Second-Order language with propositions expressed by its First-Order sentences. Since the ramified Second-Order theory is in fact *essentially* undecidable—has, that is, no decidable consistent extension—this result is independent of any debatable question about the semantic interpretation of Russell's logic: on any interpretation for which ramified Second-Order Logic is sound, it is impossible to identify all the Second-Order propositions with propositions expressed by First-Order sentences.

For First-Order Logic extended by the addition of predicate modifiers or term-forming operators, a relevant measure of expressive power is that of definability in particular languages of the type in question. In the light of the arguments of Davidson 1965, we restrict our attention to languages with finite vocabularies: finitely many predicates for pure First-Order languages (we may, as is well-known, assume without loss of generality that there are no individual constants or function symbols), finitely many predicates and predicate modifiers (predicates and term-forming operators) for the other language types. Consider, then, an interpreted language, with a finite vocabulary, of one of the richer types. Certain subsets of the domain of interpretation are defined by formulas of the language with one free variable. As a preliminary attempt at formulation, we could say that these languages are stronger if, for one particular such interpreted language, there is no finite set of predicates, defined over the domain of its interpretation, such that each of these subsets is defined by a purely First-Order formula in these predicates. This formulation, however, is too crude: as it stands, the existence of such a finite set of predicates is trivial. The interesting case is that in which the domain of the interpretation is infinite (if it is finite, it has only finitely many subsets). In that case, the syntax of the language can be isomorphically mapped (in infinitely many ways!) into the domain. Choose its image under one such mapping, and add enough predicates to define it, to express the usual syntactic concepts, and to allow each formula of the language to be uniquely specified: the single primitive predicate of "protosyntax" from the last chapter of Quine 1940 will suffice. Now add one more predicate: a dyadic "true of" predicate, interpreted so as to relate (the image in the domain of) each formula with a single free variable to all and only those objects which are members of the subset of the domain it defines. Now each subset of the domain definable by a formula of the original language is defined by a formula of pure First-Order Logic employing only the protosyntactic and true-of predicates.

The problem is clear enough. We wanted a definition of when the expressive power—the conceptual resources, so to speak—of the original language could be *concentrated* in a finite number of predicates, but the syntactic and semantic predicates described above are imported from the outside: nothing in the argument just rehearsed suggests that the new predicates are definable in the original language, and indeed, by a form of Tarski's theorem on the indefinability of truth, we can see that they aren't.[8] The correct statement of our measure of expressive power, then, will be that an extension of First-Order Logic is stronger than pure First-Order Logic if, for some interpreted language of the extended type, it is not the case that there are finitely many predicates *definable in that language* such that every subset of the domain of interpretation defined by a formula of that language is also defined by a purely First-Order formula in those predicates.

A predicate modifier is an operator attaching to a (simple or complex) predicate, of some number of argument places, to form a new, complex, predicate of the same (in the case of analogues of English adjectives and adverbs) or a greater (in the analogues of prepositions) number of argument places, the extension of the new predicate so formed being in general different from that of the original predicate. Since the application of predicate modifiers is iterable, a finite vocabulary of predicates and predicate modifiers can give the effect of an infinite number of distinct predicates. (As Terence Parsons observed long ago, since the usual completeness proofs for First-Order Logic apply to languages with arbitrary sets of predicates, construing the results of applying predicate modifiers to predicates as new predicates allows us to extend Gödel's completeness theorem to the language with predicate modifiers.)

Any example, therefore, of a First-Order language with denumerably many predicates which cannot all be defined by First-Order means from finitely many predicates definable in the language can be turned into an example to show that predicate modifier language is of greater expressive power than pure First-Order language. For a simple, though artificial, example, consider an interpreted language whose domain of interpretation contains the finite strings of its own symbols and is closed under the formation of finite sequences, and which has enough predicates to express all the usual syntactic notions concerning it. (Yes—another appeal to Tarski's theorem is coming up!) Add a single monadic predicate F, and a single predicate

---

8. There are subtleties about Tarski's theorem that are often overlooked (cf. Gupta 1982) but none that give hope of defining predicates like those described in the general case.

modifier μ. Interpret F, unmodified, to be true of precisely the true sentences of the language in which neither F nor μ occurs, μF to be true of true sentences containing at most unmodified occurrences of F, μ^{n+1}F as true of true sentences containing at most n iterations of the operator μ, and give the applications of μ to any other predicates trivial, throwaway, interpretations. If there were finitely many predicates definable in this language which sufficed to define every set definable in it, the fragment of the language admitting just enough iterations of μ to define these predicates would contain its own truth definition.

Variable-binding term-forming operators, such as the familiar set-abstraction and definite description operators, or Church's notation of λ-abstraction, are far more common in logical *practice* than the rather perfunctory treatment of their theory in standard textbooks would suggest. Sometimes, in the context of a theory formalized in a language containing such an operator, the operator is *eliminable*.[9] One familiar example is the fact that, in virtue of extensionality, set abstracts can be eliminated: $\{x: ...x...\}$ is simply the unique y such that

$$\forall x(x \in y \leftrightarrow ...x...).$$

As should by now be a familiar point, however, not all such operators are eliminable. If we do not posit extensionality (so our abstraction terms are better thought of as standing for properties or attributes than for sets), there is no guarantee that the abstraction terms can be eliminated in favor of any predicates definable in the language. Now, any, otherwise First-Order, interpreted language with an ineliminable variable-binding term-forming operator is an example showing that First-Order languages with such operators are, in yet another sense, stronger than pure First-Order languages: such a language does not allow the definition of a finite set of predicates sufficient to identify the denotata of arbitrary given terms, something the enriched language does trivially! To show that languages with such operators are richer than pure First-Order languages in the sense we have defined (*i.e.*,

---

9. One way of looking at the conceptual analysis of the notion of a *model* of Church's λ-calculus in chapter 11 of Hindley and Seldin 1986 is as a proof that, when propositional connectives and quantifiers are added to the λ-calculus to turn it into a First-Order theory, predicates can be defined by the use of which the λ-operator is eliminable, thus allowing the use of standard model-theoretic methods in the study of the λ-calculus.

that of perhaps defining more subsets of the domain than can be defined by First-Order formulas in definable predicates), another argument is needed. For that, however, it suffices to note that (at least if we assume infinite domains of interpretation) an operator like the μ of the previous paragraph can be reconstrued in terms of a predicate and a term-forming operator. Simply add such an operator—for definiteness I will write it using the braces of set-abstraction—so any predicate you want to apply the predicate modifier to can be "nominalized", and rewrite, *e.g.*, μFx as xμ{y:Fy}, with μ reconstrued as a dyadic predicate. (Adopting such a reconstrual in general for predicate modifiers used in the semantic representation of natural languages would raise familiar questions of ontological commitment, etc.,[10] but that does not affect its employment here, to make a purely formal point about two types of language.)

There are, then, important differences between pure First-Order Logic and these extended formalisms. The existing literature of mathematical logic does not, to my knowledge, contain any adequate discussion of the extended logics, perhaps because languages with these added features are of comparatively little use in the analysis of mathematical theories and structures. The model theory of mathematical systems, however, is not the only "customer" for logic: linguistics, cognitive science, and various branches of philosophy are also in the market, and perhaps need a different product.[11]

References

Ajtai M., 1988, 'The Complexity of the Pigeon Hole Principle,' *Proceedings of the 29th Annual IEEE Symposium on the Foundations of Computer Science*, White Plains (NY), pp. 346–355.

Anderson A. R., and Belnap N. D., 1962, 'The Pure Calculus of Entailment,' *Journal of Symbolic Logic* 27, 19-52 (incorporated in Anderson & Belnap 1975).

Anderson A. R. and Belnap N. D., 1975, *Entailment*, vol. I, Princeton: Princeton University Press.

Boolos G., 1984, 'Don't Eliminate Cut,' *Journal of Philosophical Logic* 13, 373-78.

---

10. See Davidson 1967, Parsons 1970, and Taylor 1985 for discussion.
11. This paper stems from reflection on natural deduction. In consideration of his sometimes under-rated contributions to logical theory, and more personally of his having first taught me natural deduction, I dedicate it to the memory of the late Professor F. B. Fitch.

Boolos G., 1987, 'A Curious Inference,' *Journal of Philosophical Logic* 16, 1–12.

Buss S. R., 1987, 'Polynomial Size Proofs of the Propositional Pigeonhole Principle,' *Journal of Symbolic Logic* 52, 916–17.

Cellucci C., 1988, 'Efficient Natural Deduction,' in G. Cellucci and G. Sembin (eds.), *Nuovi problemi della logica e della filosofia della scienza*, Bologna: CLUEB, pp. 29–57.

Van Dalen D., 1983, *Logic and Structure* (2nd ed.), Berlin: Springer-Verlag.

Davidson D., 1965, 'Theories of Meaning and Learnable Languages,' in Y. Bar-Hillel (ed.), *Logic, Methodology, and Philosophy of Science: Proceedings of the 1964 International Congress*, Amsterdam: North-Holland, 1965, pp. 383–94; reprinted in D. Davidson, *Inquiries into Truth and Interpretation*, Oxford: Clarendon Press, 1984.

Davidson D., 1967, 'The Logical Form of Action Sentences,' in N. Rescher (ed.), *The Logic of Decision and Action*, Pittsburgh, University of Pittsburgh Press, pp. 81–95; reprinted in D. Davidson, *Essays on Action and Events*, Oxford: Clarendon Press, 1980.

Fine K., 1983, 'The Permutational Principle in Quantificational Logic', *Journal of Philosophical Logic* 12, 33–37.

Fine K., 1985, *Reasoning with Arbitrary Objects*, Oxford: Basil Blackwell.

Fitch F. B., 1952, *Symbolic Logic: An Introduction*, New York: Ronald Press.

Garey M. R. and Johnson D. S., 1979, *Computers and Intractability*, San Francisco: Freeman.

Gentzen G., 1934, 'Untersuchungen Über das logische Schliessen,' *Mathematische Zeitschrift* 39, 176–210, 405–431; Eng. tr. 'Investigations into Logical Deduction,' *American Philosophical Quarterly* 1 (1964), 288–306; 2 (1965), 204–218; reprinted in G. Gentzen, *Collected Papers*, Amsterdam: North-Holland, 1969.

Gupta A., 1982, 'Truth and Paradox,' *Journal of Philosophical Logic* 11, 1–60; reprinted in R. L. Martin (ed.), *Recent Essays on Truth and the Liar Paradox*, New York: Oxford University Press, 1983.

Hazen A. P., 1992, 'Interpretability of Robinson Arithmetic in the Ramified Second-order Theory of Dense Linear Order,' *Notre Dame Journal of Formal Logic* 33, 101–11.

Hindley J. R. & Seldin J. P., 1986, *Introduction to Combinators and λ-Calculus*, Cambridge: Cambridge University Press.

Hintikka K. J. J., 1970, *Logic, Language-Games, and Information*, Oxford: Clarendon Press.

Hodges W., 1983, 'Elementary Predicate Logic,' in D. Gabbay and F. Guenthner (eds.), *Handbook of Philosophical Logic, Vol. I: Elements of Classical Logic*, Dordrecht: Reidel, pp. 1-131.

Kripke S.A., 1972, 'Naming and Necessity,' in D. Davidson and G. Harman (eds.), *Semantics of Natural Language*, Dordrecht: Reidel, pp. 253-352; reprinted with introduction as S. A. Kripke, *Naming and Necessity*, Cambridge (Mass.): Harvard University Press, 1980.

Martin-Löf P., 1984, *Intuitionistic Type Theory*, Naples: Bibliopolis.

Parsons C. A., 1980, 'Mathematical Intuition,' *Proceedings of the Aristotelian Society* 80, 145-68.

Parsons T., 1970, 'Some Problems Concerning the Logic of Grammatical Modifiers,' *Synthese* 21, 320-34; reprinted. in D. Davidson and G. Harman (eds.), *Semantics of Natural Language*, Dordrecht: Reidel, 1972.

Prawitz D., 1965, *Natural Deduction*, Stockholm: Almqvist & Wiksell.

Quine W. V., 1940, *Mathematical Logic*, New York: Norton.

Quine W. V., 1969, 'Existence and Quantification,' in W. V. Quine, *Ontological Relativity and Other Essays*, New York: Columbia University Press.

Sellars W., 1962, 'Naming and Saying,' *Philosophy of Science* 29, 7-26; reprinted. in W. Sellars, *Science, Perception, and Reality*, London: Routledge & Kegan Paul, 1963.

Sher G., 1991, *The Bounds of Logic: a Generalized Viewpoint*, Cambridge (Mass.): MIT Press.

Smullyan R., 1968, *First-Order Logic*, New York: Springer-Verlag.

Stockmeyer L., 1987, 'Classifying the Computational Complexity of Problems,' *Journal of Symbolic Logic* 52, 1-43.

Taylor B., 1985, *Modes of Occurrence: Verbs, Adverbs, and Events*, Oxford: Basil Blackwell.

Tarski A., 1986, 'What Are Logical Notions?' *History and Philosophy of Logic* 7, 143-54.

Thom P., 1977, 'Termini Obliqui and the Logic of Relations,' *Archiv für Geschichte der Philosophie* 77, 143-55.

Thomason R. H., 1970, *Symbolic Logic: An Introduction*, New York: MacMillan.

Urquhart A., 1987, 'Hard Examples for Resolution,' *Journal of the Association for Computing Machinery* 34, 209-19.

Urquhart A., 1995, 'The Complexity of Propositional Proofs,' *Bulletin of Symbolic Logic* 1, 425-67.

Philosophy Department
University of Melbourne
Parkville, VIC 3052
Australia

ARNOLD KOSLOW
The Implicational Nature of Logic: A Structuralist Account

1. Introduction

Our account of logic begins with the study of *implication relations* on arbitrary non-empty sets. These relations are characterized by a slightly emended version of Gentzen's structural rules of inference—only they are now viewed as general conditions for the concept of an implication relation, rather than as rules governing some particular rule of inference. The result is an abstract theory of implication that includes familar proof-theoretic and semantic examples, but extends far beyond them. It is this extension that allows there to be implication relations that hold not only between elements that have a syntax or a semantic value, but as well between those that do not.

In Section 2 we shall describe a variety of implication relations. From those examples it should be clear that implication relations may involve sets, objects that in some sense have parts, Tarskian theories, belief states, as well as more familiar fare. Indeed, it can be shown that any set with at least two members has an implication realtion on it. Thus the theory of implication relations is radically topic neutral. Some writers have required that the conditions for implication relations are not only true, but are known *a priori*. We shall argue that this is incorrect; some implication relations hold true, but it is not known *a priori* that they do. Let us say that an *implication structure* is any non-empty set with an implication on it. We shall take such structures to be central to logical theory.

Since the description of implication structures will not involve any reference to the logical operators, there is a real question of how they can be understood in such an abstract setting. In Section 3 we shall provide specific definitions for each of the logical operators (e.g. conjunction, disjunction, negation, and the hypothetical) as special kinds of functions that map the implication structure to itself and we shall do this in a way that relies only upon the implication relation of a structure.[1] The logical operators can be defined on anything for which there is an implication relation. It is an old dogma that the logical operators confer propositional status on anything that they involve. On the present account that dogma is rejected. Thus our theory of the logical operators matches the generality of the theory of implication relations.

Given our account of the various logical operators, a natural question concerns the universal laws of logic. What are the implications which hold in all implication structures? The general picture that is developed in Section 4 is this: The implications which hold in all structures for which the logical operators are all defined are exactly those which hold intuitionistically. In contrast, there is a special sublass of implication structures such that the implications which hold in all of them are precisely the ones which hold classically. In this sense it is intuitionism which is more general than classical logic. This result will be used to place the nature of the conflict between classical and intuitionistic logic in a new perspective.

In Section 5 we shall explain how a general theory of modal operators is available without relying on anything other than the concept of an implication relation. We shall do so without appeal to truth or possible worlds. Modal operators on structures will be defined as special kinds of functions that map a structure to itself, and they are characterized by conditions that involve only the implication relation of that structure. Most, if not all the known modal operators satisfy those conditions. There are several applications of this theory that we shall develop. With their aid one can recover all the systematic organization that Kripke provided for the familiar modals, without any reliance on possible worlds. We shall also explain why it is that van Fraassen's concept of supervaluational truth is a modal notion, and also explain why counterfactual conditionals (unlike material conditionals) have modal character.

Finally, in Section 6 we shall consider an application that is connected to our account of the logical operators. According to that account, each logical

---

1. Space does not allow for a discussion of universal and existential quantification, and identity. For details see Koslow 1992, Chapters 20 and 21.

operator is associated with a characteristic condition on the members of a structure. Two requirements hold: the value of the operator for any argument satisfies the characteristic condition, and the value of the operator is implied by any member of the structure that satisfies the condition. For example, if λ is a logical operator (with one argument) and C is its characteristic condition, then for any element A in the structure, $\lambda(A)$ (if it exists) satisfies the condition C, and if any B in the structure satisfies C, then B implies $\lambda(A)$.

Given this uniform way of treating the logical operators, one might wonder whether there are any predicates that could be studied in exactly the same way as the operators. We shall argue that the predicate "is a natural number" is such a case. Thus, even if various reductive attempts fail, nevertheless there is something logical about about "is a natural number" in this sense: when we treat it at all, we do so in just the same way as the logical operators.

2. Implication Structures

The notion of an *implication relation* is characterized by the following conditions. Let S be any nonempty set. An implication relation $\Rightarrow$ on the set S is any relation on S such that

(1) *Reflexivity*: $A \Rightarrow A$, for all A in S.
(2) *Projection*: $A_1, A_2, ..., A_n \Rightarrow A_k$, for any k = 1, ..., n.
(3) *Simplification* (sometimes called *Contraction*): If $A_1, A_1, A_2, ..., A_n \Rightarrow B$, then $A_1, A_2, ..., A_n \Rightarrow B$, for all A_i and B in S.
(4) *Permutation*: If $A_1, A_2, ..., A_n \Rightarrow B$, then $A_{f(1)}, A_{f(2)}, ..., A_{f(n)} \Rightarrow B$, for any permutation f of $\{1, 2, ..., n\}$.
(5) *Dilution*: If $A_1, A_2, ..., A_n \Rightarrow B$, then $A_1, A_2, ..., A_n, C \Rightarrow B$, for all A_i, B, and C in S.
(6) *Cut*: If $A_1, A_2, ..., A_n \Rightarrow B$, and $B, B_1, B_2, ..., B_m \Rightarrow C$, then $A_1, A_2, ..., A_n, B_1, B_2, ..., B_m \Rightarrow C$.[2]

---

2. Elliott Mendelson, noting that Reflexivity follows from Projection, Dilution follows from Projection and Cut, and Projection follows from Reflexivity, Dilution, and Permutation, has shown that Projection, Simplification, and Permutation are independent from the other axioms.

(The A_i will be referred to as antecedents, and B as the consequent of $A_1, A_2, \ldots, A_n \Rightarrow B$.) These six conditions are based upon Gentzen's "structural" rules of inference.[3] They are, for Gentzen, a special subset of rules of inference that do not involve any logical complexity that the members of S may have.[4] Because of this connection with Gentzen's structural rules, the six conditions may be somewhat familiar. However, there is a difference: instead of thinking of these rules as concerning some specific concept of implication, as Gentzen seems to have done, we have taken them to be precisely the conditions for any relation to be an implication relation.

An *implication structure* $I = (S, \Rightarrow)$ is any non-empty set S, together with an implication relation $\Rightarrow$ on it. If $I = (S, \Rightarrow)$ is an implication structure, we shall say that any C in S is a *thesis* of the structure if and only if (iff) it is implied by every member of S. And A is an *antithesis* of the structure iff it implies every member of the structure.

Several natural questions arise: (1) What makes these conditions an abstract theory of implication relations? (2) If this is to be the basis of a theory of logic, what account can one give for the usual logical operations? (3) There has been no mention of truth in the conditions for an implication relation. What role does it have in a structuralist setting? (4) What is the status of the conditions on implication relations? Are they supposed to hold necessarily or be known *a priori*? (5) Modal logics ought to be given some account in a structuralist theory, but it's not clear how that is to be done, given that there is no reference to modality or to possible worlds in this description of implication relations. All of these questions can be resolved, we think, by using only the simple resources available in implication structures.

2.1 Examples

The six conditions for implication relations do not determine any one implication relation uniquely. That is a virtue, since it opens the way for many different kinds of applications. As we shall see, familiar logical systems are implication structures. They, of course, are part of the story, but they are certainly not the whole story. Let's look at several examples of implication

---

3. Gentzen 1934.
4. Gentzen 1932, and Koslow 1992 for a bit of the history of this idea in the works of P. Hertz and D. Scott.

structures. An even wider range of the various kinds of implication structures can be found in Koslow 1992.

a. Bisection Implication. This is a type of implication relation which shows that *any* non-empty set S with at least two members has an implication relation on it. Let a *bisection of S* be defined as an ordered pair $\tau = (K, L)$ of two non-empty subsets of S such that their intersection is empty and their union is S itself. The *bisection implication* $\Rightarrow^\tau$ is defined as follows:

$A_1, A_2, ..., A_n \Rightarrow^\tau B$ iff some A_i is in K or B is in L.

All the members of K are equivalent: they imply each other by this particular implication relation. All the members of L are equivalent, and every member of K implies every member of L.

We can strengthen the notion of a bisection implication if we are dealing with an implication structure and not just some non-empty set. If $I = (S, \Rightarrow)$ is an implication structure, then a *strong bisection* $\tau = (K, L)$ on I is a bisection of S for which L is closed under the implication relation of I. That is, if $A_1, A_2, ..., A_n$ are in L, and $A_1, A_2, ..., A_n \Rightarrow B$, then B is in L. A *strong bisection implication* is a bisection implication based upon a strong bisection. Then we have the rather remarkable result:

> *Strong Completeness* (Lindenbaum-Scott). Let $I = (S, \Rightarrow)$ be a non-trivial implication structure (at least two members of S are not equivalent with respect to $\Rightarrow$). Then $A_1, A_2, ..., A_n \Rightarrow B$ iff $A_1, A_2, ..., A_n \Rightarrow^\tau B$ for all strong bisection implications $\Rightarrow^\tau$ of the structure I. [5]

This result enables us to introduce the notion of a truth-value assignment. It looks initially impossible to have anything like truth-value assignments in an abstract setting, where the members of a structure may not even be truth bearers. Nevertheless, here is how it can be done:

Let $I = (S, \Rightarrow)$ be an implication structure, and let $\tau = (K, L)$ be any strong bisection on I. To each such τ, there is a mapping T_τ of S to the set $\{K, L\}$ defined as follows:

For every A in S, $T_\tau(A) = L$, if A is in L, and $T_\tau(A) = K$, if A is in K.

These mappings are the *truth-value assignments* on the structure. They assign the K's and L's of strong bisections instead of the traditional t's and

---

5. For a simple proof of this result, see Koslow 1992, pp. 50–51.

f's, and we shall sometimes say that T_τ assigns "true" to A if A is in L, and "false" if A is in K. With their help one can give a clear description of the extensionality of the various logical operators and determine the exact conditions under which each of them is or is not extensional (cf. also § 5.2).[6]

With this terminology in place, we can now see from the strong-completeness result above, that $A_1, A_2, \ldots, A_n \Rightarrow B$ holds iff every truth-value assignment that makes each of the A_i's true, also makes B true. Thus the familiar apparatus of assigning truth-values is obtainable in the general structuralist setting.[7]

b. Relative Implication. Sometimes we may wish to single out some of the members of a structure for a special role. Suppose that we thought of them as always being available as an antecedent in any implication. Given the structure $I = (S, \Rightarrow)$, and the special element T of S, we could form a new structure, I^T, relativized to T, as follows: Let $I^T = (S, \Rightarrow^T)$, and define $A_1, A_2, \ldots, A_n \Rightarrow^T B$ as $T, A_1, A_2, \ldots, A_n \Rightarrow B$. The relativized implication $\Rightarrow^T$ is an extension of (or extends) $\Rightarrow$ in the sense that if $A_1, A_2, \ldots, A_n \Rightarrow B$, then $A_1, A_2, \ldots, A_n \Rightarrow^T B$, for all $A_1, A_2, \ldots, A_n$ and B in S. The new relation is easily seen to be an implication relation. It provides a simple example of an implication relation that isn't truth preserving. Even if the implication relation $\Rightarrow$ on S preserves truth in the sense that if any true antecedents imply B, then B is also true, it needn't be the case that $\Rightarrow^T$ preserves truth. The reason is simply that if $A_1, A_2, \ldots, A_n \Rightarrow^T B$, then $T, A_1, A_2, \ldots, A_n \Rightarrow B$. So even if all the A_is are true, that will not yield the truth of B. The notion of relativized implication can be defined for any subset of the implication structure, not just to a single member of it.

It would be a mistake to think of all implication structures as confined to sets of truth-bearers, and as truth-preserving on them. For there are structures on sets of truth-bearers, where the implication relation (as above) fails to be truth-preserving. A more important example of this possiblity is the

---

6. The idea for replacing the assignments of t and f by membership in a specified set is, I believe, due to Scott 1974. For a full account of extensionality (or non-extensionality) of the various logical operators see Koslow 1992, Ch. 19.
7. It is proved in Koslow 1992, Ch. 19, that the logical operators are extensional iff their L and K values distribute in exactly the same way that the usual ts and fs distribute in the standard classical systems. Thus a disjunction is assigned the value L iff both disjuncts are assigned the value L.

dual of an implication relation, discussed below. But it would also be a mistake to think that the structuralist view has no room for the familiar syntactic (proof-theoretical) and semantic (model-theoretical) accounts of logic. These familiar theories are special examples of implication structures. That is,

c. Deducibility and Logical Consequence as Implication Relations. The familiar notions of deducibility ⊢ and logical consequence ⊨, are special cases of implication relations. A deducibility relation $A_1, A_2, ..., A_n \vdash B$ is usually specified on a well-defined set of sentences S (relative to axioms (if any) and rules). Define the implication relation $\Rightarrow^\vdash$ on S such that $A_1, A_2, ..., A_n \Rightarrow^\vdash B$ holds iff ⊢ $(A_1 \wedge A_2 \wedge ... \wedge A_n) \to B$. The relation of semantic consequence ⊨ on a set of sentences S (B is a semantic consequence of some sentences iff every model of those sentences is also a model for B), can also be associated with an implication relation on S: $(A_1, A_2, ..., A_n \Rightarrow^\vDash B$ holds iff ⊨ $(A_1 \wedge A_2 \wedge ... \wedge A_n) \to B$.

d. Dual Implication Relations. Given any structure I = (S, ⇒), we can define a new structure, its dual, which is based upon the same set S, together with a new implication relation ⇒^, *the dual of* ⇒. The dual implication, enables one to give a general account of the dual of operators on S, and of the duals of the logical operators in particular. This in turn enables one to study the dual of negation with surprising results, which we shall describe below. The most compact description of the dual is that

> For any $A_1, A_2, ..., A_n$ and B in S: $A_1, A_2, ..., A_n \Rightarrow^\wedge B$ iff for every T in S, if all the $A_i \Rightarrow T$, then $B \Rightarrow T$.

In the case of implications that have single antecedents, $A \Rightarrow^\wedge B$ iff $B \Rightarrow A$. That is, the dual of ⇒ is just its converse. So, of course, if any A and B are equivalent with respect to an implication relation, they are also equivalent with respect to its dual. Once we have defined the various logical operators, it can be proved that $A_1, A_2, ..., A_n \Rightarrow^\wedge B$ iff $B \Rightarrow (A_1 \vee A_2 \vee ... \vee A_n)$. There is an equivalent definition of dual implication relations that gives the "converse feature" a more central place.[8]

---

8. ⇒^ is that implication relation on S that extends all the implication relations ⇒* on S such that $A \Rightarrow^* B$ iff $B \Rightarrow A$.

We turn to two examples of implication relations that could not possibly be thought of as sentential, propositional, or truth-bearing. One concerns implication relations on objects, and the other concerns sets.

e. Mereological Implication. Suppose that S is a set of individuals or objects in the sense that they satisfy a whole-part relation P(x, y) (x is a part of y), such that for all x, y, and z in S, (1) (Reflexivity) P(x, x), and (2) (Transivity) If P(x, y) and P(y, z), then P(x, z) (every part of a part is a part). This is a very weak part of what usually passes for Mereology; for example, nothing is assumed about fusion, or identity. Nevertheless it is possible given this weak formulation to define a mereological implication relation:

For all x, y, ..., z and u in S: x, y, ..., z $\Rightarrow_p$ u iff for all w in S, if P(w, x) and P(w, y) and ... and P(w, z), then P(w, u) (everything that is a part of x, y, ... and z, is a part of u).

f. Set Theoretical and Tarskian Implication Relations. Suppose that S is a collection of sets, and for any $X_1, X_2, ..., X_n$, and Y in S, we define a relation as holding between them iff $X_1 \cap X_2 \cap ... \cap X_n \subseteq Y$. If the set S is closed under intersections (if for example, S is the set of all subsets of some set Z), then the subset relation on S is an implication relation. There are, of course many other implication relations that can be provided for sets of sets.

One of the most interesting is *Tarskian Implication*. By a *(Strong) Tarskian Theory* of a structure I = (S, $\Rightarrow$), we mean any subset U of S that is strongly closed under the implication relation $\Rightarrow$. (That is, if $A_1, A_2, ..., A_n \Rightarrow B$, and all the A_is are in U, then B is in U). We can now define a *Tarskian Implication Relation*. Let U, V, ..., Z, with or without positive numerical subscripts, range over the Tarskian theories of the structure I. Let T be the set of all the theories of I. The Tarskian implication relation $\Rightarrow^T$ is given by

$$U_1, U_2, ..., U_n \Rightarrow^T V \text{ iff } U_1 \cap U_2 \cap ... \cap U_n \subseteq V.$$

Thus, if I is an implication structure, the Tarskian implication structure is the set T of all the Tarskian theories of I, together with the implication relation $\Rightarrow^T$ on it.

g. Quasi-Orders and Implication Relations. There is a whole family of implication relations that can be constructed from quasi-orders (preorders). We mention this possibility because they have a role in a later discussion of whether the conditions on implication relations are *a priori* (we think not). Quasi-orders (or pre-orders) are binary relations that are reflexive, and transitive. The relation ≤ on the real numbers, ⊆ on any collection of sets, "at least as tall as", "at least the same temperature as", and any equivalence relation (reflexive, symmetric and transitive) are all quasi-orders. For one's favorite quasi-ordering relation R, on a set S, one could always construct an implication relation $\Rightarrow^R$, on that set such that $A \Rightarrow^R B$ iff $R(A, B)$. More generally,

R is a quasi-order on a set S. Define $\Rightarrow^R$ as follows: For any $A_1, A_2, ..., A_n$ and B in S, $A_1, A_2, ..., A_n \Rightarrow^R B$ iff $R(A_i, B)$, for some A_i.

h. Epistemic Implication Relations. P. Gärdenfors (1984) has offered an account of "propositions" that was designed to provide a basis for logic that rested upon his account of the dynamics of belief revision. Gärdenfors' account begins with some set of states S, the states of belief of an agent, and considers a set P (I shall call them "G-propositions") which is a subset of S^S (the set of all functions from S to S) satisfying two constraints: its members are idempotent (for all f in S, ff=f), and commutative (for all f and g in S, fg=gf, where fg is functional composition). According to his theory, we are supposed to understand "The proposition f is accepted as known, in the belief state K" as the condition that for f in P, and K in S, "f(K) = K". Gärdenfors then defines what he calls a consequence condition between any two G-propositions:

f $\Rightarrow$ g iff for all states of belief K, if f is accepted as known in state K, then g is accepted as known in state K.

That is, the universal conditional $(K)[(f(K) = K) \rightarrow (g(K) = K)]$ holds. It follows easily that for any G-propositions f and g in P, f $\Rightarrow$ g iff f = gf (Gärdenfors' Principle (C)). It's this connection of f $\Rightarrow$ g with the universal conditional that makes it an epistemic relation. However it is not at all clear what drives the definition of the G-propositions. Taking G-propositions as functions on belief states is supposed to emphasize the role that they play in transforming some belief states to others, but it leaves the requirements of idempotency and commutativity unmotivated.

Here is a way of addressing the matter that exploits the structuralist perspective. In order to get something "logical" going, we have to have an implication relation. Start with Gärdenfors' Principle (C), generalized, to account for multiple antecedents:

For any functions $f_1, \ldots, f_n$ and g, that map S to S, define a relation between them as follows: $f_1, \ldots, f_n \Rightarrow g$ iff $gf_1 \ldots f_n = f_1 \ldots f_n$.

One can then prove that this relation among functions is an implication relation iff the functions are idempotent, and commute with each other. This way of placing the implication relation first, and then letting the logical operators be defined (as we do below) makes the particular logical structure that rests on it look quite natural (given the special implication that is used).[9] The fact that the logical operators can be defined for G-propositions does not make them sentential, truth bearing, or propositional.[10]

2.2 Substructual Relations

There is a vast and serious literature that studies what happens when only some of the six structural conditions are used.[11] Thus one might consider those subrelations of implication relations for which (say) reflexivity, or monotonicity (I mean the failure of the Dilution condition; this usage is not universal) and so forth might fail. Here is a very natural substructural relation that changes none of the logical operators, and uses a standard notion of implication: Let $\Rightarrow$ be some standard implication relation (say a classical deducibility relation of sentential logic) and let $\neg$ be classical negation.

Contrastive implication ($\Rightarrow^C$) is defined as follows: $A_1, A_2, \ldots, A_n \Rightarrow^C B$ iff $A_1, A_2, \ldots, A_n \Rightarrow B$, and not: $A_1, A_2, \ldots, A_n \Rightarrow \neg B$.

Thus a group of As contrastively implies B iff those As imply B, but fail to imply the negation of B. Contrastive implication is an interesting and very natural substructural notion. It is nonmonotonic, and both reflexivity and the cut condition fail. Nevertheless,

$\Rightarrow^C$ is *adjunctive*: if some things contrastively imply B, and contrastively imply C, then they contrastively imply $B \wedge C$.

---

9. Gärdenfors (private correspondence) regards the implicational underpinning as an acceptable way of organizing the results of his article.
10. Indeed, it is possible to provide an implication structure directly onto the set of belief states, so that the logical operators apply directly to them. For a fully developed theory of this kind, cf. Levi 1991.
11. For a good view of recent problems and the relevant literature in substructural logic, see Schröder-Heister and Dosen (eds.) 1993.

$\Rightarrow^C$ is *transitive*: if A contrastively implies B, and B contrastively implies C, then A contrastively implies C.

It also has the interesting property that contradictions contrastively imply nothing, nor are they implied by anything so that they are in a sense rendered "contentless" according to a now deviant tradition in the history of logic dating perhaps back to Aristotle.[12]

Our aim is to show how the logical operators can be defined relative to whatever implication relation there may be on a structure. The behavior of the logical operators with respect to subrelations of implication relations, is a task that is beyond the present study.

2.3 The Status of the Conditions for Implication Relations

We have been concerned thus far with a description of the variety of relations that are implicational. It is worthwhile addressing a philosophical question about the status of the Gentzen conditions for implication relations. There is no doubt that in his earliest publication on the matter, Gentzen thought of these conditions as covering examples which included not only those which were obviously "logical" (examples which covered not only sentences, propositions and properties), but also included cases which do not seem to have logical character such as a relation between events which involve causation. Our account is also meant to have this kind of generality. Whatever relation satisfies the six conditions is an implication relation, and logic proceeds by defining its key operations with respect to implication relations whatever they may be.

The philosophical question can be put this way: isn't there a condition that has been omitted? Suppose that some specific relation R satisfies the six conditions. Isn't there an additional requirement: the fact that R satisfies those conditions be known *a priori*?[13] Even if one granted that the conditions for being an implication relation are *a priori* it does not follow that it is an *a priori* matter that any specific relation satisfies those conditions. The conditions seem to me to be a way of singling out a concept for study; it does not follow that it is an *a priori* matter that some particular item is an instance of that concept. On the contrary, there are particular implication

---

12. For more details, see Priest 1997.
13. Peacocke 1976 has argued forcefully for this requirement. That argument is rejected in Koslow 1992, pp. 170–73.

relations for which not all the implication conditions for them can be known *a priori*. An example: Let R be the quasi-ordering relation "x has at least the *same temperature* as y". By the observation in 2.1(g), we can define an implication relation $\Rightarrow^R$. In particular, the Cut condition for $\Rightarrow^R$ requires that it is transitive. And so, the symmetric relation R(x, y) ∧ R(y, x) (x and y have the same temperature) is also transitive. Thus the fact that $\Rightarrow^R$ satisfies the Cut condition requires that

> For any x and y, if x and y have the *same temperature*, and x and z have the same temperature, then y and z have the same temperature.

Far from being known *a priori*, this law is known as the zero-th law of classical thermodynamics, and is regarded as one of the fundamental laws of that theory.[14] So, for at least some implication relations, the six conditions are not known *a priori*. In fact, since the zero-th law is contingent, and not logically necessary, the example also shows that some of the six conditions for $\Rightarrow^R$ are contingent.

3. The Logical Operators

Up until now we have been concerned with a simple abstract theory of implication relations. Nothing has been said about the logical operators, and it isn't obvious how they get into the picture. Our claim however, is that they can all be defined using only the resources that are available in any implication structure. That is our next concern. But before we do that it is worth emphasizing two points about the kind of structuralism that we advocate. The first point is this: unlike most varieties of structuralism developed in the current philosophy of mathematics, we do not require that the members of an implication structure be individuated by the implication relation on it. For us, a non-empty set S can have (as we have seen) a variety of implication relations on it. The identity or non-identity of the members of the set does not shift with the implication relation. Though we cannot argue the point here, a view which requires such a shift seems to us to be incoherent. The second related point is that we do not assume that the members of a structure have no properties other than those that can be pro-

---

14. Cf. J. C. Maxwell 1877 who distinguishes this law from the Euclidean claim that things that are identical to the same thing are identical to each other (which he describes as a triviality), and maintains that this law is the fundamental basis of the science of thermometry.

vided by the implication relation of that structure. For example the quasi-ordering relation "is at least as tall as" can be an implication relation on a set of people. That does not mean that those people don't have mass.[15]

Let $I = (S, \Rightarrow)$ be an arbitrary implication structure. Since we do not in general have any syntactical or semantic notions available in implication structures, we shall define the various logical operators as functions that map S (or the Cartesian product $S \times S$) to S, that satisfy certain conditions that are characteristic of each of the various logical operators. The conditions are all of the same type, and the definitions have a uniform character to them. The basic idea, roughly speaking, is to associate a special kind of condition to each logical operator, and the value of the operator will then meet two requirements: it will satisfy that condition for the operator, and it will be the (implicationally) weakest member to satisfy that condition in the sense that the value of the operator will be implied by anything that satisfies the condition for that operator. We shall sometimes refer to the second requirement as the minimizing condition for the operator. In this way one can sort out the conjunctions, disjunctions, negations, and hypotheticals (if any) of any structure. It will not be generally true that conjunctions, disjunctions, hypotheticals, and negations of members of a structure will always exist in that structure. Moreover, it is not assumed that interaction of the operators will always be well defined. Lastly, each of the operators is defined in a "pure" manner—that is, without any reference to any of the other operators.

We first present a simple form of the definitions. The official (parameterized) version is a generalization that will be described below, once the simple form is given. Let $I = (S, \Rightarrow)$ be an implication structure.

a. The *Hypothetical Operator* ($H_\Rightarrow$) is a function mapping $S \times S$ to S[16] such that for any A and B in S,

---

15. The claims about individuation and the lack of any properties not provided by the relations of a structure are dominant in many structuralist theories of mathematics. Jonathan Kastin, in an unpublished paper, has developed some very powerful arguments against those claims.
16. A subtle, but not important point: Here we defined the operator as having values in S. However since there may be several equivalent hypotheticals with antecedent A and consequent B, it would be better (as in Koslow 1992) to say that H(A,B) is a subset of S whose members satisfy conditions H_1 and H_2. That set may be empty in some structures.

(H_1) $A, H_\Rightarrow(A, B) \Rightarrow B$, and
(H_2) $H_\Rightarrow(A, B)$ is the (implicationally) weakest member of S that satisfies the first condition. That is, for any T in S, if $A, T \Rightarrow B$, then $T \Rightarrow H_\Rightarrow(A, B)$.

It follows immediately that any two members of S that are hypotheticals with antecedent A and consequent B are equivalent. In fact, the same result can be proved for all of the logical operators. The first condition is familiar enough as a version of Modus Ponens (MP). Clearly (MP) does not suffice, for there may be non-equivalent members of the structure which also satisfy the first condition. The second condition requires that the hypothetical be the (implicationally) weakest member of the structure that satisfies the first condition. So, on any implication structure, the hypothetical operator is determined by the implicational features of the structure, without any dependence on the nature of the particular objects in S.

But things run even deeper. The first condtion corresponds to Gentzen's Elimination Condition for the conditional ($\rightarrow$), but the surprising thing is that our minimizing condition corresponds exactly to Gentzen's Introduction Condition for ($\rightarrow$) when one's concern is narrowed to the familiar logical systems that he studied. And this holds true for all the logical operators. There will, for each of the other logical operators, and for the first-order quantifiers, be two conditions for each operator. For a characteristic condition Σ (which, as we will explain below, is a filter condition), the first operator condition says that a value of the operator satisfies Σ, and the second operator condition says that the value of the operator is the implicationally weakest member to satisfy Σ. In each case they turn out to be, in this abstract setting, the counterparts of Gentzen's Elimination and Introduction Conditions.

In what follows, I shall just suppress the reference to the implication relation $\Rightarrow$, and write "H(A, B)" instead, still keeping the functional notation for this and the other logical operators. We do not have enough space to indicate the range, and the ease with which various results about the hypothetical can be proved. Here is a typical example:

In any implication structure, for all A and B: $B \Rightarrow H(A, B)$.
Proof: $B, A \Rightarrow B$ (by Projection). Therefore $B \Rightarrow H(A, B)$, by (H_2).

This result, together with a similar one that shows that the negation of any A implies H(A, B) might lead one to believe that the hypothetical is in fact just the material conditional. This is not so. In some structures, H(A, B) will be equivalent to the disjunction of the negation of A with B, but in other structures, it will not. Here is an example of a simple implication structure in which Peirce's law, H(H(H(A, B), A), A) ([((A→B)→A)→A] more familiarly) is not a thesis. Let S ={A, B, C}, and let the implication relation on S be indicated by the single arrows in the diagram below:

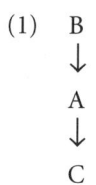

(1)   B
      ↓
      A
      ↓
      C

Using the two conditions for hypotheticals, a straightforward calculation shows that H(A, B) is just B, H(B, A) is C, and H(C, A) is A. Therefore H(H(H(A, B), A), A) is A. However, A is not a thesis of the structure (it is not implied by every member).

In the preceding structure the various hypotheticals all exist. However, as we indicated earlier, it is not true in all structures, that the hypothetical of every two members exists. Here is a simple example: Let S = {A, B, C, D}, where the implication relation on S is indicated as follows:

(2)   A   C
      ↓   ↓
      B   D

Although A and B are members of the structure, the hypothetical H(A, B) does not exist in this structure (even though A implies B). The reason is that H(A, B) (if it exists) is the (implicationally) weakest member of S for which A, T ⇒ B, by the minimizing condition for hypotheticals. However, since A ⇒ B, all the members of S satisfy this condition. Therefore, if H(A, B) exists in this structure, it must be the weakest of all the members of S—but there is no (implicationally) weakest member of S.

Although the definition of the hypothetical operator seems very natural, nevertheless, in this case, as with the other operators, something fundamental is missing, without which transitivity [H(A, B), H(B, C) ⇒ H(A, C)], contraposition [(H(A, B) ⇒ H(N(B), N(A))] (where "N(A)" indicates the value which the negation operator N has for the item A), exportation, and interchange all fail. As for the other operators, it is also easy to see that without the same additional requirement, closure under conjunction would fail, and so would the implication from A ∧ (B ∨ C) to (A ∧ B) ∨ (A ∧ C). These failures are doubly surprising. First because one would have thought that the definitions of the logical operators, familiar as they are, would suffice, and second, that these results about the hypothetical, conjunction, and distribution are a dividing line, on one side of which we find classical and intuitionistic logics, and on the other side, counterfactual logics (failure of transitivity, contraposition, exportation etc.), non-adjunctive, certain epistemic logics, and various logics of quantum mechanics. It doesn't matter for the moment whether you find yourself on one side of the line or the other. The structuralist account of logic makes it easy to see what the difference is for all these cases. It is of course a serious matter whether you endorse the additional assumption or not. In our account of the logical operators, we do.

What is the assumption? It is one that is usually made but goes little noticed. It is that the two (simple) conditions for the hypothetical still hold in the presence of arbitrary additional assumptions. The idea can be expressed this way: Let $I = (S, \Rightarrow)$ be an implication structure. If $A_1, A_2, ..., A_n$ are any members of S, then for any A and B in S, (1) $A_1, A_2, ..., A_n, A, H(A, B) \Rightarrow B$, and (2) for any T in S, if $A_1, A_2, ..., A_n, A, T \Rightarrow B$, then $A_1, A_2, ..., A_n, T \Rightarrow H(A, B)$. We shall call this operator the *parameterized hypothetical*. It is the official account. And it can be expressed more compactly this way:

> Let $I = (S, \Rightarrow)$ be an implication structure, let Γ be any finite subset of S, and let $\Rightarrow^\Gamma$ be the implication relation $\Rightarrow$ relativized to Γ (in the sense of 2.1.b). Then for any A and B in S,
> (HP_1) $A, H(A, B) \Rightarrow^\Gamma B$, and
> (HP_2) For any T in S, if $A, T \Rightarrow^\Gamma B$, then $T \Rightarrow^\Gamma H(A, B)$.

This is of course more general than the simpler (initial) version, requiring as it does that the hypothetical operator act not only in the simple (initial) way with respect to the implication relation $\Rightarrow$ of the structure, but act in the simple initial way with respect to all the relativized implication relations $\Rightarrow^\Gamma$ of the structure (for finite Γ).

b. The *Conjunction Operator* $C_\Rightarrow$ is a function that maps $S \times S$ to S which satisfies the following conditions:

(C_1) $C_\Rightarrow(A, B) \Rightarrow A$, and $C_\Rightarrow(A, B) \Rightarrow B$, and
(C_2) $C_\Rightarrow(A, B)$ is the weakest member of S to satisfy the first condition. That is, if $T \Rightarrow A$, and $T \Rightarrow B$, then $T \Rightarrow C_\Rightarrow(A, B)$.

The parameterized version of conjunction is obtained by replacing "$\Rightarrow$" by the relativization of $\Rightarrow$ to Γ (i.e. $\Rightarrow^\Gamma$) for any finite subset Γ of S, and requiring that the two conditions hold for all $\Rightarrow^\Gamma$. The parameterized versions of the remaining logical operators are obtained in the same way from their simple versions.

The features of conjunction are as one might expect. There is one important result that parameterization yields: In any implication structure in which $C_\Rightarrow(A, B)$ exists for some A and B in S, we have A, B $\Rightarrow C_\Rightarrow(A, B)$. (Proof: By the parameterized version, for any finite subset Γ of S, and any T in S, if $T \Rightarrow^\Gamma A$ and $T \Rightarrow^\Gamma B$, then $T \Rightarrow^\Gamma C_\Rightarrow(A, B)$. Take T to be A, and $\Gamma =$ {A, B}. Then, since $A \Rightarrow^\Gamma A$ and $A \Rightarrow^\Gamma B$, we have $A \Rightarrow^\Gamma C_\Rightarrow(A, B)$. Therefore A, B, $A \Rightarrow C_\Rightarrow(A, B)$, and by Permutation and Simplification, A, $B \Rightarrow C_\Rightarrow(A, B)$.)

Some structures may have conjunctions; others may not, and the failure may occur in two different ways. Either there isn't anything in the structure which satisfies condition C_1, or there are several and no weakest among them (failure of C_2). To illustrate the three possibilities, here are three simple structures:

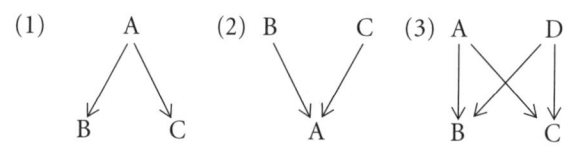

(1) A ↙ ↘ B C   (2) B ↘ ↙ C A   (3) A ↓ ↘ B D ↙ ↓ C

In structure (1), A is obviously the conjunction of B and C. In (2) there is no conjunction of B with C because condition C_1 fails. In (3), A implies both B and C, and so too does D. But neither A nor D implies the other, and so there is no weakest member of S which implies both B and C (C_2 fails). Consequently, there is no conjunction of B and C in this structure.[17]

c. The *Disjunction Operator* $D_\Rightarrow$ on an implication structure I = (S, $\Rightarrow$) is such that

(D_1) For any T in S, if $A \Rightarrow T$ and $B \Rightarrow T$, then $D_\Rightarrow(A, B) \Rightarrow T$, and

---

17. There is an interesting use to which the right hand structure can be put. It is often said that statements like (1) "He put on his parachute and (he) jumped" and (2) "He jumped and (he) put on his parachute" are not conjunctions of the embedded statements. "And" it is said, means "and then", indicating a temporal sequence. If one thought (for whatever reason) that neither (1) nor (2) implied each other, but that each implied (3) "He put on his parachute" as well as (4) "He jumped", then on our account, neither (1) nor (2) is a conjunction of (3) and (4).

(D$_2$) D$_\Rightarrow$(A, B) is the weakest member in S to satisfy the first condition. That is, for any U in S, if [for all T in S, if A $\Rightarrow$ T and B $\Rightarrow$ T, then U $\Rightarrow$ T], then U $\Rightarrow$ D$_\Rightarrow$(A, B).

Again, things are pretty much as one might expect. For example, the proof that A (and B) imply their disjunction is direct: A satisfies condition D$_1$. That is, for any T in S, if A $\Rightarrow$ T and B $\Rightarrow$ T, then A $\Rightarrow$ T. By D$_2$, A $\Rightarrow$ D$_\Rightarrow$(A, B). Similarly, B $\Rightarrow$ D$_\Rightarrow$(A, B).

d. The *Negation operator* N$_\Rightarrow$ in an implication structure I =(S, $\Rightarrow$) is such that

(N$_1$) A, N(A) $\Rightarrow$ B, for all B in S, and

(N$_2$) N(A) is the weakest member in S to satisfy the first condition. That is, if T is any member of S for which A, T $\Rightarrow$ B, for all B in S, then T $\Rightarrow$ N(A).

The present account of negation has some consequences that are worth noting. For example: In all structures in which N(A) and N(N(A)) exist, A $\Rightarrow$ N(N(A)). (Proof: From the first condition we have A, N(A) $\Rightarrow$ B, for all B, so, by Permutation, N(A), A $\Rightarrow$ B, for all B in S. However, by the second condition N(N(A)) is the weakest to do so, therefore A $\Rightarrow$ N(N(A)).)

The converse N(N(A)) $\Rightarrow$ A does not hold in all implication structures. When N(N(A)) $\Rightarrow$ A for all A in a structure I we shall say that the negation operator is *classical*, and call the structure *classical* as well. Otherwise the negation operator (and the structure) will be called *non-classical*. Consider two simple structures which illustrate the two possibilities:

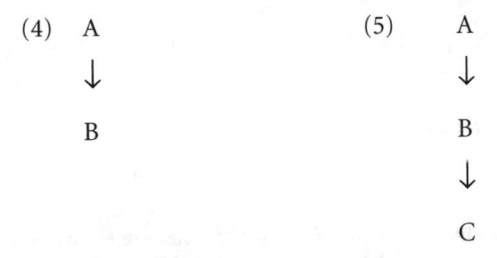

(4)   A   (5)   A
      ↓   ↓
      B   B
                       ↓
                       C

Structure (4) is classical since N(A) is B, and N(B) is A. Structure (5) is non-classical: a since N(A) is C, N(C) is A, and N(B) is A. Therefore N(N(B)) is C and C does not imply B. This simple result is a special case of a more general result that provides one way of thinking about the difference between classical and non-classical structures:

> Let I = (S, ⇒) be an implication structure and N be the negation operator on I. Let N[S] be the image of S under N (any C in S is in N[S] iff C is equivalent to the negation of some A in S). So N[S] is a subset of S. Say that N is a mapping of S *onto* S (surjective) iff N[S] = S. Then the negation operator is classical on I iff N is a mapping of S onto S.

(4) and (5) can be seen as special cases of this result. In the case of (4), the image of the set {A, B} under negation is itself, and so the structure is classical, while for (5), the image of {A, B, C} is the proper subset {A, C}. Thus (5) is non-classical. There are additional results that concern the dual of the negation operator, but in order to state them we shall first have to describe what it is for an operator to be the dual of another.

3.1 The Logical Operators and Specific Implication Relations: Examples

We have defined the various logical operators with respect to arbitrary implication relations. Here are some examples of what happens when specific implications are used:

a. When the implication relation of set theoretical inclusion (§ 2.1.f) is used on a structure of sets, then the logical operators of disjunction, conjunction, and negation are just the set-theoretical operations of union, intersection, and relative complementation.

b. When the mereological implication relation (§ 2.1.e) is used on a structure of objects, then the key concepts of the calculus of individuals are provably just the logical operators with respect to that implication relation. That is, disjunction of objects is their sum (SUM), conjunction is their product (PRO), and negation is just the operation that yields the negate (NEG) of an individual. In fact, negation turns out to be classical (every member is implied by its double negation), and the theorems and non-theorems of the calculus of individuals turn out to be just the familiar logical theses and nontheses of classical implication structures.[18]

c. When the implication relation is Tarskian implication (§ 2.1.f) on a structure consisting of Tarskian theories, then it can be proved that the algebraic operations which Tarski introduced for his calculus of systems (theo-

---

18. For the details, see Koslow 1992, Ch. 22.

ries) are exactly the logical operators on Tarskian structures.[19] That is, the conjunction of two theories is their intersection, what Tarski called "the logical sum" of two theories (the smallest theory which contains their union) is just their disjunction, and what he called "the logical complement" of a theory U (the smallest theory that contains any theory whose intersection with U is the set of logical theorems) is exactly what the negation operator yields in Tarskian implication structures. Thus, even if we didn't have the genius of Tarski to provide the appropriate algebraic operations on his theories, a study of the logical operators on a Tarskian implication structure would have led to exactly those algebraic operations.

3.2 *Logical Operators and their Duals*

We described the various logical operators as operators on arbitrary implication structures. Thus for conjunction relative to a structure $I = (S, \Rightarrow)$, we used "$C_\Rightarrow$". Although the structures may vary, the description remains the same in this sense: to obtain the conjunction operator for another structure, just use the implication relation for that structure. In passing from one structure to another, nothing changes in the description of the operator except the implication relation (and the possible shift to a new set).

We have defined the dual of an implication structure $I = (S, \Rightarrow)$ as the new structure $I^\wedge = (S, \Rightarrow^\wedge)$ (§ 2.1.d). We can now define the notion of the dual of an operator. Let O be a mapping which assigns to any structure $I = (S, \Rightarrow)$, the logical operator O_I (the logical operator O on the structure I). We shall say that $O^\wedge$ *is the logical operator which is the dual of* O iff $O^\wedge$ assigns to each implication structure I the logical operator $O(I^\wedge)$. Thus, $O^\wedge(I) = O(I^\wedge)$, or in other words, $(O^\wedge)_\Rightarrow = O_{\Rightarrow^\wedge}$. So $O^\wedge$, the dual of O, assigns to the members or pairs of members of S just the values which the operator O relativized to the dual implication relation assigns to them.

Here's what happens with conjunction. To obtain the dual of C, replace "$\Rightarrow$" in the definition of the conjunction operator by its dual "$\Rightarrow^\wedge$". We then obtain the conditions (1) $C^\wedge(A, B) \Rightarrow^\wedge A$, and $C^\wedge(A, B) \Rightarrow^\wedge B$, and (2) For any T in S, if $T \Rightarrow^\wedge A$ and $T \Rightarrow^\wedge B$, then $T \Rightarrow^\wedge C^\wedge(A, B)$. Note that for any A and B, $A \Rightarrow^\wedge B$ iff $B \Rightarrow A$. As a result, $C^\wedge(A, B)$ satisfies those conditions which hold for the disjunction of A and B in the structure $I = (S, \Rightarrow)$. It fol-

---

19. The basic paper is Tarski 1935/1936.

lows easily that the dual of conjunction on the structure I is just disjunction on I, and conversely.[20]

Unlike the case for conjunction and disjunction, the dual of negation is a much more complex matter. The dual $N^\wedge$ of the negation operator N satisfies the following conditions, which are just the conditions for N on the structure dual to I. That is

(1) $A, N^\wedge(A) \Rightarrow^\wedge B$, for all B in S, and
(2) For any T in S, if $A, T \Rightarrow^\wedge B$, for all B in S, then $T \Rightarrow^\wedge N^\wedge(A)$.

If follows from (1) and (2), that in any structure $I = (S, \Rightarrow)$ in which disjunctions always exist, that

(i) $N^\wedge N^\wedge(A) \Rightarrow A$, for all A in S, but not $A \Rightarrow N^\wedge N^\wedge(A)$.
(ii) $A \vee N^\wedge(A)$ is a thesis of I, for all A in S.
(iii) N is stronger on I than its dual $N^\wedge$. That is, $N(A) \Rightarrow N^\wedge(A)$, for all A in S.
(iv) N is identical with its dual iff the structure is classical.
(v) If N is nonclassical, then there is no sequence $N_1 N_2 \ldots N_k$ (where N_i is either N or $N^\wedge$, and $N_1 N_2 \ldots N_k(A)$ is $N_1(N_2(\ldots(N_k(A))\ldots))$), such that $N_1 N_2 \ldots N_k(A) \Leftrightarrow A$.

Some comment is called for. (i) We have already noted (3.d) that if N(A) and NN(A) exist, then $A \Rightarrow NNA$ holds in all structures, and that NN(A) will fail to imply A in some structures (even if N(A) and NN(A) exist). However, whereas NN(A) fails to imply A in general, $N^\wedge N^\wedge(A)$ will always do so. Although NN(A) will in general be implied by A, that is not the case for $N^\wedge N^\wedge(A)$ (otherwise negation will be classical). (ii) The disjunction of A and N(A) will not be a thesis in all structures. If one uses the simple structure whose graph is given in (3.a.(1)), it is evident that since N(B) is A, the disjunction of B with N(B) is just the disjunction of B with A. Now both A and B satisfy the first condition (D_1), and since the disjunction is the weakest of those, it is B. That is, $(B \vee A)$ is B. However, B is not a thesis of the structure since it is not implied by C. Therefore $(B \vee N(B))$ is not a thesis. The dual, however, is another matter. We have from the definition of the dual negation that $A, N^\wedge(A) \Rightarrow B$, for all B in S. As we noted, it can be

---

20. Cf. Koslow 1992, pp. 115–16.

proved that when disjunction exists, that this is equivalent to $B \Rightarrow (A \vee N^\wedge(A))$ for all B. Let B be a thesis of I. It follows that so too is $(A \vee N^\wedge(A))$. As for (iii), it can be proved that $N(A)$ together with $(A \vee B)$ imply B. Now $A \vee N^\wedge(A))$ is a thesis, it is implied by any member of the structure. In particular then $N(A) \Rightarrow (A \vee N^\wedge(A))$. Therefore, for all A in S: $N(A) \Rightarrow N^\wedge(A)$. A proof of (iv) and other related matters can be found in Koslow 1992.[21] As for (v) it follows easily from the fact that if N_1 is N, then $NN(A)$ is equivalent to A, and if N_1 is $N^\wedge$, then $N^\wedge N^\wedge(A)$ is equivalent to A, and in either case negation will be classical.[22]

The striking thing then is this: if an implication structure is classical, then no implicational difference exists between the negation operator and its dual, $N^\wedge$. However, if the structure is non-classical, then N is distinct from its dual, though between the two of them, a good many of the classical features are recaptured. Thus a major difference between non-classical and classical structures is that the former keeps the negation operator and its dual distinct, while the latter identifies them.

4. The Laws of Logic: Completeness and the Intuitionistic Connection

We noted that certain implication structures are classical ($NN(A) \Rightarrow A$ for all A in the structure), and others are not. What is the general picture? What, if anything, holds for all structures besides (1)–(6)? Since there can be significant differences in both the sets and the implication relations of different structures, the question of what holds in all structures needs to be refined. Given the abundance of implication structures, the quest for some common, non-trivial feature seems hopeless. Not all structures have theses (members that are implied by everything in the structure). Neither of the structures (1) and (3) in (3.b) have theses. And it is not true that every thesis of a structure is true (consider a structure of two false statements, one of which implies the other, but not conversely; the implied statement is a thesis of the structure, but false). Without some refinement, we cannot even say that in all structures, a conjunction implies its conjuncts,

---

21. Chapter 17, Theorem 17.5.
22. This proof is a bit fast. It assumes that NNN is equivalent to N (similarly for $N^\wedge$), which follows easily from the fact that if $A \Rightarrow B$, then $N(B) \Rightarrow N(A)$ (similarly for $N^\wedge$).

since some structures don't have conjuncts for all A and B in them. It looks like there is an enormous price to pay for stripping structures of syntax and semantics. Nevertheless, there is an exact answer that relates what implications hold in all structures with Intuitionism.

Let L be a formal language of the sentential calculus, specified in the usual way by its sentential letters, logical connectives, and its formulas.[23] Let $I^* = (S, \Rightarrow)$ be any implication structure in which conjunctions, disjunctions, negations, and hypotheticals always exist. We want to associate to each formula X (of L) a member of S. Let f be any function which maps the sentential letters of L to the members of S, and extend f to a function that maps each formula X of L to some member $I^*_f(X)$ in S. It is easy to show that $I^*_f(X)$, the counterpart of X, under f, always exists in S. We shall say that $I^*(X)$ is a thesis of the structure I^* if and only if, for all f, $I^*_f(X)$ is a thesis of I^*. Let "$\vdash_{ISC} X$" indicate that X is a theorem of the Intuitionistic Sentential Calculus,[24] and "$\vdash_{CSC} X$" indicate that X is a theorem of the Classical Sentential Calculus. Then there are two completeness results that sum up the situation:

(1) If X is any formula of L, then $I^*(X)$ is a thesis of every implication structure $I^* = (S, \Rightarrow)$ iff $\vdash_{ISC} X$.

(2) If X is any formula of L, then $I^*(X)$ is a thesis of every classical implication structure $I^* = (S, \Rightarrow)$ iff $\vdash_{CSC} X$.[25]

The picture then is this: There are implication structures of interest which may not be closed under some of the logical operators. If we consider all the implication structures for which the logical operators have values in them, then it is precisely the intuitionistic theorems which are theses in all of them. If we restrict the class of structures to the smaller class of structures that are classical (that is $NN(A) \Rightarrow A$ for all A in them), then it is precisely the theorems of the classical sentential calculus which are theses in all those structures. It is in this sense that intuitionistic logic is the correct logic for

---

23. The results which follow are stated for sentential logic, and are easily extended to cover first-order quantification by using a language appropriate for first-order quantification, and the notion of an extended implication structure (cf. Koslow 1992).
24. As formulated by, say, Heyting 1956.
25. These results can be extended to the intuitionistic and the classical predicate calculus.

arbitrary implication structures, and is more general than classical logic, which is correct only for the narrower class of classical structures.

4.1 Remarks

Several observations are in order. In a way one might think that this result settles the matter in favor of intuitionistic logic. True enough, it is intuitionism that prevails in all structures, and classical logic is restricted to a narrower class. This places the burden on the classical logician. Why would one want to be restricted to the narrower class? Why would one exclude some structures as out of bounds for the logical operators? Surely a reason has to be given for such a choice.

It is not a choice of whether negation is classical or non-classical on a structure. For any particular structure, that matter is not up to us. Consider the two simple structures from § 3.d:

(4) A   (5) A
     ↓   ↓
     B   B
                     ↓
                     C

As we have seen, the negation operator is classical in structure (4), and non-classical in (5). Why would the classical logician admit that (4) is a structure but deny that (5) is? It's hard to see what objection a classical logician would have against (5). The intuitionist on the other hand has no need to exclude the first structure, which is just a substructure of the second. In fact, this example is just a special case of a general situation: given any non-classical structure I = $(S, \Rightarrow)$, one can define a substructure $I^* = (S^*, \Rightarrow^*)$ of it which is classical.

If generality were the sole consideration, the non-classical, intuitionistic position has the advantage. It does not seem to me to be the business of logic to close off the consideration of structures which may be useful or fruitful ways to discuss problems or state theories. Yet this is just what the advocate of using classical negation everywhere would do. Of course this is a comparison of the two positions from a structuralist perspective, and it isn't at all clear that an intuitionist would take that perspective.

There is another way of comparing classical and intuitionistic views from a structuralist perspective. It considers intuitionism in a way that is closer to how it was presented by its historical founders. The idea is that intuitionists like Brouwer and Heyting were interested in a special subject. Although Heyting may have used sentential variables p, q, etc. in his formalization of the intuitionistic sentential calculus, they did not range over sentences or propositions. Heyting thought that they ranged over mathematical tasks or problems, or they could also be thought of as ranging over Husserlian-like "expectations" and "fulfillments" (here he followed a phenomenological interpretation due to O. Becker).[26] The various logical constants were defined in such a way that complex mathematical tasks (or complex expectations) could be formed out of others. It is not difficult to see this as a description of a special implication structure, where the logical operations, as they defined them for this special subject matter also satisfy the conditions we gave for the logical operators. Negation on such a structure is of course not classical. In this special structure of obvious importance, the members of the set S are certainly not sentential or propositional.[27] With its variables ranging over mathematical tasks, problems, or expectations, it certainly violates the usual requirement of topic neutrality. In this regard, the Classical Sentential Calculus (which can also be regarded as an implication structure) would have a clear advantage as a "logic", over the "historical" intuitionistic view, which appears to be a theory with a very specific subject matter.

5. Modal Operators

The main idea is to obtain a simple and unifying characterization of most, if not all of what has figured as modal, and to do so by relying not upon truth, possible worlds, or indeed upon anything other than the abstract notion of an implication structure. The theory of the modal opera-

---

26. An excellent collection and discussion of the relevant papers, translated for the first time, is Mancosu 1997.
27. Although it is misleading, on this historical version, to read p,q,... as sentential variables, it might have been helpful to Heyting to do so. He is reported to have said that he arrived at his formalization of the Intuitionistic Sentential Calculus by going down the list of theorems of Russell and Whitehead. Cf. Mancosu 1997. If true, this might account for the use of what looked like sentential variables in his formalization.

tors has the same generality as implication structures and the logical operators on them. Modal operators, like the logical operators, are relativized to implication relations. We hope with this proposal to shed some light on why all our familiar modals are non-extensional, and to recover the dramatic systematization that Kripke gave to familiar modals without using possible worlds semantics. Moreover, the proposed account makes it very clear (if that is needed) why the study of modal operators is the natural next step after the study of implication.

In what follows, we shall assume for simplicity that the logical operators are always defined in the structures.[28] We shall say that any function ϕ that maps S to S, is a *modal operator on the structure* I iff it satisfies these two conditions (we shall use greek letters for the modal operators, though occasionally we shall use the more familiar boxes and diamonds as well):

(M_1) For any A_1, ..., A_n, and B in S, if A_1, ..., $A_n \Rightarrow B$, then $\phi(A_1)$, ..., $\phi(A_n) \Rightarrow \phi(B)$ (we shall say that ϕ *distributes* over $\Rightarrow$).

(M_2) ϕ does not distribute over $\Rightarrow^\wedge$, the dual of $\Rightarrow$. That is, for some A_1, ..., A_n, and B in S, A_1, ..., $A_n \Rightarrow^\wedge B$ holds, but $\phi(A_1)$, ..., $\phi(A_n) \Rightarrow^\wedge \phi(B)$ does not.

Thus, we think of a modal operator as a function which maps a structure to itself. Not every function has modal character, and the role of the preceding two conditions is to distinguish those particular functions which are modal from those which are not. Such a description has a mathematical clarity, but it also provides an important reason for studying the modal operators. Even if one were the kind of philosopher who took any departure from extensional logic and idioms as an admission of defeat, there would still be good reason to study the modal operators. They are a special class of invariants of the implication relation. Since implication is central to logic, what is more natural than the study of those conditions under which implication is preserved despite transformations in the items to which implication applies? Modal logic, on our account, is just such a study.

There is a natural question of why these two conditions; why not just M_1? Occasionaly it has been suggested that M_1 is the hallmark of modal-

---

28. For a development of the theory without these restrictions, see Koslow 1992, Part IV.

ity.[29] However M_1 alone is insufficient. There are many operators that satisfy it, which clearly fail to be modal. The operator which assigns to any A its conjunction with some fixed C is a simple example. Clearly some condition in addition to M_1 is needed. We propose M_2. It does get the job done, though its full import is an extended matter.[30]

Several immediate consequences should be noted. We shall say that φ *distributes over disjunction* iff for all A and B, $\phi(A \lor B) \Rightarrow \phi(A) \lor \phi(B)$, and that a modal operator φ is a *necessitation modal* on I iff for all A in S, if A is a thesis of I, then so too is φ(A).

(1) If the implication structure always has disjunctions, then M_2 holds iff there exist A and B such that $\phi(A \lor B) \Rightarrow \phi(A) \lor \phi(B)$ fails.

This form of M_2 is the easiest one to apply. If the structure is classical and φ is a necessitation modal, then M_2 is equivalent to

(2) For some A, $\phi(A) \lor \phi(\neg A)$ is not a thesis of I.

---

29. For example, David Lewis motivates his possible worlds analysis of truth in fiction this way: "I have already noted that truth in a given fiction is closed under implication. Such closure is the earmark of an operator of relative necessity, an intensional operator that may be analyzed as a restricted universal quantifier over possible worlds." (Lewis 1978, reprinted 1983, p. 264).
30. A fuller discussion can be found in Koslow 1992. As indicated below, it is partly a matter of noting that M_2 is satisfied by most, if not all the familiar modal operators, and that it does yield the result that all modal operators are non-extensional. Moreover, any operator which is a necessitation operator (the value of the operator for any thesis is also a thesis) which satisfies M_1 but not M_2 will be such that possibility always implies necessity. This would violate the modal square of opposition. If in addition necessity implied possibility, then there would be a collapse of necssity with possibility, something which M_2 rules out (cf. Lewis 1973, p. 137, on "Prussian Deontic Logic"). Finally, another way of looking at the situation when M_2 fails is this: if a Kripkean semantics is available (so that for some accessibility relation R, □(A) is true in any possible world U iff if A is true in all worlds V accessible from U), then it can be shown that M_2 fails iff the accessibility relation is a function (that is if for every U, V, and W, if URV and URW, then V = W). Here is a simple example: suppose that the accessibility relation is just identity. It follows that $\Box(A) \Leftrightarrow A$, so that we have "collapse" of the modal, or in our terminology, no modal at all. For further discussion see Koslow 1997.

All the familiar normal modal systems in the literature use a box ($\Box$) that satisfies the modal conditions M_1 and M_2. (Each of those modal systems can be thought of as an implication structure, with its deducibility relation providing the implication relation. The mapping which takes each formula A to $\Box$A will satisfy the two conditions on modality.[31]) It is an immediate consequence of M_1 and M_2 that

(3) For all A and B, $\phi[H(A, B)] \Rightarrow H(\phi(A), \phi(B))$ (more familiarly, $\Box(A \to B) \Rightarrow (\Box A \to \Box B)$)

(4) For all A and B, $\phi(A \wedge B) \Leftrightarrow \phi(A) \wedge \phi(B)$.

To prove (3), notice that since A, $H(A, B) \Rightarrow B$, it follows by M_2 that $\phi(A)$, $\phi[H(A, B)] \Rightarrow \phi(B)$. Therefore, by H_2, $\phi[H(A, B)] \Rightarrow H(\phi(A), \phi(B))$. (4) is equally obvious.

There is one point that should be taken care of immediately. It looks as if possibility ($\Diamond$) does not satisfy the first condition of modality, since it is not generally true that $\Diamond(A), \Diamond(B) \Rightarrow \Diamond(A \wedge B)$. That is certainly the case. And the reason for the difference between $\Box$ and its dual $\Diamond$, is that if $\Box$ is a modal with respect to $\Rightarrow$, then its dual is a modal operator with respect to the dual implication relation $\Rightarrow^\wedge$. So it is important to take seriously the fact that an operator is defined as modal on a structure, relative to the implication relation on that structure. Shifting to a different implication relation risks the loss of modal character. Nevertheless it is possible to miss this difference between modals and their duals, if one considers only implications with single antecedents.[32]

We have taken the modal operators to be functions of a special sort. That aspect raises some interesting philosophical issues. Let us first define two special kinds of modals. We shall say that a modal operator ϕ is a T-*modal* on the structure $I = (S, \Rightarrow)$ iff for all A in S, $\phi(A) \Rightarrow A$, and ϕ is a K_4-*modal* operator iff $\phi(A) \Rightarrow \phi\phi(A)$. Define a operator on I to be *onto* I if and only if, for every A in S, there is some A* in S such that $A \Leftrightarrow \phi(A^*)$. Then

---

31. See Koslow 1992, Part IV, for details. In fact the two conditions include more than the normal modals, since it is not assumed that a modal operator has to be a necessitation modal.

32. Even though ϕ is a modal with respect to $\Rightarrow^\wedge$, it will distribute over $\Rightarrow$ in the single antecedent cases. Thus, suppose that $A \Rightarrow B$. Then $B \Rightarrow^\wedge A$. Since ϕ is a modal with respect to $\Rightarrow^\wedge$, we have $\phi(B) \Rightarrow^\wedge \phi(A)$. Therefore $\phi(A) \Rightarrow \phi(B)$.

(5) If ϕ is a modal operator on I that is also onto I, then ϕ cannot be both a T-modal and a K_4-modal.[33]

This can be a problem for an intuitionist account of mathematical statements that assumes that a certain collection or implication structure of mathematical statements all have a special necessary character. Those statements cannot be marked with a special modal $ϕ_I$ such that each statement is equivalent to $ϕ_I(A^*)$ for some statement A* in the structure. There would be a problem of expressing the necessary character of all the statements of the structure, while retaining the T and K_4 character of that kind of necessity.[34] A similar kind of difficulty can be raised against a certain kind of mathematical platonist as well.[35]

5.1 Modal Existence and Non-existence

Since the modal operators have been described as special kinds of functions that map structures to themselves, there is a question of whether any structures have modals on them. It is possible to give a very simple necessary and sufficient condition for the existence of a modal operator on an implication structure:

> There is a modal operator on I = (S, ⇒) iff there are at least two members of S neither of which implies the other.[36]

This explains why the structure which has just two members t and f (where f implies t but not conversely) has no modal operators on it. This general result can be sharpened in the special case of classical implication structures.

---

33. Suppose that for every A in S, there is some A* such that A ⇔ ϕ(A*). By the T and K_4 conditions, we have ϕ(A*) ⇔ ϕϕ(A*). Therefore A ⇔ ϕ(A), for all A in S. So ϕ fails to be a modal. The equivalence of A with ϕ(A) for all A is sometimes referred to as "modal collapse".
34. I first learned of the implication of this result for intuitionism from Charles Parsons.
35. At any rate, the kind of platonist who thinks that all the statements of, say, arithmetic have a necessary character which can be indicated by an equivalent modal statement.
36. Let C be the disjunction of A and B, neither of which implies the other. For any E, define ϕ(E) to be C, if C ⇒ E, and to be A otherwise. For details see Koslow 1992, pp. 259–60.

We shall say that a structure is *syntactically incomplete* iff there is some A_0 in it such that neither A_0 nor its negation is a thesis. Then

> If I is a classical implication structure, then there is a modal operator on it iff it is syntactically incomplete.

From this we see that the implication structure $I_{CSC} = (S, \vdash_{CSC})$, where S is the language of the Classical Sentential Calculus and $\vdash_{CSC}$ is the standard deducibility relation on it, has a necessitation modal on it. So there is a necessitation modal operator on the structure associated with the Classical Sentential Calculus. Of course this does not mean that the modal is representable, expressible, or definable in the Classical Sentential Calculus, or in the implication structure associated with it. Its resources are too meager for that task. Nevertheless, as a function mapping the structure to itself, the modal does exit.

5.2 The Non-extensionality of the Modal Operators

With the help of truth-value assignments on structures (§ 2.1.a) we can now define the notion of the extensionality of an operator ϕ on I. Let O be an operator of one argument (the case for several arguments is easily defined).

> O is *extensional* on I iff for any truth-value assignment τ on I, and any A and B in S, if A and B are assigned the same value by τ, then O(A) and O(B) are also assigned the same value by τ.[37]

Now it is no news that modal operators are non-extensional. That goes without saying, but it has also gone without explaining. It is possible, however, to prove (making essential use of the second condition of modality) that all the modal operators are non-extensional. i.e.

> If ϕ is a modal operator on $I = (S, \Rightarrow)$, then ϕ is non-extensional on I.[38]

---

37. One can strengthen the notion of a strong assignment to a *normal* truth-value assignment (a discovery by Bernstein, Carnap and Church) by requiring that L be closed under implication, and that, symmetrically, K be closed under the dual implication relation of the structure. This insures in effect that if two members are assigned "false" (i.e., K), then their disjunction will also be false.
38. The proof is simple, but rather long. See Koslow 1992, 261–2.

5.3 Specific Modals[39]

There are some concepts, already in place as it were, that are modal, but do not seem to have been widely recognized as such. Our description of the modal operators makes their modal character evident. Here are two examples:

a. *Non-classical Double Negation.* Classically, double negation is just the identity operator on a structure, and in that case the operator ϕ_{NN} which assigns NN(A) to each A in S is certainly not a modal operator. So, if ϕ_{NN} is modal on a structure, the structure cannot be classical. Much more interesting is the fact that on certain non-classical structures, the double negation operator will be modal. That is

> Let I = (S, ⇒) be a non-classical implication structure that contains some A_0 such that $N(A_0) \vee NN(A_0)$ is not a thesis of I, then ϕ_{NN} is a modal operator on I.

The condition in this theorem holds for intuitionistic structures, so that the intuitionistic double negation is a modal operator.[40] The double negation modal obeys an unusual combination of modal laws: (1) it is a necessitation modal, (2) for every A: A ⇒ ϕ_{NN}(A), (3) it is a K_4-modal, and (4) it is an S_5-modal (◊A → □◊A). It fails to be (5) a T-modal, (6) a D-modal (□A → ◊A), and (7) a B-modal (A → □◊A).

---

39. The Gödel-Löb model (G-L) is an example of a modal operator that was originally used in a highly syntactic context, since it has roughly the sense of "It is provable in Peano Arithmetic that …". Nevertheless it can be described in the present abstract context as any modal operator ϕ such that for any A and B in the structure, if ϕ(A),B ⇒ A, then ϕ(B) ⇒ ϕ(A). It can be shown that this formulation is equivalent to the usual one for which ϕ((ϕ(A)→A) ⇒ ϕ(A), for all A. It can also be shown that if I is a classical structure, then there is a G-L modal operator on I iff there is some non-thesis G of I whose consequence set (all those A's which are implied by G) is incomplete with respect to negation (there is some C such that neither it nor its negation are implied by G). For proofs, see Koslow 1992, pp. 279, 283–4.
40. Here an important distinction should be observed. Not every non-classical structure is intuitionistic. The example in the text in which A implies B and B implies C (and none of the converses hold) is non-classical since B is not implied by its double negation. Nevertheless, N(E) ∨ NN(E) is a thesis for all E in this structure. It is therefore not intuitionistic.

b. *The Power Set Operator as Modal.* The power set operation which maps a set to the set of all its subsets is familiar and central to set theory. Surprisingly, it has a feature which marks it as modal. I shall use a structure simpler than ZF set theory to illlustrate the point:

> Let I = (S, ⇒), where S is a set of sets that is closed under finite intersections and unions, closed under the power set operation $\wp$, and has at least two members A^* and B^* neither of which is a subset of the other. Let the implication relation on S be the subset relation. That is, for any sets $A_1, ..., A_n$, and B in S: $A_1, ..., A_n \Rightarrow B$ iff $A_1 \cap ... \cap A_n \subseteq B$. Then $\wp$ is a modal operator on I.

Clearly, $\wp$ distributes over implication on this structure. The disjunction of any two sets is easily seen to be their set theoretical union (∪), and there are sets in the structure, namely A^* and B^*, such that $\wp$ does not distribute over their union. For suppose that $\wp(A^* \cup B^*) \subseteq \wp(A^*) \cup \wp(B^*)$. Let a be a member of A^* that is not in B^*, and b be a member of B^* that is not in A^*. The set {a, b} is a member of $\wp(A^* \cup B^*)$, so it is a member of $\wp(A^*) \cup \wp(B^*)$. But {a, b} can't be a member of $\wp(A^*)$ for then b would be a member of A^*. Similarly, it can't be a member of $\wp(B^*)$. Consequently, $\wp$ is a modal operator and it is easily seen that

(1) $\wp$ is not a T-modal if some member of S is not a member of itself.
(2) $A \Rightarrow \wp(A)$ iff A is transitive (every member of A is a subset of A).
(3) $\wp$ is a K_4-modal iff every member of S is transitive.

It is not news that certain standard mathematical notions are modal. The closure operation for certain topological spaces is an obvious example. The power set operation is another.

5.4 Kripke Systematization without Possible Worlds Semantics

It was a great landmark of modern logic when Kripke provided a systematization of modal theory with the aid of possible worlds semantics. Readers may wonder whether all that systematization will be lost in the present account of the modal operators. The positive result is that the systematization remains, without the use of possible worlds and accessibility relations. All that is needed are implication structures and their resources.

A *(weak) Tarskian theory*[41] (more briefly, a theory) of $I = (S, \Rightarrow)$ is any subset of S that is weakly closed under implication (if A is in T, and $A \Rightarrow B$, then B is also in T). We shall now introduce the notion of an accessibility relation on these theories by defining this notion separately for modals and their duals. Let U, V, W, ..., with or without numerical subscripts, range over the theories of I. For any theory U, define $\phi^{-1}U$ to be a subset of S such that A is in $\phi^{-1}U$ iff $\phi(A)$ is in U (similarly for $\sigma^{-1}U$). Let ϕ be a modal operator on I, and σ be its dual. Then a binary relation R^ϕ (R^σ) is an *accessibility relation* for ϕ (σ) such that

(1) $UR^\phi V$ iff $\phi^{-1}U \subseteq V$, and
(2) $UR^\sigma V$ iff $V \subseteq \sigma^{-1}U$.[42]

The accessibility relation is tailored to each modal operator, and we have a pair of such relations for a modal and its dual. The reason for the separate conditions is due to the use of (weak) theories for the accessibility relation. If one assumed that U, V, etc. were maximal consistent subsets of S (a strong assumption which we do not make), and that negation is classical, then only one accessibility relation is needed. The Kripke systematization for T-modals can now be expressed this way:

> Let ϕ be a modal operator on any implication structure I. Then ϕ is a T-modal on I iff R^ϕ is reflexive.

The story for the other modals is similar. The usual connection between K_4-modals and transitivity of the accessibility relation, Y-modals (those for which $\phi\phi(A) \Rightarrow \phi(A)$ for all A), and density, D-modals (those for which $\phi(A) \Rightarrow \sigma(A)$ for all A), and seriality, B-modals (those for which $A \Rightarrow \phi\sigma(A)$ for all A), and symmetry, S_5-modals (those for which $\sigma(A) \Rightarrow \phi\sigma(A)$ for all A), and the Euclidean Condition, can all be proved quite easily.[43] In fact we can strengthen the account along structuralist lines by defining accessibility relations to hold among strongly (as against weakly) closed theories of the structure. It is then possible to define the notion of a *model* on a structure: Instead of defining models on a Kripke Frame $\langle W, R \rangle$ where W is any set of

---

41. This is in contrast with the notion of a strong Tarskian theory of section 2.1(f).
42. It should be noted the these definitions only make sense if $\phi^{-1}U$ and $\sigma^{-1}U$ are theories. However is is easy to show that they are theories if U is.
43. See Koslow 1992, Ch. 35, for the details.

possible worlds together with an accessibility relation R on it, we use instead the particular frame ⟨T, R⟩ on a structure I, that consists of the set T of all *strongly* closed theories of I, together with an accessibility relation R on those theories. Models on I are then defined by functions which assign sets of theories (subsets of T) to each member of S, subject to certain conditions. It is then possible again to recover all the previous results systematizing the modals, this time including even the standard result connecting G-L modals with well-capped transitive R.[44]

5.5 Some Philosophical Modals

There are some problems that involve deep philosophical issues on which this account of the modal operators might shed some light.

a. *Truth as a Modal Operator.* We have elsewhere studied truth as an operator on implication structures.[45] The operator we there called a truth operator was characterized by its implicational properties. We assumed that (1) T(A) ⇒ A, for all A (reading "T(A)" roughly as "It is true that A"), (2) T distributes over the implication relation, and (3) it is a necessitation operator. These conditions fall short of the *Tarskian Equivalence Condition* that T(A) ⇔ A for all A. If we characterize *Bivalence* (BP) as the condition that "T(A) ∨ T(¬A)" is a thesis, and the *Law of Excluded Middle* (LEM) as the condition that "T(A ∨ ¬A)" is a thesis of the structure, it can be proved that even for truth operators weaker than Tarskian,

(1) In any classical structure, T is modal iff Bivalence fails.

More generally,

(2) In any structure (classical or not), if LEM holds, but BP fails, then T is modal.

So, by (1) the price of giving up Bivalence has a steeper price that even Quine reckoned. By (2) Bas Van Fraassen's supervaluational account of truth is modal, since LEM holds, but BP fails for the operator "It is supervaluationally true that".

---

44. For the details see Koslow 1992, Ch. 36.
45. See Koslow 1992, Ch. 33, and Feferman 1984.

It is also possible to explore the possibilities for a non-modal notion of truth.[46] Let's define a *truthlike operator* on a structure as any operator that

(a) distributes over the implication relation,
(b) distributes over the dual of the implication relation (so that it isn't modal),
(c) preserves the theses of the structure (if A is a thesis of I, so too is T(A)), and
(d) preserves the antitheses of I (if A is an antithesis of I, so too is T(A)).

Truthlike operators include a host of concepts widely employed in philosophy generally and they behave beautifully with respect to the logical operators.[47] They form a natural class of operators which belong to what one might call the implicational tradition of truth. It can be shown that what distinguishes a Tarskian operator from all its truthlike cousins is this: Truthlike operators satisfy the Tarski Equivalence condition iff they are extensional.

b. *Conditionals: The Intuitionistic Case.* It is possible to show that the hypothetical in any classical structure is extensional. It is also possible to show that in non-classical structures, and in particular those that are Intuitionistic, the hypothetical is not extensional.[48] Our account of modals helps to explain why there is non-extensionality in the non-classical case.

Consider the conditional C → A in a non-classical structure, and in particular, the prefix "If C, then" (or "C →", or the operator H_C which assigns to each A the value H(C, A)). For every C in an implication structure, H_C distributes over the implication relation. In classical structures, H_C also distributes over disjunction. On classical structures, therefore, H_C is not a modal operator. On the other hand, in some non-classical structures, H_C is a modal for some Cs. Let us say that an operator ϕ_C which to each A assigns C → A is a *conditionalization operator*. So we know that

> If there is a conditionalization operator that is modal on a structure, then the structure is non-classical.

---

46. For the details, and the motivation for studying the truthlike operators, see Koslow 1998.
47. In a classical structure, it can be proved that T(¬A) ⇔ ¬T(A) for all A. And for the other logical operators, it can be proved that T[O(A,B)] ⇔ O(T(A),T(B)).
48. This is proved in Koslow 1992, p. 177.

The converse doesn't hold for all non-classical structures. Nevertheless, if I is a special kind of non-classical structure then we can do better.

If I is *strongly non-classical* (that is, for some A_0 and B_0 in it, $(A_0 \to B_0) \vee (B_0 \to A_0)$ is not a thesis), then there is a conditionalization modal on I (namely $\phi_{(A_0 \vee B_0)}$).[49]

In particular, it follows that since Intuitionistic structures are strongly non-classical, there will be C's such that ϕ_C is modal. Thus for certain C's, the conditionals $C \to A$ (for all A) are all equivalent to the application of a modal operator to A, i.e. $\phi(A)$.

Now, since we know that all the modal operators are non-extensional, that explains why, in particular, the hypothetical in Intuitionistic (and in all strongly non-classical) structures is non-extensional.

c. *Conditionals: The Counterfactual Case.* Counterfactual conditionals have a modal aspect to them, and material conditionals do not. This seems to me to be an accurate intuition of a significant difference between them, and the present account of the modals can be used to explain the difference.

Consider D. Lewis' account of counterfactuals.[50] His favorite axiomatization, VC, of these conditionals is an extension of the Classical Sentential Calculus to which the new connective $\Box\to$ (boxarrow) is added ("$A\Box\to B$" has the intended reading: If A were the case, then B would be the case). In addition to Modus Ponens, there is a new rule (D), and some axioms that govern the boxarrow. We can recast the logical system VC as an implication structure $I^{VC} = (S, \Rightarrow^{VC})$, where S is the set of formulas of the theory VC, and the implication relation on it is given by $A_1, A_2, ..., A_n \Rightarrow^{VC} B$ iff $\vdash_{VC}(A_1 \wedge A_2 \wedge ... \wedge A_n) \to B$. What is important for the discussion of modality is his rule (D) which can be formulated this way:

(D) For any C, if $A_1, A_2, ..., A_n \Rightarrow^{VC} B$, then $C\Box\to A_1, C\Box\to A_2, ..., C\Box\to A_n \Rightarrow^{VC} C\Box\to B$.

The modality of counterfactuals is easy to see, given the structure I^{VC}. It involves focusing upon the operator associated with each antecedent of a

---

49. A proof can be found in Koslow 1992, pp. 308–10.
50. See Lewis 1979. Lewis believes (private correspondence) that T. Sprigge simultaneously (1973) and independently had the same idea, and that it should be called the Lewis-Sprigge theory. I confine myself here to Lewis' 1979 account.

counterfactual conditional. For each A in S, let $\Box_A$ be an operator on S, which to any C in S assigns "A$\Box\!\!\to$C". Thus "A$\Box\!\!\to$C" can be written as "$\Box_A(C)$", the value of the operator $\Box_A$ for C. Our claim is this:

> For some A's in S, $\Box_A$ will be a modal operator on I^{VC}, and for some A's in S, $\Box_A$ will fail to be modal.

The question of which $\Box_A$s are modal and which are not has an exact solution. First it should be noted that every $\Box_A$ satisfies M_1, the first condition of modality. That much is guaranteed by rule (D). We now have to consider which of the $\Box_A$s satisfies M_2, the second condition of modality.

It is well known that VC does not validate the law of Conditional Excluded Middle (CEM):

(CEM) For every A and B in S, (A$\Box\!\!\to$B) ∨ (A$\Box\!\!\to\neg$B) is a thesis.

Let us say that A *satisfies* CEM iff for all B in S, (A$\Box\!\!\to$B) ∨ (A$\Box\!\!\to\neg$B) is a thesis. It follows that $\Box_A$ distributes over disjunctions iff A satisfies CEM. Since $\Box_A$ distributes over implication ($\Rightarrow^{VC}$), it follows that

> $\Box_A$ is a modal operator on I^{VC} iff A does not satisfy CEM.

Thus, for example, since theses and antitheses satisfy CEM (since counterfactuals with theses as antecedents are equivalent to their consequents, and counterfactuals with antitheses as antecedents are theses), their associated operators will fail to be modal. Attending either to the prefix "A$\Box\!\!\to$" or to the operator $\Box_A$, the modality of the counterfactual A$\Box\!\!\to$B is right up front as it were.

Our intention in these brief remarks was to show how our account of the modals, when combined with one powerful theory of of counterfactuals can be used to account for some of the salient features of counterfactuals. For example it explains why the counterfactual "A$\Box\!\!\to$B" is non-extensional in those cases when $\Box_A$ is modal: on our account of them, all modals are non-extensional operators.[51] In addition the obvious fact that material condi-

---

51. Of course, if $\Box_A$ is not modal (for example, if A is a thesis), then the counterfactual A$\Box\!\!\to$B may still be non-extensional, depending on B. For example, in the case of embedding, where B is itself a counterfactual conditional C$\Box\!\!\to$D, and $\Box_C$ is modal then the counterfactual A$\Box\!\!\to$(C$\Box\!\!\to$D) may be non-extensional.

tionals do not in general imply their corresponding counterfactuals can also be explained.⁵²

If for all A and B, if $A \to B \Rightarrow^{VC} \square_A(B)$, then the two conditionals are equivalent (since in I^{VC}, every counterfactual $A\square\!\to B$ implies $A\to B$). Since for material conditionals, $A \to (B \vee C)$ is equivalent to $(A \to B) \vee (A \to C)$, it follows that $\square_A$ distributes over disjunctions. Thus $\square_A$ fails to be modal.

In particular, for any A^*, you cannot have $A^*\!\to B \Rightarrow^{VC} A^*\square\!\to B$, for all B, without losing the modal character of $\square_{A^*}$.

Although our discussion of the modal character of counterfactuals depended upon the system VC, it did not depend upon all the details of that particular theory. The part of the theory that yields the modality can be isolated (as a theory of proto-conditionals) and the specific modal character of the modal depends upon specific axioms of VC (for example, the modal is a necessitation modal and a K_4-modal, but it is not a T-modal, and it is a D-modal iff the antecedent of the counterfactual is not vacuous.⁵³).

6. Logical Operators and Logical Predicates: "is a natural number"

We turn finally to a more speculative note. All of the logical operators discussed were defined in a special way. To each member (or pair of members) of an implication structure there was associated a condition $\Sigma_A(T)$ (or $\Sigma_{A,B}(T)$). The condition was a *filter condition* (that is, if $\Sigma(T)$, and $R \Rightarrow T$, then $\Sigma(R)$). To each such condition, we associated a logical operator ϕ as follows: For any A in the structure, the value of the operator for the argument A satisfies the condition $\Sigma_A(T)$, and it is the (implicationally) weakest member of S to so so (if it exists). That is,

(1) $\Sigma_A(\phi(A))$, and
(2)   For any T in S, if $\Sigma_A(T)$, then $T \Rightarrow \phi(A)$.

---

52. Sometimes of course a material conditional will imply the corresponding counterfactual. This will happen, for example if the consequent if a thesis. The question raised here is whether this can happen for all material conditionals.
53. For details, see Koslow 1996.

Thus in the particular case of negation, the condition $\Sigma(T)$ for the negation of A was that A, $T \Rightarrow C$ for all C, so that the first condition for the negation operator N is that A, $N(A) \Rightarrow C$ for all C, and the second, minimizing condition for negation, is that for all T, if A, $T \Rightarrow C$ for all C, then $T \Rightarrow N(A)$.

(1) expresses a generalized Elimination condition for $\phi(A)$ $(N(A))$ in a general structuralist setting, and (2) expresses a generalized Introduction condition for $\phi(A)$ $(N(A))$. The restriction to filter conditions for the logical operators may seem puzzling, perhaps an artifact of the definitions. But in fact there is a possible explanation. There is good reason to think that when Gentzen proposed the pairing of Introduction and Elimination conditions for each of the logical operators, he had in mind that the second condition, the Introduction condition, was a kind of "definition", as he says, and that in the "ultimate analysis" the Elimination condition would be a consequence of the Introduction condition.[54] These are dark sayings, difficult to justify. However, if the second condition were definitional, the conditional should at the very least be replaced by a biconditional. Once that is done, it follows immediately that the Elimination condition follows from the modified Introduction Condition, and it also follows from the modified Introduction Condition that the condition Σ associated with the operator has to be a filter condition. So the use of filter conditions in an account of the logical operators seems central. Why this is so needs a deeper analysis of them. But analysis or not, filter conditions and minimizing conditions seem to be at the heart of the matter.

We don't have to wait for that deeper analysis to raise the possibility of asking whether there are any *predicates* that have the same logical character that the logical operators have. After all, the logical operators are functions of a special kind, and predicates can also be thought of as a special kind of function. Indeed, we have argued elsewhere that identity can be studied in exactly the same way as the logical operators discussed here, where a filter condition is described, and the Elimination condition is the principle of substitutivity.[55]

We shall sketch an account which shows that the predicate "is a natural number" can be treated in exactly the same way as the logical operators, with generalized Elimination and Introduction conditions, where the Elimi-

---

54. Gentzen, 1934.
55. For details see Koslow 1992, Ch. 21.

nation condition for the predicate "is a natural number" turns out to be the principle of mathematical induction. This result has a significant implication. It indicates that there is something logical about "is a natural number", where the justification for this is not some logicist reduction. Rather the idea is that this predicate is treated in just the way that we treat the logical operators. It is logical in the same way that they are. This idea I believe was first stressed by C. Parsons, in reflecting upon earlier work by W. Tait and Per Martin-Löf, he noted the similarity of treatment of "is a natural number" and the logical connectives.[56] This point is one that should hold whatever the particular logical setting or reduction there might be for the predicate.

Here is a sketch using an implication structure that is based upon a modification of a standard formalization of Peano Arithmetic. Take a standard axiomatization of PA[57] that uses the constant "0", " ' " (the successor function), addition, multiplication, and identity, and an axiom schema for the principle of mathematical induction. The modified version PA* consists in adding two predicate constants, $N(x)$ and $R_0(x)$ to the vocabulary and adjusting the notion of a formula of the language, leaving out the axiom schema of mathematical induction, and adding an axiom (1), and an axiom schema (2). Let us say that a one-place predicate T is *inductive* (Ind(T)) iff $T(0) \wedge (\forall x)(T(x) \rightarrow T(x'))$. The axiom (1) and axiom schema (2) to be added are:

(1) $R_0(0) \wedge (\forall x)(R_0(x) \rightarrow R_0(x'))$. That is, Ind($R_0$), and
(2) $(\forall x)[(\text{Ind}(R) \wedge R_0(x)) \rightarrow R(x)]$, for all R (where Ind(R) contains no free occurrences of x).

Corresponding to the system PA*,[58] we now form the implication structure

---

56. Parsons 1983, p. 175.
57. The one in Mendelson 1997 will do nicely.
58. A word about the particular form of PA*: The predicate R_0 is, by (1) and (2) given those features which we would like "is a natural number" to have, and the predicate N(x) is also added to the vocabulary. As in the case of the logical connectives and operators, the Elimination and Introduction conditions are sup-

I^{PA^*} [59] on the language of PA*, with the implication relation $\Rightarrow^{PA^*}$ defined this way: for any $A_1, ..., A_n$ and B: $A_1, ..., A_n \Rightarrow^{PA^*}$ B iff the universal closure of $[(A_1 \wedge ... \wedge A_n) \rightarrow B]$ is a theorem of PA*, and for any predicates P(x) and Q(x), we write "P $\Rightarrow^{PA^*}$ Q" as shorthand for "$(\forall x)(P(x) \rightarrow Q(x))$ is a theorem of PA*". It's clear that $\Rightarrow^{PA^*}$ is an implication relation on the language of PA*, and that A is a theorem of PA* iff A is a thesis of I^{PA^*}. Now let us define a condition Σ on any one-place predicate T:

$$\Sigma(T): \text{Ind}(R) \Rightarrow^{PA^*} (\forall x)(T(x) \rightarrow R(x)), \text{ for all R},$$

(where Ind(R) contains no free occurrences of x). In effect this condition says that T satisfies the condition Σ iff for every R, R's being inductive implies that all T's are R's. (If we were doing this set theoretically, the condition would say that the set T is a subset of every inductive set). Given the definition of $\Rightarrow^{PA^*}$, an equivalent formulation of $\Sigma(T)$ is Ind(R), T $\Rightarrow^{PA^*}$ R (the universal closure of $[\text{Ind}(R) \wedge T(x)] \rightarrow R(x)$ is a theorem of I^{PA^*}, and therefore the universal closure of $\text{Ind}(R) \rightarrow (\forall x)(T(x) \rightarrow R(x))$ is a theorem of I^{PA^*} since there are no free occurrences of x in Ind(R)).

Now we note that $\Sigma(T)$ is a filter condition on the structure I^{PA^*} (Suppose that $\Sigma(T)$, and let S be any predicate such that S $\Rightarrow^{PA^*}$ T. Then Ind(R) $\Rightarrow^{PA^*}$ $(\forall x)(T(x) \rightarrow R(x))$, for all R, and $(\forall x)(S(x) \rightarrow T(x))$ is a thesis of I^{PA^*}. It follows that Ind(R) $\Rightarrow^{PA^*} [(\forall x)(T(x) \rightarrow R(x)) \wedge (\forall x)(S(x)] \rightarrow T(x))]$, for all R. Therefore Ind(R) $\Rightarrow^{PA^*} (\forall x)(S(x) \rightarrow R(x))$, for all R. Consequently, $\Sigma(S)$.)

---

posed to provide all the information about the operator or connective. So too inthe case of N(x), the idea is that the relevant information about it will be given by a (filter) condition which it satisfies, and a minimizing condition. Consequently no new axioms are added that concern N(x). The Introduction and Elimination conditions are supposed to determine which (if any) of the predicates of the language satisfy them. It turns out of course that R_0 satisfies the introduction and elimination conditions for N(x) and, up to equivalence, is the only predicate that satisfies them. It would be nice to have a more intuitive version of first-order arithmetic that uses "is a natural number". As far as I know, none of the present versions of formalized PA do so.

59. The implication structure will be an extended implication structure which incorporates first-order quantifiers. A sketch of how a first-order theory of quantification can be converted to an extended implication structure is contained in Koslow 1992, pp. 200–201.

We can now describe two conditions for the predicate "N(x)" using the filter condition $\Sigma(T)$:

(E) $\Sigma(N)$.

(I)   For all T, if $\Sigma(T)$, then $T \Rightarrow^{PA^*} N$.

The Elimination condition (E) for N says that $\text{Ind}(R) \Rightarrow^{PA^*} (\forall x)(N(x) \to R(x))$ for all R (equivalently, $\text{Ind}(R), N \Rightarrow^{PA^*} R$). This is a form of the principle of mathematical induction. The Introduction condition (I) for N says that the predicate N is implicationally the weakest to satisfy the Elimination Condition. A number of consequences follow readily: (1) Ind(N) is a thesis of I^{PA^*} (it follows from (E) and (I) that $R_0 \Leftrightarrow^{PA^*} N$; and since $\text{Ind}(R_0)$ is a thesis of I^{PA^*}, so too is Ind(N)), and (2) $(\forall x)(S(x) \to N(x))$, $\text{Ind}(S) \Rightarrow^{PA^*} (\forall x)(S(x) \leftrightarrow N(x))$. These are the usual results. What is not usual is that by using these conditions for "N(x)" we obtain a result that we had for the logical operators: *uniqueness*.

We know that if there are two members of an implication structure that satisfy the same conditions for (say) conjunction, then they are equivalent with respect to the implication relation on that structure. Similarly, suppose that there are two predicates, "N(x)" and "N'(x)", which satisfy the same conditions. Then the two predicates are equivalent. More exactly,

Suppose that in the implication structure I^{PA^*}, there is a predicate "N'(x)" such that

(1)   E(N): $\text{Ind}(R) \Rightarrow^{PA^*} (\forall x)(N(x) \to R(x))$, for all R.

(2)   I(N): For all T, if $\text{Ind}(R) \Rightarrow^{PA^*} (\forall x)(T(x) \to R(x))$ for all R, then $T \Rightarrow^{PA^*} N$.

(3)   E(N'): $\text{Ind}(R) \Rightarrow^{PA^*} (\forall x)(N'(x) \to R(x))$, for all R, and

(4)   I(N'): for all T, if $\text{Ind}(R) \Rightarrow^{PA^*} (\forall x)(T(x) \to R(x))$ for all R, then $T \Rightarrow^{PA^*} N'$.

Then $N \Leftrightarrow^{PA^*} N'$ (equivalently, $(\forall x)(N(x) \leftrightarrow N'(x))$ is a theorem of PA*).

The proof goes as follows: From (2) we get [If $\text{Ind}(R) \Rightarrow^{PA^*} (\forall x)(N'(x) \to R(x))$ for all R, then $N' \Rightarrow^{PA^*} N$] by substitution. But the antecedent is just (3). So $N' \Rightarrow^{PA^*} N$. From (4) we get [If $\text{Ind}(R) \Rightarrow^{PA^*} (\forall x)(N(x) \to R(x))$ for all R, then $N \Rightarrow^{PA^*} N'$] by substitution. But the antecedent is just (1). So $N \Rightarrow^{PA^*} N'$. Therefore $N \Leftrightarrow^{PA^*} N'$.

This result is easily explained: If Σ is a filter condition, then [E(N) and I(N)] iff for all T, Σ(T) *iff* T$\Rightarrow^{PA^*}$ N. So if we have E(N), I(N), E(N'), and I(N'), then it follows for all T that T$\Rightarrow^{PA^*}$ N iff T$\Rightarrow^{PA^*}$ N'. Consequently, N $\Leftrightarrow$ N'.

Sooner or later, in any logical theory, one has to deal with the notion of implication. In the present theory it is sooner. The resources of an abstract concept of implication are incredibly rich. With its use, an account of the logical operators as well as the modals unfolds. Results that were once closely linked to languages that assumed some syntactic or semantic regimentation are now available without those constraints. It is not just a case of familiar results recovered. There are a host of new observations and explanations that the theory offers. Some of these we have described; still others can be found in *A Structuralist Theory of Logic*, and others still remain to be discovered.[60]

References

Boolos G., 1979, *The Unprovability of Consistency, An Essay in Modal Logic*, Cambridge: Cambridge University Press.

Feferman S., 1984, 'Toward Useful Type-Free Theories, I', *Journal of Symbolic Logic*, 49, 75–111; reprinted in R. L. Martin (ed.), *Recent Essays on Truth and the Liar Paradox*, Oxford: Oxford University Press, 1984, pp. 237–87.

Gärdenfors P., 1984, 'The Dynamics of Belief as a Basis for Logic', *The British Journal for the Philosophy of Science* 35, 1–10.

Gentzen G., 1932, 'Über the Existenz unabhängiger Axiomensysteme zu unendlichen Satzsystemen', *Mathematische Annalen* 107, 329–50; Eng. trans. as 'On the Existence of Independent Axiom Systems for Infinite Sentence Systems', in *The Collected Papers of Gerhard Gentzen*, M. E. Szabo ed., Amsterdam: North-Holland, 1969, pp. 29–52.

Gentzen G., 1934, 'Untersuchungen über das logische Schliessen', *Mathematische Zeitschrift* 39, 176–210, 405–31; Eng. trans. as 'Investigations into Logical

---

60. Parts of this paper were read at Columbia University, King's College London, and the Moral Science Club, Cambridge. Many thanks to the participants of those meetings. I am especially indebted to Jody Azzouni, Horatio Arlo Costa, Jonathan Kastin, Jerrold Katz, Hugh Mellor, Elliott Mendelson, and Graham Priest for their help along the way.

Deduction', in *The Collected Papers of Gerhard Gentzen*, M. E. Szabo ed., Amsterdam: North-Holland, 1969, pp. 68–131.

Heyting A., 1956, *Intuitionism: An Introduction*, Amsterdam: North-Holland.

Koslow A., 1992, *A Structuralist Theory of Logic*, Cambridge: Cambridge University Press.

Koslow A., 1996, 'Counterfactuals, Proto-conditionals, and Modality', unpublished ms.

Koslow A., 1997, 'Modal Failure', unpublished ms.

Koslow A., 1998, 'Truthlike and Truthful Operators', in G. Sher and R. Tieszen (eds.), *Between Logic and Intuition: Essays in Honor of Charles Parsons*, Cambridge: Cambridge University Press, in press.

Levi I., 1991, *The Fixation of Belief and Its Undoing*, Cambridge: Cambridge University Press.

Lewis D., 1978, 'Truth in Fiction', *American Philosophical Quarterly* 15, 37–46; reprinted in D. Lewis, *Philosopical Papers*, Vol. I, Oxford: Oxford University Press, 1983, pp. 261–275.

Lewis D., 1979, *Counterfactuals*, Cambridge, MA: Harvard University Press.

Mancosu P. (ed.), 1997, *From Brouwer to Hilbert, The Debate on the Foundations of Mathematics in the 1920s*, Oxford: Oxford University Press.

Maxwell, J. C., 1877, *Matter and Motion*; reprinted with notes and appendices by J. Larmor, New York: Dover, 1952

Mendelson E., 1997, *Introduction to Mathematical Logic* (4th ed.), Chapman & Hall.

Parsons C., 1983, *Mathematics in Philosophy*, Ithaca: Cornell University Press.

Peacocke C., 1976, 'What is a Logical Constant?', *The Journal of Philosophy* 73, 221–40.

Priest G., 1997, 'Connexivist Logic', unpublished ms.

Schröder-Heister P. and K. Dosen (eds.), 1993, *Substructural Logics*, Oxford: Clarendon Press.

Scott D., 1974, 'Completeness and Axiomatizability in Many-Valued Logic', in L. Henkin *et al.* (eds.), *Proceedings of the Tarski Symposium*, Providence: American Mathematical Society, pp. 411–35.

Tarski A., 1935/1936, 'Grundzüge des Systemenkalküls', *Fundamenta Mathematicae* 25, 503–26 (Part I); 26, 283–301 (Part II); Eng. trans. by J. H. Woodger: 'Foundations of the Calculus of Systems', in A. Tarski, *Logics, Semantics, Metamathe-*

matics, Papers from 1923 to 1938, Oxford: Clarendon Press, 1956 (2nd edition ed. by J. Corcoran, Indianapolis: Hackett, 1983), pp. 342–383.

The Graduate Center,
City University of New York
and Brooklyn College
New York, NY USA

Manuel Pérez otero and
Manuel García-Carpintero
The Ontological Commitments of Logical Theories

1. Introduction

This paper is partly inspired by a well-known debate between Ruth Barcan Marcus, Terence Parsons and W. V. O. Quine in the sixties, concerning the extent to which Quantified Modal Logic ('QML' henceforth) is committed to "essentialism"; the issue nevertheless goes back to the origins of "analytic philosophy", to the reflections of Frege, Russell, and the earlier Wittgenstein on the nature of logic. By elaborating on a suggestion by Quine, we purport to show that there is a relevant and interesting way to look at the ontological commitments of logical systems such that they are stronger than they are usually taken to be.

In the more usual way of looking at the issue—adopted by writers like Marcus and Parsons—the commitments of logical theories are just those explicitly acquired by their theorems, the class of logical truths they determine. These may be called "the description-commitments", for they are captured in the body of claims which can be taken to fulfill the *descriptive* goals of a logical theory: at the very least, a logical theory aims to lay down in a precise and systematic way a set of sentences and arguments expressed in a language, or fragment thereof, thus *describing* the set of logical truths and logically valid arguments in the fragment. Developing the suggestion by Quine we will argue, however, that a separate, and usually stronger set of commitments can be distinguished from the description-commitments of a given logic. We will refer to them as "the explanation-commitments", for in our view they are required for the successful fulfillment of the *explanatory* concerns of logical theories, as pursued nowadays. A logical theory should not merely characterize a set of sentences and arguments; it should also make manifest what it is that distinguishes the members of the class from other sentences and arguments in the fragment, improving on the intuitive means through which we come upon the notion of logical theories in the first place.

It is in pursuing this second goal (as it is pursued contemporarily by the logical theories we accept) that the commitments we are interested in are acquired; or so we will try to show. Although the explanation-commitments of a given logical theory do not need to be explicitly stated by theorems of the theory (they only need to manifest themselves when the logical theory is contemplated, as it were, "from outside", at a metatheoretical level), the theory is still committed to them as much as if they were.

We will not confine our discussion to QML; instead, we will establish what we take to be an illuminating analogy by giving first an example of the distinction between description-commitments and explanation-commitments applying to the best established and least controversial logical system, First Order Logic ('FOL' henceforth). In fact, in our view it is clearer that a distinction along the lines sketched should be made and applied in the first-order case than that the distinction can in fact be used to vindicate Quine's attribution of essentialism to QML. The main objective of the paper is therefore to argue for the former, and only secondarily and tentatively—taking for granted a fair number of arguable assumptions—for the latter.

We begin our examination in section 2 by placing the issues we want to address in the context where they originated in contemporary times: the Quinean charge that QML is committed to a form of "essentialism", and Parsons' rejoinder to it. In section 3, we elaborate on the distinction between describing and explaining as applied to logical theories, so far only outlined. We develop the idea of explanation-commitments in section 4 on the basis of the promised analogy with FOL, and conclude with a few remarks about essentialism in the last section.

2. Parsons and Quine on the Ontological Commitments of QML

QML originated with the development of different formal (axiomatic) systems in the forties. It has to do with the validity and logical truth, respectively, of arguments and sentences involving the interaction of modal operators, '□' and '◊', with the logical expressions of FOL. In particular, the class of well-formed sentences of QML includes sentences in which modal operators appear inside the scope of quantifiers; that is to say, sentences like '$\exists x\,(\square\,\Phi(x))$'[1] involving "quantifying into" modal contexts.

From the beginning, QML was rejected by its harshest critic, Quine. In Quine's work on the subject, we can discern three different types of argument against it. First, there is the use of the "slingshot", the form of argument—first sketched by Frege and then developed by Church, Gödel and Quine himself—to conclude that any linguistic context (as discerned in "logical" syntax) admitting free substitution of coreferential singular terms (crucially including definite descriptions among the singular terms) and replacement of logically equivalent formulas is truth-functional. A related second form of criticism from Quine is a general objection to the intelligibility of any form of "quantifying into" a position in logical syntax regarding which the principles of substitutivity and existential generalization, as usually understood, do not apply in their full generality. As Smullyan 1948 made clear, however, these two arguments can be resisted by treating descriptions as quantifiers in the manner of Russell's theory of descriptions. In reaction to this defense of QML, Quine elaborated the last type of objection, the one we are interested in here. Quine now argues that, in any case, accepting the semantic correctness of "quantifying into" positions governed by modal operators would commit us to Aristotelian essentialism; this is a doctrine he assumes (and takes his readers to assume with him) to be nonsense.

The first explicit pronouncement by Quine on this issue can be found in Quine 1953b; the revised version of 'Reference and Modality', Quine 1953a, includes a similar claim. He there characterizes Aristotelian essentialism as the view that some attributes of some entity are essential to it, while other attributes of that same thing are only accidental to it; this, independently of the way we refer to the object, or conceptualize it. He takes this to be

---

1. Throughout the paper, we use simple quotation-marks as ambiguously expressing either ordinary quotation, or the form of quasi-quotation usually expressed with Quine's corner-quotes. We trust that in each particular case the context will include enough information to disambiguate.

embodied in the truthfulness of sentences like (1), for some open formulae '$F(x)$' and '$G(x)$':

(1) $\exists x \, (\Box F(x) \wedge G(x) \wedge \neg \Box G(x))$

A plausible example could be

(2) $\exists x \, (\Box\, x > 5 \wedge$ there are exactly x planets $\wedge \neg \Box$ there are exactly x planets$)$

QML, says Quine, is committed to something even stronger, namely,

(3) $\forall x \, (\Box F(x) \wedge G(x) \wedge \neg \Box G(x))$

for some open formulae '$F(x)$' and '$G(x)$'. To show this, it is enough to take as '$F(x)$' '$x = x$' and '$x = x \wedge p$', in which 'p' is some contingently true sentence, as '$G(x)$'. There have to be such sentences as 'p'; otherwise, '$\Box$' would be vacuous, and modal logic would lack interest. (See Quine 1953b, 175–6.) As regards the other aspect of essentialist claims mentioned above—the independence of their truth from the "modes of presentation" or linguistic resources by means of which we refer to the objects at stake—it is taken by Quine to be manifested by the fact that in QML modal expressions are not predicates of fully-fledged sentences (the "first grade of modal involvement"), but genuine operators, forming in particular open formulae out of open formulae.

These days, after the work of writers such as Putnam, Wiggins and especially Kripke, Aristotelian essentialism may not be such a loathsome symptom of philosophical blunder. It was of course otherwise in the fifties and sixties. We will, in any case, leave the issue aside, and concern ourselves only with the question of whether or not Quine was right in his contention that QML involves the doctrine in some way.

Some writers argued to the contrary; Parsons (1969) is a case in point. In Parsons' argument, it is not sentences instantiating schema (1) that are taken to express essentialism, but rather sentences instantiating the following schema:

(4) $\exists x_1 ... \exists x_n \, (\pi_n x_n \wedge \Box F(x_1 ... x_n)) \wedge \exists x_1 ... \exists x_n (\pi_n x_n \wedge \neg \Box F(x_1 ... x_n))$

where $\pi_n x_n$ is a conjunction of formulae (the same for both conjuncts) of the form '$x_i = x_j$' or '$\neg x_i = x_j$' for each $1 \leq i < j \leq n$ which does not entail, for any i, '$\neg x_i = x_i$'.[2] Parsons' essentialist sentences, thus, assert that some attributes are necessary to some objects and not necessary to others. The reader may perhaps perceive more clearly the contrast between Parsons' and Quine's formulations of essentialism by considering the following schematic case of (4) closer to (1): $\exists x \,\Box F(x) \land \exists x \,\neg \Box F(x)$.

Parsons' formulation of essentialist claims is not without problems. Instead of asserting a distinction between essential and accidental properties of objects, as was the case with Quine's version, Parsons' formulation asserts that some properties are such that some objects have them essentially, while others have them accidentally. This, however, is even compatible with the "collapse" of modal distinctions: (4) is consistent with the truth of the schema '$\Box p \leftrightarrow p$', which would entail that modal operators make no discrimination not already made without them. However, Quine's version has problems of its own. His essentialism is compatible with the possibility excluded by Parsons' formulation, i.e. that all objects have exactly the same essential properties. Fine (1989), however, describes a way to specify the truth-conditions of QML's sentences which is compatible with this form of "essentialism", but should not be objected to by anybody accepting the usual model-theoretic characterization of logical truth—which Quine does. (See Fine 1989, pp. 206–210 and 258.)

With characteristic verbal ingenuity, Quine described the Aristotelian distinction between essential and accidental attributes as "invidious". That invidiousness in attempting to discriminate, *de re* and for some objects but not others, a proper subclass of their attributes as essential might perhaps be better captured by means of the conjunction of (1) and (4). In any case, taking a stand on this debate would have little bearing on the conclusions of this paper. The reader may choose whatever formulation he or she finds preferable—Quine's, Parsons', or the conjunction of the two—for our main contentions apply equally to the three of them.

---

2. Parsons (1969), 77. Parsons considers languages without constants; otherwise, a more elaborated formulation would be needed. We have slightly modified Parsons' description of the formula (4). He requires that $\pi_n x_n$ does not include, for any i, j, '$x_i = x_j$' and '$\neg x_i = x_j$'. This, however, does not secure what appears to be its intended goal, that $\pi_n x_n$ does not entail any formula '$\neg x_i = x_j$'. Parsons' condition would be satisfied (against what appear to be his intentions) if, for instance, $\pi_n x_n$ were '$x_1 = x_2 \land x_2 = x_3 \land \neg x_1 = x_3$'. We are thankful to our colleague, Ramón Jansana, for pointing this out to us.

Having thus enunciated the schema that he takes to be common to essentialist claims, Parsons proceeds to distinguish three ways in which a logical system could in some way be committed to them (Parsons 1969, pp. 77–8): (i) some instances of (4) are theorems of the system; (ii) the system entails some instances of (4), given some obvious non-modal facts; (iii) the system allows for the meaningful formulation of some instances of (4).

The semantics for the modal systems that Parsons presupposes is the classic semantics developed by Kripke, as in Kripke (1963). Every model is determined by a set of possible worlds, with a highlighted member (the actual world), an accessibility relation between the worlds, and a function assigning to every predicate and world an appropriate extension in the domain of the world; this interpretation can be extended, in the usual way, so as to obtain a truth-value with respect to every possible world for every formula, relative to an assignment to the variables. A *logical truth* is a sentence true in every world in every model. (See the details in Parsons 1969, p. 86, and Kripke 1963, pp. 64–6.)

The existence of *maximal* models can be proved (Parsons 1969, p. 87): these are models that, for every consistent set of non-modal sentences, include a possible world with respect to which they all are true. It can also be proved that no instance of (4) is true in any possible world in a maximal model. Thus, there is no commitment to essentialism in Parsons' sense (i). Moreover, if we take (as Parsons does) sense (ii) to entail that the system has as theorem a sentence of the form $\alpha \rightarrow \beta$, in which α is an obvious non-modal truth and β an instance of (4), it also follows that QML is not committed to essentialism in sense (ii); for, $\{\alpha\}$ being a consistent set, there is a maximal model containing a possible world with respect to which α is true, while β, as we have indicated, is false with respect to that world (and any other in the model). Finally, says Parsons, QML is certainly committed to essentialism in sense (iii); but the anti-essentialists need not be worried about this, if they sensibly limit themselves to contending the falsehood of essentialism rather than seeking to render it non-sensical. They are even free to take the negation of every instance of (4) as an axiom of their world-theory, so that no essentialist claim is true in any possible world of any model (Parsons 1969, p. 85).

Parsons thus connects the ontological commitments of a logical system to the explicit contentions of its set of logical truths. He is not alone in doing so. Ruth Barcan Marcus, one of the philosophers most deeply involved in the development of QML, appears also to have conceded relevance to Parsons' criteria (i) and (ii) in deciding the ontological commitments of QML. This is what she has to say on the issue in Marcus 1981—a good survey of the development to that date of philosophical issues related to QML: "In what sense committed? Granted such [essentialist] sentences are well-formed, is every model of a modal system committed to the truth or more strongly, the validity of essentialist sentences?" A few lines below she indicates that Parsons 1969 has shown that there are models consistent with the falsity of any sentence making an essentialist claim (Marcus 1981, p. 285).

Parsons' and Marcus' notion of the ontological commitments of a logical system is a reasonable one, and they seem right to contend that, in that sense, QML is not committed to essentialism. In the next section, however, we develop the distinction between describing and explaining for logical theories, in order to pave the way for our later demonstration of another way of looking at the issue in which things are not so clear.

3. The Constitutive Goals of Logical Theories

Logic may not only be approached as a solely mathematical enterprise; it can also be taken as a *scientific* pursuit. We use 'scientific' instead of 'empirical' for lack of a better word, since the use of the word 'empirical' would be a solecism in view of the fact that logic, even when not purely mathematical, may well be in a well-defined sense *a priori*. The solecism, however, is tempting; because the contrast we mean is similar to the one existing between purely mathematical geometry and empirical geometry, or between purely mathematical physics and empirical physics. Purely mathematical geometry provides precise characterization of "spaces", establishes that these "spaces" possess certain properties of interest to well-regarded practitioners of the art, proves consequences of their possessing those properties equally interesting to those practitioners, and so on. These theoretical activities are pursued without any commitment to the "spaces" being in fact spaces in which physical entities interact or spaces of which we have sensory representation; the correct theoretical characterization of this space is the concern of physical geometry. Analogously, purely mathematical physics consists in the precise characterization of "physical systems", "gravitatory fields", and so on, establishes that they possess some properties that well-regarded theoreticians find interesting, proves consequences of this, and so on; while empirical physics aims to offer accurate characterizations of actual physical systems, actual gravitatory fields, etc. No disrespect is intended by reserving "scientific" for the latter members of pairs like these; we believe that the former members only constitute a genuine body of knowledge (and are thus indirectly "scientific", in the etymological sense of that much abused word) to the extent that it is reasonable to pursue them in the hope (which, of course, may not be realized) that the information thus acquired will be important for the adequate development of the concerns of the latter members.

Purely mathematical logic characterizes "logical systems" precisely: "languages" are defined, their "syntax" and "semantics" given in a precise way; deductive relations are established, and are proved to have certain properties (particularly having to do with the interaction of relations of deducibility and a relation of "logical consequence"). It then defines properties of those systems that mathematical logicians find interesting, and proves consequences of the fact that systems have or lack those properties. Scientific logic, on the other hand, is concerned with actual cases, in our assertions and arguments, of logical validity, and subsidiarily of logical truth. As in every other similarly interesting case, we cannot offer at the outset a philosophically acceptable explication of these properties. We can only provide paradigm instances (arguments and thoughts expressed in our vernacular languages, among them some of the ones used by purely mathematical logicians when they present their systems and argue about their properties) and a rough, "intuitive" characterization. In our view, this rough characterization would involve three features, perhaps conceptually related. Firstly, logically valid arguments *necessarily preserve truth* (necessarily, either some of the premises are not true, or the consequence is true), and logical truths are necessarily true. Secondly, these facts can be recognized or known *a priori*. Thirdly, logical validity and logical truth depend on the semantic properties of relatively *structural* traits of the sentences and sequences of sentences involved.

Because this last feature will play an important role in our argument, we will elaborate on it. The structural traits whose semantic significance is essential for logical validity and logical truth consist mainly of the following (this is of course no attempt at a definition): firstly, expressions by means of which complex sentences are built out of less complex phrases (like 'and', 'or', 'for all' and so on) in a well-determined, systematic way, and secondly, logico-syntactical traits of the expressions conforming elementary sentences, also structurally relevant to their well-formedness. Among the latter traits are those distinguishing *referential expressions, n-adic predicates, kind-terms, propositional expressions*, and so on; also, traits like those indicating when two expression-instances are intended to make the same truth-conditional contribution (say, to have the same reference) and when they are not so intended.

It is very important not to confuse the structural traits themselves with their semantic significance, a mistake which is more likely in the case of the logico-syntactical traits of the expressions conforming elementary sentences. In order to avoid confusion, it may help to note that here as elsewhere the same semantic fact may be expressed by two different formal means. For instance, in natural language the fact that two predicate-instances are intended to make the same truth-conditional contribution is usually expressed by using instances of the same type. In languages used in logical systems the same applies to "constants", the equivalent in those languages of referential expressions. But in natural languages this is not always the case. For instance, the fact that a given referential expression is intended to make the same referential contribution as that made by a previously used indexical is not indicated in natural language by using an indexical of the same type, but by using anaphoric expressions. This is thus a case in which the same semantic fact (co-reference of two expression-occurrences) is indicated by two different structural means.

By the (perhaps artificial) device of counting the logico-syntactical traits of proper names, basic predicates, etc., as separate *expressions* in their own right, we can conveniently summarize the third feature of our "intuitive" characterization of logical truth and logical validity by saying simply that these properties depend on the semantics of structural expressions ("logical constants"). The reader should remember henceforth, though, that "logical constants", in the present understanding, include not only separate expressions like conjunction, negation, existential quantification and so on, but also syncategorematic features of expressions like monadic predicatehood, etc. Now, part of the reason why the three features constituting our intuitive characterization of logical truth and logical validity are rough is that they are expressed in terms of concepts, like *necessity, aprioricity* and *structurality,* which are themselves as much in need of illumination as those that we are characterizing by means of them, *logical validity* and *logical truth*. Moreover, while the characterization remains at this intuitive, rough level, there is no denying that, at the end of the day, we may have to abandon the assumption that logical truth and logical validity, so understood, are genuine properties having instances and making discriminations. But there is no denying, either, the strong *prima facie* presumption that the sets of logical truths and logically valid arguments constitute non-empty proper subclasses of the sets of significative thoughts and purportedly argumentative sequences of thoughts.

Philosophers of science distinguish two separate domains in which the comparative virtues of theories provided to account for the facts in a given field may be measured: *description* and *explanation*. One theory may be descriptively as adequate as another, while failing to be as explanatory. A typical example lies in the contrast between Newton's theory applied to celestial mechanics and Kepler's laws: the degree to which Newton's theory improves on Kepler's laws regarding the adequate description of the motions in the planetary system, if in fact it does, cannot quite match the degree to which the former improves on the latter at the level of providing adequate explanations.

The structural character of logical truth and logical validity makes it possible to classify sets of instances of these properties relative to the structural traits on whose semantic significance their being logical truths or logically valid arguments depends. This is how the distinction arises between propositional logic, first-order logic and, of course, QML. Scientific logic makes use of the logical systems studied in mathematical logic. This follows the usual scientific strategy of considering "frictionless worlds"; it allows for the clear-cut isolation of the specific properties on which the facts to be explained depend, according to the theory, abstracting them away from other properties in conjunction with which they may well appear always instantiated in the actual world, perhaps even lawfully so. It is, in a nutshell, a way of setting the really explanatory facts into relief and making the explanation perspicuous. Thus, the sentences of languages devised by logicians are supposed to "formalize" corresponding sentences of natural languages expressing the relevant thoughts and arguments. At the very least, the formalization should render perspicuous the logically relevant structural traits of corresponding sentences in the vernacular.[3]

---

3. For the remarks about the relationship between natural and formal languages we are indebted to discussions with our colleague Josep Macià, and to his MIT doctoral dissertation.

By these means, the theories provided by scientific logic achieve one of their goals: they can present, in a systematic and clear manner, the set of logical truths and logical consequences "in virtue of" a specified class of logical constants. In some cases (those where a *complete* deductive calculus is available), this can even be done in a purely formal, syntactical way. It can even be done without bothering to make explicit the semantic significance of the structural traits isolated in devising the artificial language, nor the extent to which its sentences *translate* the sentences in the vernacular they formalize, preserving some of the semantic properties that go into the individuation of the thoughts the vernacular sentences express. Now, unlike the goal we will describe presently, achieving this goal can be properly characterized as obtaining only a higher or lower degree (relative to the perspicuity, simplicity, etc., of the system) of *descriptive* adequacy. Something is missing if this alone is achieved—something which is to be expected from a truly scientific logical theory.

QML is, in fact, a well-known case in which the descriptive goal was first pursued in a purely syntactical way. David Kaplan points to the contrast we want to highlight in this passage:

> What we have done, or rather what we have sketched, is this: a certain skeletal language structure has been given, here using fragments of English, so of course an English reading is at once available, and then certain logical transformations have been pronounced valid. Predicate logic was conducted in this way before Gödel and Tarski, and modal logic was so conducted before Carnap and others began to supply semantical foundations. The earlier method, especially as applied to modal logic (we might call it the run-it-up-the-axiom-list-and-see-if-anyone-deduces-a-contradiction method), seems to me to have been stimulated more by a compulsive permutations-and-combinations mentality than by a true philosophical temperament" (Kaplan 1969, pp. 208–209).

What is achieved when a semantic interpretation (like the possible-worlds semantics for modal logic, or the model-theoretic semantics for FOL) is provided, which would be definitively missing if the set of logical validities and logical truths were merely characterized syntactically? What is it that a "true philosophical temperament" requires in addition? Newton's celestial kinematics constitutes an improvement in explanatory adequacy, in that it provides a better account of properties on which the already well-characterized movements in the Solar System depend. Similarly, we would gain in explanatory adequacy in the field covered by logical theories if, in addition to a simple, clear characterization of a given set of logical validities, we also had an account of what makes a given argument belong in that set. Because we start with a rough, merely "intuitive" answer to this, such an improvement, we suggest, would have mainly to do with showing, in clearer and more precise terms than those of the rough intuitive presentation of the logical properties, how the three features intuitively characterizing logical truths and logically valid arguments do indeed capture real properties, having instances and making discriminations.

This inevitably requires a detailed examination of the relevant semantic properties, and cannot be given while remaining at a purely formal level; this is therefore why the purely combinatorial method described by Kaplan is insufficient for explanatory purposes. Achieving some degree of explanatory adequacy in the field covered by logical theories has to do with tracing illuminating connections among the three features, which clarify why they hang together. In previous work (cf. García-Carpintero 1993 and 1996a), one of us has argued that the adequacy of the model-theoretic definition of the logical properties, whose acceptance is widespread at least regarding FOL, depends on the semantic account of the relevant structural traits that flows from the truth-theoretical semantics usually provided for first-order languages. Given the classical logical empiricist analysis of a priori knowledge as semantic knowledge (the "metasemantic" account in Peacocke 1993 is a contemporary variation we find appealing), the structurality of logical truth and logical consequence would be enough (as indicated in the work just mentioned) to account for their aprioricity. This, traditionally, would also have been considered sufficient to account for the necessity of logic, but contemporary Kripkean sophistication indicates that the relations between a priori knowledge and necessity are to be handled with more care than previously thought. Still, an account of modality along the lines of Peacocke 1997 would connect the structurality of the logical properties with the modal ways in which they apply.

This is a sketchy answer to the question of what is missing from an explanatory viewpoint when the validities are only syntactically characterized. It allows, however, for the distinction between description- and explanation-commitments we seek to establish.

4. The Explanation–Commitments of Logical Theories

Let us go back now to the debate that pitted Quine against critics like Parsons and Marcus regarding the ontological commitments of QML.

This is what Quine had to say about criticisms such as those in the course of a discussion (much discussed these days, for not directly related reasons) with Føllesdal, Kripke, Marcus and McCarthy:

> I've never said or, I'm sure, written that essentialism could be proved in any system of modal logic whatever. I've never even meant to suggest that any modal logician ever was aware of the essentialism he was committing himself to, even implicitly in the sense of putting it into his axioms. I'm talking about quite another thing—*I'm not talking about theorems, I'm talking about truth, I'm talking about true interpretation*. And what I have been arguing is that if one is to quantify into modal contexts and one is to interpret these modal contexts in the ordinary modal way and one is to interpret quantification as quantification, not in some quasi-quantificatory way that puts the truth conditions in terms of substitutions of expressions—then in order to get a coherent interpretation one has got to adopt essentialism [...] But I did not say that it could ever be deduced in any of the S-systems or any system I've ever seen. (Quine *et al.* 1962, p. 32; our italics).

Our goal in this section is to develop, on the basis of the proposal put forward in the previous section, Quine's suggestion that there is a further way of looking at the ontological commitments of logical theories that have to do with truth, or with true interpretation, rather than with the set of logical truths.

As indicated at the outset, we want to use an analogy with FOL to present our view. To that end, consider the following question: to what extent is FOL ontologically committed to the existence of individuals? On the face of it, a smooth working of the analogy would require the following: that, on the one hand, the existence of individuals were not a description-commitment of FOL, in that no instance of the schema '$\exists x\, F(x)$' is a theorem of FOL; while, on the other hand, there was a sense, linked to the explanatory aims of FOL, in which that was indeed the case. Unfortunately, the first requirement is not satisfied, which prevents the smoothness of the analogy; for '$\exists x\, x = x$' is a logical truth of FOL. That, however, is a consequence of relatively superficial facts, of theoretical decisions that could be modified without affecting the substance of the issues; and the analogy is, we believe, the best to be had, and so we are prepared to suffer its superficial lack of smoothness. A non-empty domain is always assumed in devising the semantics for first-order languages; it is this decision that has the consequence we have mentioned. However, the decision is taken just for reasons of expediency. (Perhaps, we would suggest, adopting it is also facilitated by the dim perception that, *in some sense*, we are committed to the truth of

'$\exists x\, x = x$'. The reasons that we are about to elaborate, although not strictly speaking logical, are after all substantially akin to logical reasons: they make the claim, in a reasonably broad sense, *analytical*.) Nothing of substance would change if empty domains were accepted; it is only that things would necessarily be more complicated. Empty domains, on the other hand, seem clearly conceivable, so that no instance of the schema '$\exists x\, F(x)$' should be counted, strictly speaking, as logically true. We will therefore assume, to pursue our analogy, that FOL is not committed to the existence of individuals at the level that Parsons and Marcus discuss. Deep down, the existence of individuals should not count as a theorem of FOL.

We can now proceed with our analogy. When FOL is considered not only as a theory that achieves descriptive goals (perspicuously systematizing the logical truths and logical validities "in virtue of" the first-order logical constants—including, remember, the structural traits), but also as a theory that achieves explanatory goals, the ontological commitment to individuals does indeed arise. The reason is this. Logical truth and logical validity are defined model-theoretically, as truth in all models and truth-preservation in all models, respectively. This definition achieves explanatory goals, only in so far as it is based on a certain semantic analysis. A crucial semantic fact according to this semantic analysis is that sentential expressions signify truth-conditions; and it is in addition essential to the explanatory power of the analysis that it carefully separates the relatively abstract truth-conditional import of the logical constants from the more specific *import* of non-logical expressions. We obtain different "models" by keeping the semantic significance of the logical constants fixed while taking all possible variations in the semantic significance of the non-logical expressions compatible with that fixation, as permitted by set-theory—the theory we assume as a meta-theoretical tool to represent truth-conditional determinants. That is to say, we keep fixed semantic facts such as the following, which, though abstract, definitely shape truth-conditions: there is a domain of individuals (possibly empty, we are now assuming); referential expressions (variables and constants) can only take values in this domain, the same value for every instance of the same expression-type (it may or may not be different for instances of different expression-types); n-adic predicate expressions represent subclasses of n-tuples of members of the domain, the same subclass for every instance of the same expression-type. Other semantic features change from model to model: the identity and number of the specific individuals in the domain, the values in that domain of referential and predicative expressions.

This semantic analysis, which is an essential correlate of the model-theoretic account, is directly provided, by stipulation, for the artificial language of FOL; however, if the claims in the previous section are correct, the fulfillment of the explanatory goals of the theory forces us to think that they are presumed to apply, too, (even if in a messy way) to the sentences by means of which we express the thoughts and arguments whose logical properties we want ultimately to account for. This assumption should be validated via the formalization relation. The structural traits of first-order sentences we have called "logical constants" have correlates in vernacular sentences (or thought-vehicles) whose semantic significance is presumed to be accurately represented by the semantic significance of the corresponding traits in the first-order expressions that translate them. The fact that this correlation exists (required for the theory to be explanatory, in the sense developed in the preceding section) has consequences which are not particularly momentous; indeed, the fact that they are not is intimately related to the enormous intuitive plausibility of FOL, which even critics like Etchemendy acknowledge.[4] But even if the consequences are not momentous, they do not need to show up among FOL's theorems; and that is what really matters for our point.

It is one of these humble consequences that our analogy depends on. Our world-theory includes, for instance, the assumption that sentences like 'Empedocles, who is a person, leapt' and 'someone leapt' are meaningful, and indeed are so in such a way that the former logically entails the latter. FOL accounts for this, after formalizing the premise of the argument as, say, '$P(e) \land L(e)$' and its conclusion as '$\exists x(P(x) \land L(x))$'. Now, when FOL is *applied* to explain the presumed validity of arguments such as these, it is part of the semantic analysis—on whose accuracy whatever explanatory value FOL may have as a scientific theory depends—that expressions like

---

4. Disposing of Etchemendy's criticisms of the model-theoretic account in Etchemendy 1990 was the main purpose of García-Carpintero 1993. Pérez Otero takes a different line of criticism in Pérez Otero (forthcoming). For other criticisms, see the doctoral dissertations of Mario Gómez Torrente at Princeton, 1996, "Tarski's Definition of Logical Consequence. Historical and Philosophical Aspects", and of Josep Macià at M.I.T., 1997, "Natural Language and Formal Languages".

'Empedocles' have structural traits corresponding to those of first-order constants.

To be sure, while it is very easy to describe the structural traits at stake in the case of first-order languages, nothing short of the resources of mature psycholinguistic theories would be needed to give an accurate characterization of the corresponding features of referential expressions in natural languages. The relevant structural features of a first-order expression like '*e*' above consist of how expressions like '*e*' combine with some *n*-adic predicate and *n*-1 expressions of the same category as '*e*' to form well-formed elementary sentences; it is also relevant that quantified variables occupy those same positions, i.e., that '*e*' instantiates positions governed by quantifiers. Even if we still know little about the syntax of natural language, it is enough to know that a much more complicated story (involving, say, the role of a level of "logical form" vis-à-vis other levels of syntactic representation) would be required to characterize the corresponding structural trait of 'Empedocles'. This is in part why the recourse to artificial languages is so serviceable.

The explanatory value of applying FOL presupposes additionally that the structural traits of 'Empedocles' corresponding to those of '*e*' also have an analogous semantic significance. This means that those structural facts regarding 'Empedocles' which correspond to the facts just described—those which the character of '*e*' as a constant of FOL amount to—possess, according to the semantic analysis which is an essential part of FOL's explanation, a determinate semantic significance. They contribute to shaping the truth conditions of the sentences in which the expression appears, by indicating that this expression signifies *an individual*: a member of the domain, a potential member of some *n*-tuples discriminated by some predicates in the language, and the sort of entity whose assignment as semantic value to a constant makes inferences of the form "$P(e)$, therefore $\exists x P(x)$" and "$\forall x P(x)$, therefore $P(e)$" truth-preserving.[5] Nothing more is required by the explanation given by FOL; nothing more, for instance, regarding the identity of that entity. From a logical point of view, this "Empedocles" may be anything we can correctly take to be an individual. But this much is indeed required.

It is in this way that by accepting FOL as an explanatory theory, one that applies explanatorily to some inferences in the vernacular, we commit our-

---

5. We are putting aside the issue of how a free logic should handle the relevant inferences.

selves to the existence of individuals. This ontological commitment can be properly described as "pragmatic", in that it arises not solely from the logical theory, but from it together with the *use* to which we put the theory, from the *application* we make of it. It does not show up at the level of the theorems (the set of logical truths characterized by the theory), because the theorems are the truths *required* by the meanings of the logical constants, and to quantify over an empty domain is compatible with those meanings. From a logical point of view, the only requirement deriving from the semantics of quantifiers is the existence of a proper domain; nothing more specific is required regarding the identities and number of its members. In particular, the empty domain is a possible domain of quantification; this is why there is no (deep) commitment to the existence of individuals asserted by the theorems. But the commitment does appear when we take into account some of the claims we want to make—or at least to take to be meaningful—over and above the claims that are logically true, given the semantics that the explanatory applicability of FOL to them requires us to attribute to them.

This ontological commitment is meager at least on two counts. Firstly, the individuality to whose instantiation FOL is thus committed is a very abstract property, shared by Empedocles with numbers, ghosts, gods and devils, cardinal virtues, events, etc. Secondly, the commitment to individuals like Empedocles is not a commitment to their ultimate, metaphysically irreducible individuality. For all that the explanatory adequacy of FOL commits us to, phenomenalism or even solipsism may still be true. FOL may explain perfectly adequately the facts about logical truth and logical consequence in virtue of the first-order logical constants, even if Empedocles is ultimately a "logical construct" out of the really ultimate particulars, which are in fact the sense data of one of the authors of this paper at the time of conceiving this very sentence: he would still be an individual of the proper sort.[6]

Moreover, nothing hangs on granting a referent to 'Empedocles' itself, as the possibility of empty domains we are contemplating should make clear. That is to say, the commitment we are emphasizing does not arise specifically from any given sentence including referential expressions which we take to be meaningful and able to take part in first-order inferences in a particular context. In any particular case—like, for instance, that constituting

---

6. For rather similar views, see Stalnaker 1984, pp. 57–8.

our example—we might be considering an empty domain without realizing it, regarding which the presuppositions for meaningfully using referential expressions would not be in fact satisfied. The ontological commitment is better seen as arising from applying FOL to our whole world-theory, the set of claims we are epistemically justified in accepting. It arises when we consider the *intended* model in its totality, "the" model for our complete world-theory, given the beliefs about its nature we can ourselves take to be most justified. It is logically permitted that we are quantifying over an empty domain in specific contexts; some sentences we take to be meaningful may fail to be so; but we obviously do not take the intended model to have an empty domain. This much seems safe, even if it is not (deeply) logically the case: that we are justified in using some referential expressions, when stating our current world-view. The commitment we have been highlighting arises from the explanatory application of FOL to sentences (thoughts) for which this justification is correct.

The reader has probably anticipated that the commitment to the existence of individuals is not in our view the only explanation-commitment of first-order logic.[7] There is also, for instance, a commitment to the existence of domains; and another to the existence of "conditions", which discriminate n-tuples of members of a given domain. If we take seriouly the theory we use to present these facts, these are ultimately commitments to sets. Of course, these commitments are as meager as the one we have been mostly discussing so far. For instance, the commitment to "conditions" is not a commitment to universals in any philosophically interesting sense. It is not a commitment to attributes, natural or objectively explanatory properties, or the like. For it is just conditions that may well be expressible only with "wildly disjunctive"

---

7. In his criticism of the model-theoretic account in Etchemendy 1990, Etchemendy makes much of the fact that for this account to make intuitively correct predictions about validity, it is committed to the existence of infinite domains. As indicated in García-Carpintero 1993 and more clearly in Pérez Otero (forthcoming), it is important to make clear, as Etchemendy does not, that the correctness of the model-theoretic account in no way requires to take the claim at stake as, strictly speaking, *logically* true. On the other hand, the account can be taken to be committed to the "analyticity" of the claim, in some broad sense. But this cannot be taken so easily to discredit the account; not, certainly, on the basis of Etchemendy's considerations. We take the ontological commitment in question to have a similar status to the other commitments we are discussing here.

open sentences that we are committed to, by the explanatory application of FOL to the meaningful claims by means of which we would establish our world-view. On the other hand, this also vindicates the distinction between description-commitments and explanation-commitments, for it is even clearer that the sort of second-order commitments to domains and conditions on them we have been describing in this paragraph cannot be properly expressed by FOL-sentences, let alone by its logical truths.

Entry 5.552 of the *Tractatus* includes the very much quoted contention that logic "is prior to the question 'How?', not prior to the question 'What?'." With most other interpreters, we read this as the contention for which we have been arguing: logic as such (which Wittgenstein, we believe, takes to go no further than first-order logic) is committed to the existence of "objects" (the 'What?'), although it is not committed to any specific objects or number of them (this is a matter left for the application of logic, *Tractatus* 5.557), nor to the nature of the state of affairs in which objects enter (the 'How?'). In justification for this, Wittgenstein offers the following characteristically enigmatic argument: "And if this were not so, how could we apply logic? We might put it in this way: if there would be a logic even if there were no world, how could there be a logic given that there is a world?" (Wittgenstein 1921, 5.5521) The following interpretation by paraphrase, which we cannot justify here on the basis of its internal coherence with the text or otherwise,[8] provides a reading of the cryptic argument which brings it close to the one we have been elaborating so far.

"*There is a world*; that is to say, we have a representational system which allows for the construction of claims, the conditions for whose truth are satisfied or are not satisfied given the states of an independent reality. Now, a necessary condition for there being a *real logic* is that *it has application* to that representational system which we have. A real logic must account for logical relations among claims belonging to our representational system, logical relations which obtain precisely in virtue of their truth conditions. A real logic should account for the *validity* of certain inferences involving the claims mentioned, for the fact that, if the truth conditions of all the premises in an argument are satisfied, the truth conditions of the conclusion must be satisfied too. Suppose, however, that *there would be a logic even if there were no world*; i.e., suppose that the only "logic" to be had is a purely

---

8. But see García-Carpintero 1996b, ch. 9.

formal system, one in which certain sentences are pronounced valid and a certain procedure is arbitrated for them to yield more sentences also pronounced valid, all of this on the basis of purely formal traits of the sentences, entirely independently of their semantic interpretation, of facts about the truth conditions of the sentences at stake. Then, the necessary condition for a real logic could not be satisfied; for a system of this kind is unable to explain the validity of the most plainly valid inference involving claims expressed in our representational system, no matter how well they fit some of the forms pronounced valid by the "logical" system. *There would not therefore be any* (real) *logic.* But this is an absurd result. Logic should refer to semantic relations between expressions and features of the extralinguistic reality corresponding to those expressed in our representational systems (even if only to semantical relations with very abstract features, whose obtaining it is plausible to assume we know a priori)."

This argument only disparages the lack of explanatory value of a logic considered as a mere calculus, while we have been concerned to make a distinction between commitments that arise at a descriptive level versus those that arise at an explanatory level, in both cases regarding systems which are not mere calculus but incorporate also a semantics. Aside from that, however, the concern with the consequences of logic having an application to inferences involving our beliefs and their expressions in natural language is rather close.

5. QML's Commitment to Essentialism

As we indicated at the beginning, the main part of our paper ends with the establishment of a distinction we take to be interesting between two ways of looking at the ontological commitments of a logical theory, one of which, disregarded by critics of Quine like Parsons and Marcus, can be taken to be the one alluded to in the remark by Quine we quoted at the beginning of the preceding section. To establish that philosophical distinction between the description-commitments and the explanation-commitments of a logical theory (justifying that they may differ in some cases), in sum, we have argued as follows. (i) Over and above setting apart, in a precise and clear way, a class of arguments (ultimately arguments expressed in the vernacular), a logical theory should contribute to accounting for the distinction between the arguments in the class and other sequences of sentences. (ii) This requires taking very seriously the semantic account which is part of the logical theory, because the explanation at stake is ultimately given model-theoretically, relative to the distinction between expressions whose interpretation varies from model to model and expressions whose interpretation remains fixed. (iii) When we consider FOL as applied to the ordinary arguments to which we take it to apply, taking that semantic account seriously entails that there are meaningful expressions whose truth-conditional contribution is an individual.

A more arguable issue is whether the distinction can in fact be used to vindicate Quine's contention; as we would put it, the claim that essentialism is among the explanation-commitments of QML. The reason why it is more arguable is related to the fact that the status of QML as a scientific theory cannot quite compare to that of FOL. Firstly (at the descriptive level), there are many modal logics, and it is not clear that any one of them captures even approximately all and only the inferences that should be counted as valid, given the way we use modal expressions and other theoretical considerations. Perhaps we use modal expressions in logically different ways in different contexts; perhaps the usual leeway that the different indeterminacies in our usage leave to theoretical decisions in matters of regimentation is here wider than in other cases. (This makes Quine's skepticism at least understandable, whatever we think of his arguments.) Turning secondly to explanatory concerns, there are many conceptual unclarities regarding the most widely accepted semantics for QML; but the explanatory application of QML also depends on the adequacy of that semantics. It is not clear, for instance, whether the commitment to possible-worlds is a commitment to particulars as objective as we take the actual world to be, and how this would tally with the Kripkean intuition that "possible worlds are not viewed through telescopes", that conceivability is a *prima facie* more reliable guide to metaphysical possibility than the mere appearance of truth can be taken to be a guide to truth.

However, to the extent that these unclarities can be ignored and QML regarded as a genuinely explanatory logical theory, we believe that a good case can be made, following Quine, for its explanation-commitment to essentialism. Consider the following schema, combining Quine's and Parsons' formulations of essentialism:

(5) $\exists x(\Box F(x) \wedge G(x) \wedge \neg \Box G(x)) \wedge \exists x \neg \Box F(x)$

Let us grant that no instance of (5) is a theorem of QML. This only establishes that essentialism is not a description-commitment of QML. But is it an explanation-commitment? By granting that no instance of (5) is a theorem, we grant just that the semantic properties of QML's logical constants do not require their truth; we grant that, compatible with that semantics, we can contemplate models relative to which they are false. In that sense, there is no commitment either arising from the logic of modality to the truth of, say, '□ 9 > 7' or '□ no bachelor is married': there are acceptable models that falsify the claims (they are false, for instance, relative to Parsons' maximal models). In the same way that the logically relevant features of the semantics of quantifiers are compatible with an empty domain, the logically relevant features of the modal operators are compatible with models that falsify essentialist claims. What is at stake now, however, is whether, relative to the standard possible worlds semantics, the explanatory application of QML to the modal claims constituting our world-view which enter in arguments essentially involving their modal properties in fact commits us to what is asserted by instances of (5). (The way in which, analogously, the *intended* model for our world-view should validate '□ 9 > 7' and '□ no bachelor is married'.)

We take it that our ordinary use of modal expressions (modal adverbs and the subjunctive, combined with the expressions that have translations in the language of FOL) allows for many true applications of (expressions that should be translated into QML by means of) open sentences of the form '□$F(x) \land G(x) \land \neg\Box G(x)$' to some entities, and true applications of open sentences of the form '$\neg\Box F(x)$' to some other entities. Think just of a claim to the effect that an event caused some other event. Arguably, claims like this involve—relative to the semantics that comes with the application of QML—separating (causally) essential properties of the event ("it was an earthquake of such and such intensity"), properties that *it* keeps in every relevant (accessible) world, from (causally) accidental properties of *that very same* event ("it was reported on the front page of today's *El País*"), properties that *it* lacks in some accessible possible world. Moreover, it is also part of our view that there are some other events lacking the (causally) essential properties of this one; that is to say, lacking in some accessible possible world the essential properties of *that event*, the particular earthquake in question.

Besides, as Quine points out, and as our use of italics in the previous sentence intends to stress, what is involved in applying the open formula to the event is the *de re* correctness of the attribution. The open formula is intended to apply to *the event itself*, independently of how we think of it; otherwise, we would rather resort to a less committal "way of modal involvement", paraphrasing the title of Quine 1953b. That is to say, the properties by means of which the event is presented to us may well be other than the relevant essential properties; we may even ignore them, when representing it as causing some other event.

It should perhaps be stressed that the preceding is independent of whether we assume the same individuals to be in the domains of different possible worlds, or rather we reject this notion, assuming a counterpart-theoretic semantics instead. In counterpart-theoretic semantics, a "counterpart" in w' of the individual assigned to the variable x in possible world w is assigned in w' to 'x', instead of the same individual being assigned (the domains of the possible worlds are taken not to overlap), and the same goes for genuinely referential expressions. Moreover, the relation of counterparthood is supposed to be determined by qualitative facts.[9] However, it is not assumed (and could not be assumed compatibly with giving an account of modal semantics fitting our semantic intuitions) that the qualities in question constitute the very modes of presentation through which we represent the individuals assigned to the expression relative to the actual world. The ultimate (linguistic) fact of the matter, to be respected both by counterpart theorists and theorists preferring the more ordinary semantics, is that while a description functioning *de dicto* in a modal context picks up its referent in other possible worlds "qualitatively", relative to the properties conforming the description, this is not the case with variables and referential expressions.[10]

Thus, we tend to agree with Quine that, in our own terms, essentialism is indeed an explanation-commitment of QML. To put it in different words, just by making the most ordinary modal inferences involving the interaction of modal expressions and the expressions translated in first-order languages which we take to be correct (something we mortals all do, including among mortals the most no-nonsense minded scientists in the pursuit of the most

---

9. See Hazen 1979, for an adequate presentation of these issues.
10. See chapter 4 of Lewis 1986, for elaboration and illumination on these issues.

serious of their scientific concerns), we are committing ourselves to there being *de re* essential and accidental properties of objects, if and to the extent to which the explanation of the validity of those inferences provided by QML is correct. Quine takes a rather grim view of QML on account of this.[11] As the reader has probably guessed, this is not an attitude we share with him. But that is an issue we have refrained from discussing here.[12]

References

Etchemendy, J., 1990, *The Concept of Logical Consequence*, Cambridge, MA: Harvard University Press.

Fine, K., 1989, 'The Problem of De Re Modality', in J. Almog, J. Perry, and H. Wettstein (eds.), *Themes from Kaplan*, Oxford: Oxford University Press, pp. 197–272.

García-Carpintero, M., 1993, 'The Grounds for the Model-Theoretic Account of the Logical Properties', *Notre Dame Journal of Formal Logic* 34, 107–131.

---

11. We should say, on behalf of Parsons, that he does recognize some form of commitment more substantive than that captured by what we have called description-commitments, arising from the "applications" of the logical system. These further commitments may come, he suggests, from truths of a priori theories to which the logical system is intended to apply, like arithmetics, or truths which are analytic but not logical theorems. He proposes to capture those additional commitments as further axioms of the logical theory. He then goes on to argue that, even so, no commitment to essentialism would follow, if two certain assumptions are granted (see Parsons 1969, sec. IV). Let us assume, for the sake of the argument, that our explanation commitments can be considered as "analytic truths" in a wide sense, and captured the way Parsons suggests. If so, this argument of his begs the question. For one of the two assumptions Parsons needs turns out to be that any additional axioms "be closed and contain no constants" (Parsons 1969, p. 80). This ensures, by assumption, that there will not be any "quantifying into" modal operators among the additional axioms. That is, however—in the framework that Parsons has chosen—just what is at stake; what is at stake, in this framework, is whether or not the additional non-logical axioms expressing the commitments that come from the "applications" include instances of (5). In assuming, without any justification, that this is not the case Parsons blatantly begs the question.

12. The present paper develops ideas first presented in Pérez Otero (1996). We want to express our gratitude to Ignacio Jané, Ramón Jansana, Josep Macià, and Gabriel Uzquiano for comments and discussions on previous versions of this material. Financial support has been provided by research project PB96-1091-C03-03, funded by the DGES, Spanish Department of Education.

García-Carpintero, M., 1996a, 'The Model-theoretic Argument: Another Turn of the Screw', *Erkenntnis* 44, 305–316.

García-Carpintero, M., 1996b, *Las palabras, las ideas y las cosas*, Barcelona: Ariel.

Hazen, A., 1979, 'Counterpart-Theoretic Semantics for Modal Logic', *Journal of Philosophy* 71, 319–38.

Kaplan, D., 1969, 'Quantifying In', in D. Davidson and J. Hintikka (eds.), *Words and Objections*, Dordrecht: Reidel, pp. 178–214.

Kripke, S., 1963, 'Semantical Considerations on Modal Logic', in L. Linsky (ed.), 1971, pp. 63–72.

Lewis, D., 1986, *On the Plurality of Worlds*, Oxford: Basil Blackwell.

Linsky, L. (ed.), 1971, *Reference and Modality*, Oxford: Oxford University Press.

Marcus, R. B., 1981, 'Modal Logic, Modal Semantics and their Applications', in *Contemporary Philosophy. A Survey*, Vol. 1, The Hague: Martinus Nijhoff.

Parsons, T., 1969, 'Essentialism and Quantified Modal Logic', in L. Linsky (ed.), 1971, pp. 73–87.

Peacocke, C., 1993, 'How Are A Priori Truths Possible?', *European Journal of Philosophy* 1, 175–199.

Peacocke, C., 1997, 'Metaphysical Necessity: Understanding, Truth and Epistemology', *Mind* 106, 521–574.

Pérez Otero, M., 1996, 'Verdad necesaria *versus* teorema de lógica modal', *Theoria* 11, 185–201.

Pérez Otero, M., forthcoming, 'A Fallacy about the Modal Status of Logic', forthcoming in *Dialectica*.

Quine, W. V. O., 1953a, 'Reference and Modality', revised version of the paper with the same title in his *From a Logical Point of View*, in L. Linsky (ed.), 1971, pp. 24–35.

Quine, W. V. O., 1953b, 'Three Grades of Modal Involvement,' *Proceedings of the XIth International Congress of Philosophy*, Brussels, 1953, Volume 14, Amsterdam: North-Holland. Also in W. V. O. Quine, *The Ways of Paradox*, New York: Random House, 1966, pp. 158–176 (to which we refer).

Quine, W. V. O., Marcus, R. B., *et al.*, 1993, 'Discussion', in R. B. Marcus, *Modalities. Philosophical Essays*, New York: Oxford University Press, pp. 24–35.

Smullyan, A., 1948, 'Modality and Description,' in L. Linsky (ed.), 1971, pp. 88–100.

Stalnaker, R., 1984, *Inquiry*, Cambridge, MA: MIT Press.

Wittgenstein, L., 1921, *Tractatus Logico-Philosophicus*, English translation by D. F. Pears and B. F. McGuiness, Atlantic Highlands, NJ: Humanities Press, 1992.

Departament de Lògica, Història i Filosofia de la Ciència
Universitat de Barcelona
Barcelona, Spain

GRAHAM PRIEST
Validity

1. Introduction: Approaching the Problem

1.1 *The Nature of Logic*

Knowledge may well, in the last analysis, be a seamless web. Yet it certainly falls into relatively well-defined chunks: biology, history, mathematics, for example. Each of these fields has a nature of a certain kind; and to ask what that nature is, is a philosophical question.[1] That question may well be informed by developments within the field, and conversely, may inform developments in that field; but however well that field is developed, the question remains an important one, and one that will pay revisiting. It is such a revisiting that I will undertake here.

The field in question is logic, one of the oldest areas of knowledge. The nature of this has been a live issue since the inception of the subject, and numerous, very different, answers have been given to the question 'what is logic?'. To review the major answers that have been given to this question would be an important undertaking; but it is one that is too lengthy to be attempted here. What I do intend to do is to give the answer that I take to be correct. Even here, it is impossible to go into all details. Indeed, to do so one would have to solve virtually every problem in logic! What I will give is the basis of an answer. As we will see, there is enough here to keep us more than busy.

1.2 *Focusing on Validity*

What, then, is logic? Uncontroversially, logic is the study of rea-

---

1. Even when—especially when—the field is philosophy itself. See Priest 1991a.

soning. Not all the things that might fall under that rubric are logic, however. For example, the way that people actually reason may, in some profound sense, be part of the ultimate answer to the question of the nature of logic (think of Wittgenstein in the *Investigations*), but logic is not about the way that people actually think. The reason for this is simple: as a rich literature—if not common sense—now attests, people frequently reason illogically.[2] Logic does not tell us how people *do* reason, but how they *ought* to reason. We will return to the question of the 'ought', here, later. For the present, let us cede the question of how people actually reason to psychology.

The study of reasoning, in the sense in which logic is interested, concerns the issue of what follows from what. Less cryptically, some things—call them *premises*—provide reasons for others—call them *conclusions*. Thus, people may provide others with certain premises when they wish to persuade them of certain conclusions; or they may draw certain conclusions from premises that they themselves already believe. The relationship between premise and conclusion in each case is, colloquially, an argument, implication or *inference*. Logic is the investigation of that relationship. A good inference may be called a *valid* one. Hence, logic is, in a nutshell, the study of validity.

The central question of logic is, then: what inferences are valid, and why?[3] Neither the answer to this question, nor even how to go about answering it, is at all obvious. Logic is a theoretical subject, in the sense that to answer this question one has to construct a theory, to be tested by the usual canons of theoretical adequacy. And what other notions the theory may take into its sweep—truth, meaning or wot not—is part of the very problem.

1.3 Validity: a First Pass

How, then, is this central question to be answered? Doubtlessly, a valid inference is one where the premises provide some genuine ground for the conclusion. But what does that mean? Traditionally, logic has distinguished between two notions of validity: deductive and non-deductive (inductive). A valid deductive argument is one where, in some sense, the

---

2. See, e.g., Wason and Johnson-Laird 1972, esp. the places indexed under 'fallacies'.
3. There are, of course, other questions (such as, e.g., the nature of fallacies). But these all make refence back to the central question.

conclusion cannot but be true, given the premises; a valid inductive argument is one where there is some lesser degree of support. Standard examples illustrate the distinction clearly enough. One might well ask why the notion of validity falls apart in this way, and what the relationship is between the two parts. I will come back to the whole issue of inductive inference later in the essay, and give a uniform account of validity, both deductive and inductive. For the present, let us simply accept the distinction between the two notions of validity as a given, and focus on deductive validity.

2. Deductive Validity

2.1 *Proof-Theoretic Characterisation*

What, then, is a deductively valid inference? Modern logic standardly gives two, very different, sorts of answer to this question: proof-theoretic and model-theoretic (semantic). In the proof-theoretic answer, one specifies some basic rules of inference syntactically. A valid inference is then one that can be obtained by chaining together, in some syntactically characterisable fashion, any of the basic rules. The whole process might take the form of a Gentzen system, a system of natural deduction, or even (God help us) an axiom system.

Such a characterisation may undoubtedly be very useful. But as an answer to the main question it is of limited use, for several reasons. The first is that there seem to be languages for which the notion of deductive validity is provably uncharacterisable in this way. Second-order logic is the obvious example. This has no complete proof-theoretic characterisation. Given certain assumptions, the same is true of intuitionistic logic too.[4]

Possibly in these cases—especially the intuitionistic one—one might simply reject the semantic notion of validity with respect to which the proof-theory is incomplete. But even if one does this, there is a more profound reason why a proof-theoretic characterisation is unsatisfactory as an ultimate characterisation of validity. We can clearly give any number of systems of rules. Some may have nothing to do with logic at all; and those that do may give different answers to the question of which inferences are valid. The crucial question is: *which system of rules is the right one?* The natural answer at this point is to say that the rules are those which hold in virtue of

---

4. See McCarty 1991.

the meanings of certain notions that occur in the premises and conclusions. This appears to take us into the second characterisation of validity, the semantic one. Some independent account of those meanings is given, and the appropriate proof-theory must answer to the semantics by way of a suitable soundness proof (and perhaps, also, completeness proof). And indeed, I think this way of proceeding is correct.

One may, however, resist this move for a while. One may suggest that it is a mistake to understand meaning in some independent way, but that the rules themselves *specify* the meanings of certain crucial notions involved. For example, one might say that the introduction and elimination rules for a connective in a system of natural deduction, specify its meaning. The problem with this was pointed out by Prior (1960). One cannot claim that an arbitrary set of rules specifies the meaning of a connective. Suppose, for example, that one could characterise a connective, $*$ (*tonk*), by the rules: $\alpha \vdash \alpha * \beta$ and $\alpha * \beta \vdash \beta$. Then everything would follow from everything—hardly a satisfactory outcome.

Some constraints must therefore be put on what rules are acceptable. One might attempt some purely syntactic constraint. For example, it has been suggested[5] that the rules in question must give a conservative extension. This, however, will not solve the problem. Conservativeness is always relative to some underlying proof theory. For example, adding the rules for Boolean negation to a complete proof theory for positive 'classical' logic is conservative; adding them to one for positive intuitionist logic is not. One needs, therefore, at the very least, to justify the underlying proof theory. And this cannot be done by conservativeness, at least indefinitely, on pain of infinite regress.[6]

One way in which it might be thought possible to avoid this regress is explained by Sundholm 1986, p. 485ff. Suppose that we are working in a natural deduction system, and suppose that we take the introduction rule for a connective to provide a direct account of its meaning. This needs no justification: *any* introduction rule may serve to do this. The corresponding elimination rule is then justified by the fact that it is conservative with

---

5. E.g., by Belnap 1962.
6. There are other problems with applying the notion of conservativeness here. What conservatively extends what may depend on the (apparently irrelevant) fact of the order in which rules are added on. See Priest 1990.

respect to the introduction rule. In the words of Dummett, one of the people to whom this idea is due, the introduction and elimination rules are in harmony.[7] The idea can be cashed out in terms of a suitable normal-form theorem: whenever we have an introduction rule followed by the corresponding elimination rule, both can be eliminated.

The regress is not eliminated, however. For the introduction and elimination rules are superimposed on structural inferential rules; for example, the transitivity of deducibility (deductions may be chained together to make longer deductions). Such structural rules are not inevitable,[8] and the question therefore arises as to how *these* rules are to be justified. This becomes patently obvious if the proof-theory is formulated as a Gentzen system, where the structural rules are quite explicit, and for which there is now a well-advanced study of logics with different structural rules: sub-structural logics.[9] One needs to justify which structural rules one accepts (and which one does not), and there is no evident purely proof-theoretic way of doing this.

If, as the forgoing discussion suggests, one cannot justify every feature of a proof-theory syntactically, the only other possibility would seem to be some semantic constraint to which the rules must answer.[10] We are thrown back to the other kind of characterisation of validity, the model-theoretic one. So let us turn to this.

2.2 Model-Theoretic Characterisation

A deductively valid inference is, we said, one where the premises cannot be true without the conclusion also being true. A crucial question here is how to understand the 'cannot'. What notion of impossibility—and, correlatively, of necessity—is being appealed to here?

Modern logic has produced a very particular but very general way of understanding this. When we reason, we reason about many different situations; some are actual—what things are like at the centre of the sun; some are merely possible—what things would have been like had the Axis won the second world war; and maybe, even, some are impossible—what things

---

7. For full references, see Sundholm 1986.
8. For example, there is 'harmony', but not transitivity in the logic of Tennant 1987.
9. See Schröder-Heister and Dosen 1993, and also Slaney 1990.
10. In the context of *tonk*, this was suggested by Stevenson 1961.

would be like if, *per impossibile*, someone squared the circle. We also have a notion of what it is to hold in, or be true in, a situation. In talking of validity, necessity is to be explicated in terms of holding in all situations. Let us use lower case Greek letters for premises and conclusions,[11] upper case Greeks for sets thereof, and write ⊢ to indicate valid inference. Then we may define $\Pi \vdash \kappa$ as:

> for every situation in which all the members of Π hold, κ holds

There is also a corresponding notion of logical truth: κ is logically true iff it holds in all situations.

So far so good. But what is a situation, and what is it to be true in it? One could, I suppose, take it that these notions are indefinable, but this is not likely to get us very far; nor is it the characteristic way of modern logic. Using mathematical techniques, both notions are normally defined. A situation is taken to be a mathematical structure of a certain kind, and holding in it is defined as a relationship between truth-bearers and structures. Both structures and relation are normally defined set-theoretically.[12]

Thus, for example, in the case of the standard account of validity for (classical) first order logic (without free variables), a structure is a pair:

$$\mathcal{A} = \langle D, I \rangle \qquad (Q)$$

where D is the non-empty domain of quantification, and I is the denotation function. Truth in $\mathcal{A}$ is defined in the usual recursive fashion. Or in a Kripke semantics for modal logics, a structure is a 4-tuple:

$$\mathcal{A} = \langle W, g, R, I \rangle \qquad (R)$$

---

11. I shall not be concerned in this paper with what *sort* of thing premises and conclusions are, sentences, statements, propositions, or wot not. As far as this paper goes, they can be anything as long as they are truth-bearers, that is, the (primary) kind of things that may be true or false.
12. No one would suppose that situations are mathematical entities, such as ordered *n*-tuples—at the very least, in the case of actual situations. Strictly speaking, then, set-theoretic structures *represent* situations. They do this, presumably, because the situations have a structure (or, at least, a pertinent structure) that is isomorphic to that of the mathematical structure. How to understand this is a question in the philosophy of mathematics. Indeed, how to understand this sort of question is *the* central question of the nature of applied mathematics, and one I cannot pursue here.

where W is a set of worlds, g is a distinguished member of W (the 'base world'), R is a binary relation on W satisfying certain properties (to be employed in stating the truth conditions of $\Box$), and I is the denotation function, which assigns each atomic formula a subset of W (namely, those worlds at which it is true). Truth at a world $w \in W$ is again defined in a recursive fashion. And truth in $\mathcal{A}$ is defined as truth at g.

In any semantics of this kind, the recursive truth conditions for a connective or quantifier can be thought of as spelling out its meaning, thus providing something against which a proof-theoretic rule employing that notion may be judged.

Once the notions of a structure and holding-in are made precise, the definition of validity can be spelled out exactly. Let us write $\mathcal{A} \vDash \alpha$ to mean that α holds in structure $\mathcal{A}$. We may also say that $\mathcal{A}$ is a *model* of α. $\mathcal{A}$ is a model of a *set* of truth bearers if it is a model of every member of the set. Then α is a logical truth iff every structure is a model of α. And:

$$\Pi \vdash \kappa \text{ iff every model of } \Pi \text{ is a model of } \kappa \qquad (DV)$$

I take this to be the best answer to the question of when an inference is deductive validity presently on offer. Note, though, that a structure is a set-theoretic entity, and $\vDash$ is a set-theoretic relation. Thus, the right hand side of (*DV*) is a statement of mathematics. Strictly speaking, then, we have not given a final account of what it is for an inference to be valid; we have reduced the matter to that of the truth of a certain mathematical sentence. We may well ask the question of what it is for such a statement—or any mathematical statement—to be true. This is a profound question, but is far too hard to address here. One problem at a time!

2.3 Filling in the Details

(*DV*) is, in fact, only the *form* of a definition of validity. It leaves many details to be filled in. These depend, for a start, on the language employed in formulating the premises and conclusions. More importantly, the details cannot be filled in without resolving philosophical issues of a very substantial kind. This is not the place to go into these, but let me just point out some aspects of the process.

A major question to be answered is: how, exactly, are situations structured? This question cannot be divorced from that of how to define the relation of being true in a structure.[13] For example, should the truth conditions of the conditional employ an ordering relation on worlds, as occurs in Kripke semantics for intuitionist logic, a ternary relation, as occurs in many relevant logics, or none of these, as in classical logic? If either of the first two of these is correct, then the relation will have to be a part of the structure. Another example: assuming that the truth/falsity conditions for a predicate are to be given in terms of its extension (those things it is true of) and anti-extension (those things it is false of), are we to suppose that these are exclusive and exhaustive of the relevant domains (as classical logic assumes) or not (as more liberal logics may allow)? Issues of the above kind pose deep metaphysical/semantical issues of a highly contentious nature.

Many of the relevant considerations here are familiar from the literature debating intuitionist, paraconsistent, and other non-classical logics. Theoretical issues concerning meaning, truth, and many other notions, certainly enter the debate. There is also a question of adequacy to the data. We have intuitions about the validity of particular inferences. (We may well have intuitions about the validity of various *forms* of inference as well, though because of the universality implicit in these, they are much less reliable.) These act like the data in an empirical science: if the theory gives the wrong results about them, this is a black mark against it. But as with all theorisa-

---

13. Let me, in passing, note that *being true in* is quite distinct from *being true* (*simpliciter*); for these two notions are frequently confused. The latter notion is a property, or at least, a monadic predicate, and has nothing, in general, to do with sets. One might be interested in it for all kinds of reasons, which it is unnecessary to labour. The other is a relation, and a set theoretic one, at that; and the only reason that one might be interested in it is that it is a notion necessary for framing an account of validity. The two notions are not, of course, entirely unrelated. One reason we are interested in valid inferences is that we can depend on them to preserve truth, *actual* truth. Hence it is a desideratum of the notion of truth-in-a-structure that there be a structure, call it the actual structure, such that truth (period) coincides with truth in it. The result is then guaranteed. No doubt this imposes constraints on what one's account of structure should be, and on how the truth-in relation should behave at the actual structure. But one should not suppose that just because the actual structure possesses certain features (such as, for example, consistency or completeness), other structures must share those features: we reason about many things other than actuality. Similarly, recursive truth conditions may collapse to a particularly simple form at the actual structure because of certain privileged properties. But that is no reason to think that they must so collapse at all structures.

tion, the fact that a theory has desirable theoretical properties (e.g., simplicity, non-*ad-hoc*ness), may well cast doubt on any data that goes against it—especially if we can explain how we come to be mistaken about the data. (We will see an example of this concerning enthymemes a little later.) The dialectical juggling of theory against data is always a matter of good judgment (which is not to say that all judgments are equally good), and always fallible.[14]

The situation is, in fact, even more prone to dispute than I have so far said. This is because (*DV*) itself is couched in terms whose behaviour is theory-laden, such as the logical constant 'every'; and if one parses the restricted quantifier 'every *A* is *B*' in the usual way as 'everything is such that if it is an *A* it is a *B*', then the conditional is getting in on the act too. The meanings of such notions, especially 'if', are philosophically contentious.[15] An orthodox course is to take the conditional to be a material one. But if one takes the material conditional to be non-detachable, as do most relevant and paraconsistent logics, then this will hardly appeal. It should be a genuine and detachable conditional.

Another way of looking at the matter is this: it is not just the definition (*DV*) itself that is at issue, but what does and what does not follow from it. This depends on the behaviour of the 'logical constants'; that is, the valid principles

---

14. It is sometimes said that there is no determinate answer to the question of whether or not an inference is (deductively) valid. An inference may be valid in one semantics (proof theory, logic, system, etc.) but not another. Maybe this is just a way of saying that it is valid according to some particular theories or accounts of validity but not others, in which case it is unproblematic. But it is, I think, often meant as stronger than this: there is no fact of the matter as to which theory gets matters right. And if it means this, it would certainly appear to be false. Either it is true that 'Socrates had two siblings' gives a (conclusive) ground for 'Socrates had at least one sibling' or it is not. This fact is not relative to anything—unless one is a relativist about truth itself.
15. The notion of set employed in (*DV*) may also be up for grabs. The nature of work-a-day sets, such as the null set and the set of integers, may not be problematic; but the definition of validity concerns *all* structures of a certain kind; and the behaviour of such totalities is a hard issue. Even if you suppose that the totality of sets is exhausted by the cumulative hierarchy, how far "up" this extends is still mathematically moot, as is the question of whether we may form totalities that are not, strictly-speaking, sets. Throw in the possibility that there may be sets that are, e.g., non-well-founded, let alone inconsistent, and one starts to see the size of the issue.

that such constants satisfy; which is part of what is at issue in an account of validity; which is what (*DV*) gives. The issue is therefore a circular one. This does not mean that it is impossible to come up with a solution to the whole set of matters. It just means that there is no privileged point of entry: we are going to have to proceed by boot-strapping. Certainly, one can do this with 'classical logic'; one can equally well do it with intuitionist logic or a paraconsistent logic. In the end, we want a theory that, *as a total package*, comes out best under 'reflective equilibrium'. There is no short way with this.[16]

2.4 The Tarskian Account

Before we leave deductive validity and turn to inductive validity, it will be illuminating to compare the account of validity I have given with the celebrated account given by Tarski in his essay (1936).[17] In a nutshell, this is as follows. Certain words of the language are designated *logical constants*. Given a sentence, its *form* is the result of replacing each non-logical-constant with a parameter (variable). An *interpretation* is a function that assigns each parameter a denotation of the appropriate type (objects for names, extensions for predicates, etc.). A relationship of *satisfaction* is defined between interpretations and forms, standardly by recursion. An inference is valid iff every interpretation that satisfies the form of each premise satisfies the form of the conclusion. (Correspondingly, a sentence is logically true if its form is satisfied by all interpretations.)

If we identify interpretations with what I have been calling structures, and write the satisfaction relationship as $\vDash$, then the form of the Tarskian definition of validity is exactly (*DV*). It is therefore tempting to think of the two accounts as the same. And indeed they may, in some cases, amount to the same thing; but as accounts, they are quite distinct. For a start, an interpretation, as employed in the definition, is normally only *part* of a structure, e.g., the *I* of (*Q*) or (*K*). In all but the simplest cases, structures carry more information than that, e.g., the domain, *D*, in (*Q*), and the binary relation,

---

16. For a further discussion concerning the rivalry of logical theories, see Priest, to appear, section 10. Section 13 of that paper raises the question of whether or not one should be a realist about logic. This papers answers the question in the affirmative.
17. It should be noted that this is not the orthodox model-theoretic account, which occurs in Tarski's later writings. For a discussion of Tarski's views and their history, see Etchemendy 1988.

R, in (K). This will, in general, make an important difference as to what inferences are valid. For example, consider the sentence $\exists x \exists y\, x \neq y$. At least as standardly understood, this contains only logical constants. According to the Tarskian account it is therefore either logically true or logically false. In fact, it is the former, since it is true (*simpliciter*). But given standard model theory, it holds in some structures and not others, hence it is not logically true.[18]

In (1990) Etchemendy provides an important critique of the Tarskian account. It will be further illuminating to see to what extent the account offered here is subject to the same problems. Etchemendy provides two sorts of counter-examples to the Tarskian account. These concern under-generation and over-generation.

According to the Tarskian account, any valid inference is, by definition, formally valid; that is, any inference of the same form is valid. This seems to render certain intuitively valid inferences invalid. For example, given the usual understanding of logical form:

> This is red;
> hence this is coloured

is invalid, since its form is:

> x is P;
> hence x is Q

which has invalid instances.

This argument is not conclusive. One may simply agree that the original inference is invalid, but explain the counter-intuitiveness of this by pointing out that the inference is an enthymeme. It is an instance of the valid form:

> x is P;
> everything that is P is Q;
> hence x is Q

---

18. This fact is picked up by Etchemendy 1990 who points out, quite correctly, that the Tarskian account of validity has to be doctored by 'cross term restrictions' for a more orthodox result. A slightly different way of doctoring it, by making the parametric nature of quantifiers explicit, is given in Priest 1995. Note that, because of typesetting errors, all the '$\forall$'s in that paper appear as '$\supset$' or '$\supseteq$'.

and the instance of the suppressed premise here is 'everything that is red is coloured', which is obviously true.[19]

I shall not discuss the adequacy of this move here. I wish only to use the example to contrast the account of validity given here with the Tarskian one. For, modulo an appropriate account of logical form, the present account may, but *need not*, make validity a formal matter. This just depends on what structures there are. In the case at point, for example, there may be no structures where there is something in the extension of 'red' that is not in the extension of 'coloured'. We might, for example, eliminate such structures from a more general class with 'meaning postulates', in the fashion of Carnap and Montague.[20] If this is the case, the inference in question is valid, though not formally so. Of course, this path is not pursued in standard model theory, where the more general notion of structure is employed; the result of this is that the notion of validity produced is a formal one. If one takes this line, then the model-theoretic account of validity also has to employ the enthymematic strategy.

Etchemendy's second sort of counter-example to the Tarskian approach concerns over-generation. In such examples, Tarski's account gives as valid, inferences that are not so; or if perchance this does not happen, this is so only by 'luck'. Consider the sentence: there are at most two cats: $\forall x \forall y \forall z((Cx \wedge Cy \wedge Cz) \supset (x = y \vee y = z \vee z = x))$. Provided that there are at least three objects *in toto*, this is not a logical truth; but if not, it is. In this case, presumably, the account gets the answer right. But if the universe is finite, with, say, $10^{10^{10}}$ objects, the account is going to give the wrong answer for: there are at most $10^{10^{10}}$ cats. Moreover, whether or not something is a logical truth ought not to depend on such accidental things as the size of the universe.

One may meet Etchemendy's criticism by pointing out that the totality of all objects is not restricted to the totality of all physical (actual) objects, but comprises *all* objects, including all mathematical objects, all possible, and maybe all impossible, objects too. Not only is this so large as to make

---

19. See Priest 1995.
20. See Carnap 1952, and Montague 1974, esp. p. 53 of Thomason's introduction. In fact, orthodox model theory employs meaning postulates for the logical constants. The recursive truth conditions select one denotation for each logical constant from amongst all the syntactically possible ones.

every statement of the form 'there are at most i cats' (where i is any size, finite or infinite) not a logical truth; but this result does not arise because of some 'lucky contingency'. There is nothing contingent about the totality of all objects.[21]

An objection similar to Etchemendy's might be made against the account of validity offered here. An inference is valid if it is truth preserving in all situations. Couldn't this give the wrong answer if there are 'not enough situations to go around'; and even if there are, should such a contingency determine validity? The answer to this is the same, and even more evident. The totality of situations is the totality of *all* situations: actual, possible, and maybe impossible too. It doesn't make sense to suppose that there might not be enough. Nor is the result contingent in any way. The totality of all situations is no contingent totality.

But the point may be pressed. The official definition is given, not in terms of situations, but in terms of the mathematical structures that represent them. Might there not be enough structures to 'go around'? One might doubt this. Structures need not be 'pure sets'. Any situation is made up of components; and it is natural to suppose that these can be employed to construct an isomorphic set-theoretic structure. Yet the worry is a real one. One of the situations we reason about is the situation concerning sets. Yet in Zermelo Fraenkel set-theory, there is no structure with the totality of sets as domain. Hence this set-theory can not represent that situation. This does not show that (*DV*) is wrong, however. It merely shows that *ZF* is an inadequate vehicle for representation. A set theory with at least a universal set is required. There are may other reasons for being dissatisfied with *ZF* as a most general account of set. See Priest 1987, ch. 2.

3. Inductive Validity

3.1 *Form vs. Content*

We have seen that the model-theoretic account of validity that I have offered is different from the Tarskian account. But, so far, we have not seen any definitive reason to prefer it to that account. The model-theoretic account is more powerful and more flexible, for sure, but as long as the enthymematic move is acceptable, we have seen no cases where this extra

---

21. See Priest 1995, pp. 289–91. Etchemendy has some other examples of over-generation, but these are less persuasive, *ibid.*

power and flexibility *must* be used. However, an argument for this may be found by looking at the question of inductive validity. In due course, I will also give a model-theoretic definition of inductive validity. But let us approach these issues via a different question.

Theories of deductive validity took off with Aristotle, and are now *highly* articulated. Theorisation about inductive validity is, by comparison, completely under-developed. Why? A standard answer, with a certain plausibility, is as follows. Deductive validity is a purely formal matter. Hence it is relatively easy to apply syntactic methods to the issue. By contrast, if an inference is inductively valid, this is not due to its form, but to the *contents* of the claims involved, a matter which is susceptible to no such simple method.

The issue is, however, not that straightforward. For a start, as we have seen, it may not be the case that deductive validity is a matter of form. That just depends on how other details of the account pan out. Moreover, it is not immediately clear that inductive validity is not a matter of form either. The inference:

x is P;
most Ps are Qs;
hence x is Q

is a pretty good candidate for a valid inductive form. (It is certainly not deductively valid.) It is true that an inference such as:

Abdul lives in Kuwait;
hence Abdul is a Moslem

is frequently cited as a valid inductive inference, and one that is not formally valid on the usual understanding of what the logical constants are. But it is not at all clear that this is so. Just as in the deductive case, we may take it to be an enthymeme of the above form with suppressed premise: most people who live in Kuwait are Moslems.

Despite this, inductive validity is not, in fact, always a formal matter. This, I take it, is one of the lessons of Goodman's new 'riddle of induction'.[22] Consider an inference of the following form (plausibly, one for enumerative induction):

---

22. As explained, for example, in ch. 3 of Goodman 1979.

$Ea_1 \wedge Ga_1, ..., Ea_n \wedge Ga_n / \forall x(Ex \rightarrow Gx)$

If E is 'is an emerald' and G is 'is green', this inference seems quite valid. If, on the other hand, G is 'is grue' (that is, a predicate which, before some (future) time, t, is truly applicable to green things, and truly applicable to blue things thereafter), it is not. It is well known that there is no syntactic way of distinguishing between the two inferences. For though 'grue' is, intuitively, a defined predicate, 'green' can be defined in terms of grue and bleen (a predicate which, before t, is truly applicable to blue things and truly applicable to green things thereafter). Hence any syntactic construction may be dualised. What breaks the symmetry is that 'emerald' and 'green' are natural-kind terms (are projectible, in Goodman's terminology), whereas 'grue' is not. But there is no syntactic characterisation of this. Hence, inductive validity is not, in general, a formal matter. It follows, then, that no version of the Tarskian account of validity is going to be applicable to inductive validity. For as we have seen, Tarskian validity is formal validity.

3.2 Probability

How, then, are we to get a grip on the notion of inductive validity? A natural suggestion is that we should appeal to a suitable notion of probability. (Probability assignments are not, except in a very few cases, a formal matter.) Now there certainly seem to be intimate links between inductive validity and probability, but it is not clear that one can use the notion to formulate a satisfactory theory of inductive validity.

Let us restrict ourselves, for simplicity, to the one-premise case, and let us write the conditional probability of α given β in the usual way, as $p(\alpha/\beta)$. Then a first suggestion for defining inductive validity is as follows: an inference from premise β to conclusion α is valid if β raises the probability of α, i.e., if $p(\alpha/\beta) > p(\alpha)$. This will not do, however. Just consider a case where β raises the probability of α though this is still small, as in:

> John used to be a boxer;
> so John has had a broken nose

This seems quite invalid. (Most boxers have never had broken noses.)

A more plausible suggestion is that the inference is valid if $p(\alpha/\beta)$ is 'sufficiently high'—where this is to be cashed out in some suitable fashion. But this, too, has highly counter-intuitive results. Consider the case, for example, where β *decreases* the probability of α, even though the conditional probability is still high, as in:

> John used to be a boxer;
> so John has *not* had his nose broken

This inference is of dubious validity.[23]

Could an appeal to Bayeseanism solve the problem at this point? According to Bayeseans, the relevance of a premise, β, is simply that if we learn—or were to learn—that β, we (would) revise our evaluation of the probability of any statement, α, to $p(\alpha/\beta)$, where p is our current probability function. I do not wish to deny that we sometimes revise in this way, but this cannot provide a satisfactory account of inductive inference for two reasons. First, if there is nothing more to the story than this, it is tantamount to giving up on the notion of inductive inference altogether. Inference is concerned with the question of when, given certain premises, it is reasonable to accept certain conclusions. In other words, we want to be able to *detach* the conclusion of the argument, given the premises. Conditionalisation does not, on its own, give an answer to the question of when this is possible.[24] More conclusively, even Bayeseans concede that there is information that cannot be conditionalised upon.[25] For example, if α is anything such that $p(\alpha) = 1$, and if the probability function that will result from our next revision is q, then we cannot conditionalise coherently on, e.g., $q(\alpha) \leq 0.5$. For the result of conditionalisation is $q(\alpha) = 1$ (still). Yet information of this form can certainly be the premise of an inductive argument; for example, one whose conclusion is that $q(\alpha) < 0.5$. Hence inference outstrips conditionalisation.

---

23. It might be thought that what is causing the problem here is that we are trying to make inductive validity an all-or-nothing matter, when it is really a matter of degree. Hence, we may simply take the degree of validity of the inference β/α to be $p(\alpha/\beta)$. But this does not seem to help. According to this account, the inference is still an inductive inference of high degree of validity, which seems odd.
24. It might be replied that we never simply accept things: we always accept things to a certain degree. The question of detachment does not, therefore, arise. But this is just false: acceptance may be a vague notion, but there are clear cases of things that I accept, *simpliciter*, for example that Brisbane is in Australia (though I would not give this unit probablity, for standard, fallibilist, reasons).
25. See, e.g., Howson and Urbach 1993, p. 99ff.

Even if there were some way of analysing inductive validity satisfactorily in terms of probability, a more fundamental problem awaits us. Deductive validity and inductive validity would seem to have something to do with each other. They are both species of *validity*. If deductive validity is to be analysed in terms of preservation of truth in a structure, and inductive validity is to be analysed as something to do with probability, they would seem to be as different as chalk from cheese.

Maybe there is some deeper connection here, but it is not at all obvious what this could be. One might try *defining* a deductively valid inference, β/α, as one where $p(\alpha/\beta) = 1$. This has nothing to do with model theory, but one might hope that, by making suitable connections (for example, by considering a probability measure on the space of models), the definition could be shown to be equivalent to (DV). One might even jettison the model-theoretic definition of deductive validity entirely, and attempt a uniform account of validity in terms of probability. Such moves face further problems, however. For example, consider:

John chose a natural number at random;
hence John did not choose 173

On the usual understanding of probability theory, this satisfies the probabilistic account of deductive validity, but it is hardly deductively valid: the conclusion might turn out to be false. There are ways that one might try to get around this problem too, but it would certainly seem much more satisfactory if an account of inductive validity could be found which made the connection with deductive validity obvious, and which did not depend upon probabilistic jiggery-pokery.

3.3 Non-Monotonic Logic

Such an account is now available, thanks to recent developments in non-monotonic logic. An inference relation, $\vdash$, is *monotonic* if $\Pi \vdash \kappa$ entails $\Pi \cup \Sigma \vdash \kappa$. Deductively valid inferences are monotonic. For suppose that $\Pi \vdash \kappa$. If all the premises in $\Pi \cup \Sigma$ hold in a structure, then certainly all those in Π do. In which case, so does κ. On the other hand, inferences traditionally accounted inductively valid are well known not to be monotonic. Consider only:

Abdul lives in Kuwait;
Abdul went to mass last Sunday;
hence Abdul is a Moslem

The study of non-monotonic inferences, quite independently of probability theory, is one that has seen rapid and exciting developments in the last 15 years, mainly from amongst logicians in computer science departments. There are many distinctive approaches to non-monotonic inference, of various degrees of mathematical sophistication. But it is now becoming clear that at the core of theories of non-monotonicity there is a canonical construction.[26]

Let me illustrate. Consider Abdul again. What makes it plausible to infer that he is a Muslim, given only that he lives in Kuwait, is that, if he were not, he would be rather abnormal. (*qua* inhabitant of Kuwait, and not, of course, in any evaluative sense). Although the inference may not be truth-preserving, it is certainly truth-preserving in all 'normal situations'.

We can formulate this more precisely as follows. Let us suppose that we can compare situations (or the structures that represent them) with respect to their normality. Normality, of course, comes by degrees. Let us write the comparison as $\mathcal{A} > \mathcal{B}$ ($\mathcal{A}$ is more normal than $\mathcal{B}$.) > is certainly a partial order (transitive and antisymmetric); but it is not a linear order. There is no guarantee that we can compare any two structures with respect to their normality. Let us say that $\mathcal{A}$ is a *most normal* model of a set of sentences, Π, $\mathcal{A} \vDash_n \Pi$, iff:

$\mathcal{A} \vDash \Pi$ and for all $\mathcal{B}$ such that $\mathcal{B} > \mathcal{A}$, $\mathcal{B} \nvDash \Pi$

Then if we write inductive validity as $\vdash_i$, we can define:

$\Pi \vdash_i \kappa$ iff every most normal model of Π is a model of κ \hfill (*IV*)

This captures the idea that an inference is inductively valid if the conclusion holds in all models of Π that are as normal as Π will let them be. Notice how this gives rise to non-monotonicity in a very natural way. κ may well be true in all situations most normal with respect to Π, but throw in Σ, and the

---

26. See, e.g., Shoham 1988, Katsuno and Satch 1995. For an application of the construction in a paraconsistent context, where normality is cashed out in terms of consistency, see Priest 1991b.

most normal situations may be more abnormal, and not necessarily ones where κ holds.[27]

3.4 Consequences of this Account

The definition (*IV*) is the one I wish to offer. It is exactly the same as (*DV*), except that where (*DV*) has 'model' (*IV*) has 'most normal model'. The connection between the two notions is therefore patent. Where deductive validity requires truth preservation over *all* structures, inductive validity requires truth preservation over *all normal* structures (with respect to the premise set). Deductive validity is the same as inductive validity except that we don't care about normality. This is equivalent to taking > to be the minimal ordering that relates nothing to anything. We therefore have a generic account of validity. Validity is truth-preservation in all structures of a certain kind. Deductive validity is the limit case where we are talking about *all* structures, period. Otherwise put: validity is about truth preservation in all normal structures. Deductive validity is the limit case where *every* situation is to be considered normal.[28]

This account of inductive validity extends the model-theoretic account of deductive validity. Hence, all the comments that I made about filling in its details carry over to it, also. In this respect they are the same. The major technical difference between the two notions, is the fact that inductive validity makes use of the ordering >, whilst deductive validity does not. This, therefore, focuses the major conceptual difference between the two. Although the question of what structures there are is open to theoretical debate, whatever they are, they are invariant across all contexts in which we reason. The definition (*IV*) also gives us a core of universally inductively

---

27. An additional condition, sometimes called the smoothness constraint, is often imposed on the ordering <: for any α and $\mathcal{A}$, if $\mathcal{A} \models \alpha$ then there is a $\mathcal{B} > \mathcal{A}$ such that $\mathcal{B} \models_n \alpha$ (see, e.g., Katsuno and Satch 1995, Gabbay 1995). This prevents finite sets of premises that are non-trivial under deduction from exploding under induction—obviously a desirable feature.
28. It is fair to ask what happens to the boxer examples of 3.2 on this account. Both, given reasonable assumptions, turn out to be invalid, since there are normal situations where boxers get their noses broken and normal situations where they do not.

valid inferences, namely those that hold for *all* orderings.[29] But when we employ the notion of inductive validity in practice, we do not argue relative to all orderings, but with respect to one particular ordering. The ordering is not *a priori*, but is fixed by external factors, such as the world and the context. For example, the fact that to be green is more normal (natural) than to be grue is determined by nature. Or what is to count as normal may depend on our interests. In the context of discussing a religious question, a resident of Kuwait who goes to mass is not normal. In the context of discussing biological appendages, such as noses, they are (normally) quite normal.[30]

This is, I think, the heart of the difference that people have sensed between inductive and deductive validity. It is not really a matter of the difference between form and content—or if it is, what this comes down to is exactly the dependence of inductive validity on an *a posteriori* feature, the ordering >.

4. Conclusion: Validity and Truth-Preservation

4.1 *Normativity*

Let me conclude by tying up some loose ends; and let us start by returning to the question of the normativity of logic. Validly, I said, is how people ought to reason. Why? The answer is simple. We reason about all kinds of situations. We want to know what sorts of things hold in them, given that we know other things; or what sorts of things don't hold, given that we know other things that don't. If we reason validly then, by the definition of validity, we can be assured that reasoning forward preserves the first property, and that reasoning backwards preserves the second. Validly is how one ought to reason if one wants to achieve these goals. The obligation is, then, hypothetical rather than categorical.

---

29. A version of this is given a proof-theoretic characterisation in Kraus, Lehmann and Magidor 1990. The semantics include the smoothness constraint.
30. The ordering may even be subjective in a certain sense. For example, a natural thought is to take $\mathcal{B} > \mathcal{A}$ to mean that situation $\mathcal{A}$ is less probable than situation $\mathcal{B}$ (assuming this to make sense), where the probability in question is a subjective one. An ordering relation plays an important role in the semantics of conditional logics—which are, in fact, closely related to non-monotonic logics. (See, e.g., Gabbay 1995, Katsuno and Satch 1995.) The *a posteriority* of this is well recognised. See, e.g., Stalnaker 1981.

In less enlightened days, I argued against a model-theoretic account of validity of the kind given here.[31] One argument was to the effect that a model-theoretic account validates the inference *ex contradictione quodlibet*: $\alpha, \neg\alpha \vdash \beta$, which is not a norm of reasoning. This argument is just fallacious. A model-theoretic account may validate this argument; but equally, it may not. It depends, crucially, on what situations there are. If there are nontrivial but inconsistent situations, as there are in many logics, this will not be the case.[32]

A second argument was to the effect that a model-theoretic account cannot be right since, if it were, to know that an inference is valid we would have to know, in advance of using it, that it preserves truth in all situations; and hence it would be impossible for us to learn something new about a situation by applying a valid inference. This argument is equally, though less obviously, invalid. It confuses matters definitional with matters epistemological. We may well, and in fact do, have ways of knowing that a particular inference is valid, other than that it simply satisfies the definition. Particular cases are usually more certain than general truths. Compare: The Church/Turing Thesis provides, in effect, a definition of algorithmaticity. But we can often know that a process is algorithmic without having to write a program for a Turing machine. If we could not, the Thesis would not be refutable, which it certainly is.[33]

4.2 Information-Preservation

Further on the subject of truth-preservation: it is sometimes objected that a definition of validity on the basis of truth-preservation is too weak. What we often need of a notion of validity is that it preserve not truth, but something else, like information. Consider an inference engine for a computational data base, for example. We want one which extracts the information that is implicit in the data. Truth has nothing to do with it.

This argument is also far too swift. Valid inferences preserve not just truth, but truth in a structure. Given the right way of setting things up, the situation as described in the data base may well be (represented by) an appropriate structure. Structures do not have to be 'large' like classical possi-

---

31. Priest 1979, p. 297.
32. The point is made by Mortensen 1981.
33. See Priest 1995, pp. 287f.

ble worlds, but may be 'small', as in situation-semantics. (In particular, the set of things true in a situation may be both inconsistent and incomplete.) A valid inference is, then, by definition, just what we want to extract the juice from the information provided by the data-base. Provided we choose our situations carefully, a logic of truth preservation is also a logic of information-preservation.[34]

4.3 A Final Thought

This last claim is, of course, just a promissory note, and needs to be redeemed by a lot of hard work, specifying all the details that have only been hinted at above. The aim of this paper has not been to present all the details of an account of validity. That is the work of several lifetimes. The aim has just been to provide the general form of an answer to the question of what validity is. To this extent, the slack in the definition is to its advantage. The details are to be filled in, in the most appropriate way. But despite the slack, the form of the answer is far from vacuous. There are certainly other possibilities (some of which we have briefly traversed); and the fact that this answer is possible at all, is a tribute to the developments in modern model theory—of both classical and non-classical logics—of which this account can be thought of as the distilled essence.[35]

References

Belnap N., 1962, 'Tonk, Plonk and Plink', *Analysis* 22, 130–4; reprinted in Strawson (ed.) 1967.

Carnap R., 1952, 'Meaning Postulates', *Philosophical Studies* 3, 65–73.

Crocco G., L. Fariñas del Cerro, and A. Herzig (eds.), 1995, *Conditionals: from Philosophy to Computer Science*, Oxford: Oxford University Press.

---

34. For example, the logic of information that Devlin gives in 1991, section 5.5, is exactly Dunn's four-valued truth-preservational semantics of First Degree Entailment, in disguise. For further connections between model-theoretic semantics and information, see Mares 1996.
35. Talks based on a draft of this paper were given at Notre Dame University, the University of Indiana, and the conference *Logica 97* in Prague. I am grateful to those present for many helpful comments. I am particularly grateful to Paddy Blanchette, André Fuhrmann, Colin Howson, David McCarty, Gören Sundholm and Achille Varzi, for discussions that helped me to see a number of things more clearly.

Devlin K., 1991, *Logic and Information*, Cambridge: Cambridge University Press.

Etchemendy J., 1988, 'Tarski on Truth and Logical Consequence', *Journal of Symbolic Logic* 53, 51–79.

Etchemendy J., 1990, *The Concept of Logical Consequence*, Cambridge, MA: Harvard University Press.

Gabbay D., 1995, 'Conditional Implications and Non-monotonic Consequence', ch. 11 of Crocco *et al.* (eds.), 1995.

Goodman N., 1979, *Fact, Fiction and Forecast*, Cambridge, MA: Harvard University Press.

Howson C. and P. Urbach, 1993, *Scientific Reasoning: the Bayesan Approach*, 2nd ed., La Salle, IL: Open Court.

Katsuno H. and K. Satch, 1995, 'A Unified View of Consequence Relation, Belief Revision and Conditional Logic', ch. 3 of Crocco *et al.* (eds.), 1995.

Kraus S., D. Lehmann, and M. Magidor, 1990, 'Nonmonotonic Reasoning, Preferential Models and Cumulative Logics', *Artificial Intelligence* 44, 167–207.

Mares E., 1996, 'Relevant Logic and the Theory of Information', *Synthese* 109, 345–60.

McCarty D., 1991, 'Incompleteness in Intuitionist Mathematics', *Notre Dame Journal of Formal Logic*, 32, 323–58.

Montague R., 1974, *Formal Philosophy*, New Haven and London: Yale University Press.

Mortensen C., 1981, 'A Plea for Model Theory', *Philosophical Quarterly* 31, 152–7.

Priest G., 1979, 'Two Dogmas of Quineanism', *Philosophical Review* 29, 289–301.

Priest G., 1987, *In Contradiction*, Boston and Dordrecht: Martinus Nijhoff.

Priest G., 1990, 'Boolean Negation and All That', *Journal of Philosophical Logic* 19, 201–15.

Priest G., 1991a, *The Nature of Philosophy and Its Place in a University*, University of Queensland Press.

Priest G., 1991b, 'Minimally Inconsistent *LP*', *Studia Logica* 50, 321–31.

Priest G., 1995, 'Etchemendy and Logical Consequence', *Canadian Journal of Philosophy* 25, 283–92.

Priest G., to appear, 'On Alternative Geometries, Arithmetics and Logics; a Tribute to Łukasiewicz', *Proceedings of the Conference Łukasiewicz in Dublin*.

Prior A., 1960, 'The Runabout Inference Ticket', *Analysis* 20, 38–9; reprinted in Strawson (ed.), 1967.

Schröder-Heister P. and K. Dosen (eds.), 1993, *Substructural Logics*, Oxford: Clarendon Press.

Shoham Y., 1988, *Reasoning about Change*, Cambridge, MA: MIT Press.

Slaney J., 1990, 'A General Logic', *Australasian Journal of Philosophy* 68, 74–88

Stalnaker R., 1981, 'A Theory of Conditionals', in W. L. Harper (ed.), *Ifs*, Dordrecht: Reidel, pp. 41–55.

Stevenson J., 1961, 'Roundabout the Runabout Inference Ticket', *Analysis* 21, 124–8; reprinted in Strawson (ed.), 1967.

Strawson P. (ed.), 1967, *Philosophical Logic*, Oxford: Oxford University Press.

Sundholm G., 1986, 'Proof Theory and Meaning', ch. 8 of D. Gabbay and F. Guenthner (eds.), *Handbook of Philosophical Logic, Vol. III: Alternatives to Classical Logic*, Dordrecht: Kluwer Academic Publishers.

Tarski A., 1936, 'O pojciu wynikania logicznego', *Przeglad Filozoficzny* 39, 58–68; Eng. trans. by J. H. Woodger: 'On the Concept of Logical Consequence', in A. Tarski, *Logics, Semantics, Metamathematics, Papers from 1923 to 1938*, Oxford: Clarendon Press, 1956 (2nd edition ed. by J. Corcoran, Indianapolis: Hackett, 1983), pp. 409–420.

Tennant N., 1987, *Anti-Realism and Logic*, Oxford: Oxford University Press.

Wason P. C. and P. Johnson-Laird, 1972, *Psychology of Reasoning: Structure and Content*, Cambridge, MA: Harvard University Press.

Department of Philosophy
University of Queensland
Brisbane, Australia

GILA SHER
Is Logic a Theory of the Obvious?

[L]ogic is peculiar: every logical truth is obvious, actually or potentially. Each, that is to say, is either obvious as it stands or can be reached from obvious truths by a sequence of individually obvious steps. (Quine 1970, pp. 82–3)

Consider ... the logical truth "Everything is self-identical", or "$(x)(x=x)$". We can say that it depends for its truth on traits of the language ... and not on traits of its subject matter; but we can also say, alternatively, that it depends on an obvious trait, viz., self-identity, of its subject matter, viz., everything. (Quine 1954, p. 113)

1. Introduction

The idea that logic is a theory of the obvious is a puzzling idea: Is logic a theory of all obvious truths? Of only obvious truths? Of truths not necessarily obvious themselves, but obtainable from obvious truths by finitely many obvious steps? From obvious truths of what kind? (Any kind? Some specifically logical kind?) By obvious steps of what type? By steps and truths obvious to whom? Obvious in virtue of what? To understand the view that logic is a theory of the obvious we have to understand what features make its truths and inferences obvious, what features distinguish them from other obvious truths and inferences, etc. In short, to understand the view that logic is a theory of the obvious we have to know what properties *other than obviousness* are characteristic of logical truths.

In spite of this air of question-begging—or, perhaps, just because of it—the view that logic is a theory of the obvious lies behind a popular trend in the philosophy of logic. The view is commonly traced to Quine, who introduced it not to say something illuminating about logic but to discard the claim of another theory, namely, Carnap's 'linguistic' theory, to say something illuminating about it. The gist of Quine's argument is that whatever phenomena are explained by the linguistic theory, these phenomena are explained just as well by saying that logic is obvious. Since the latter statement says very little about the nature of logic, the more elaborate linguistic account is redundant.[1]

Today the claim that logic is a theory of the obvious is 'in the air', so to speak, and its influence is deeper and more subtle than in Quine. This claim is implicit in a certain prevalent attitude in the philosophy of logic: an attitude of *skepticism* towards the feasibility of a philosophical explanation of logic, combined with an attitude of *contentment* with (or at least *acquiescence* to) the absence of such an explanation. A philosophical explanation of logic, according to this attitude, is not possible, but this is no cause for alarm: such an explanation would in any case be superfluous. This special combination of criticism and acquiescence is naturally explained by the obviousness of logic. If the logical truths and inferences are obvious, there is nothing to explain: the very idea of an explanation of logic is based on a misunderstanding. By definition, the obvious cannot, need not, and should not be explained.

In this paper I would like to challenge both the claim that an explanatory account of logic is impossible and the claim that such an account is not needed. In sections 2–3 I will discuss some of the difficulties involved in an explanatory account of logic and I will show how these difficulties are naturally linked to the view that logic is obvious. In sections 4–10 I will argue that an explanatory account of logic is highly important and I will demonstrate the feasibility of such an account by constructing an outline of a concrete example. In section 11 I will conclude by showing how the difficulties motivating the skeptical approach are dealt with by the proposed account.[2]

---

1. See Quine 1954, pp. 112f; 1970, pp. 97f.
2. There are of course many exceptions to the attitude I am criticizing in this paper, and the present volume (whose designated topic is "the nature of logic") is a testimony to their existence. Still, the number of serious attempts to explain the nature of logic is relatively small and the prevalent attitude among epistemologists, philosophers of science, philosophers of language, philosophers of mathematics and philosophers of logic proper is that an explanatory account of logic is neither possible nor needed. In discussing some of the reasons motivating this approach I will not direct myself to any particular philosopher or piece of philosophical writing. Rather, I will present a series of basic difficulties facing the theorist of logic, and I will examine the possibility of responding to these difficulties. The positive account I will outline in this paper incorporates elements from Sher 1989, 1991, 1996a, 1996b, and Forthcoming.

2. Why is Logic Resistant to Explanation?

What makes logic resistant to explanation is, in my view, not the identity of its properties, but the extreme degree to which it possesses its properties. Not the *generality* of logic, but its *unbounded generality*; not the '*basicness*' of logic, but its *ultimate basicness*; not the *normative force* of logic, but its *supreme normative force*; not its *certainty*, but its *absolute certainty*. It is the excesses of logic that make it resistant to explanation.

A. *Unbounded generality.* The generality of logic is unbounded: logic applies to every subject matter and no subject matter is conceivable beyond logic. Two problematic aspects of this unrestricted generality are (1) the threat of emptiness, and (2) the impossibility of an external viewpoint on logic. Both aspects were elaborated by Wittgenstein in his *Tractatus Logico-Philosophicus*.

1. *The emptiness of logic.* The argument for the emptiness of logic can be formulated as follows: Logic applies to every subject matter (logic is 'topic neutral'), therefore, logic has no subject-matter of its own; logic is subject-less (3.031).[3] Its constants do not represent any objects, properties or relations (4.0312, 5.4, 5.42), and its statements do not say any particular thing about any particular matter. It is, however, inherent in statements with content that they say something specific about some particular matter. Therefore the statements of logic are contentless: 'all the propositions of logic say the same thing, to wit nothing' (5.43); the statements of logic are tautologous, hence empty. '[T]he propositions of logic say nothing.' (6.1–11)

By claiming that logic says nothing, Wittgenstein does not mean to say that logic is not about the world (that logic is purely linguistic). On the contrary: logical statements do show something important about the world, but *showing* is contrasted with *saying*. Logic *shows* something, but *says* nothing: 'The fact that the propositions of logic are tautologies *shows* the formal—logical—[structure] of language and the world.' (6.12) But 'what *can* be shown, *cannot* be said.' (4.1212) Logic 'displays' the logical form of reality (4.121), but what it displays cannot be described in words: 'Logic is not a body of doctrine, but a mirror-image of the world.' (6.13) But if logical statements *say* nothing, there is nothing to explain: no logical content to be

---

3. References to the *Tractatus* are given by proposition number only.

elucidated, no logical objects to be identified, no logical properties and relations to be characterized. A substantive account of logic is impossible.

2. The impossibility of an external viewpoint on logic. The unbounded generality of logic means that the laws of logic are universally applicable: nothing is excluded from logic, nothing is beyond logic. Logic governs the world in its entirety: there is no realm of being beyond logic. In Wittgenstein's words:

> Thought can never be of anything illogical, since, if it were, we should have to think illogically. (3.03)

> It is impossible to represent in language anything that "contradicts logic" (3.032).

> In order to be able to represent logical form, we should have to be able to station ourselves with propositions somewhere outside logic, that is to say outside the world. (4.12)

> [W]e cannot say in logic, "The world has this in it, and this, but not that." For that would appear to presuppose that we were excluding certain possibilities, and this cannot be the case, since it would require that logic should go beyond the limits of the world; for only in that way could it view those limits from the other side as well. We cannot think what we cannot think; so what we cannot think we cannot *say* either. (5.61)

Two related arguments can be extracted from these citations: (a) To say something substantive about logic is to exclude certain possibilities with regard to logic; but there is no realm of possibility beyond logic; hence we cannot speak substantively about logic. (b) To identify the distinctive characteristics of logic, we have to examine logic without using (or assuming) logic; but that would require stepping outside the boundaries of logic; since there is 'nowhere to stand' outside of logic, we cannot give an explanatory account of logic. There is simply no vantage point from which to explain logic.

B. Ultimate basicness. Logic lies at the foundation of all knowledge. Logic delineates the most basic forms of human thought and its expression (statements, theories), provides us with the most basic tools of valid inference, tells us what combinations of statements are permissible and what combinations are impermissible, etc. Logical form, logical inference, logical criteria of consistency, are ingredients that no system of knowledge can do without. Our system of knowledge can survive the removal of many a science, but not logic. Knowledge is not possible without logic. If we think of our total system of knowledge as a hierarchical structure in which theories higher in the structure are dependent on theories below them in the structure, then logic constitutes the base of the structure. Every science and theory is dependent on logic, but logic is dependent on none. Logic abstracts from the content of all sciences, but no science abstracts from logic. If no science is prior to logic, however, then an explanatory account of logic is impossible. If nothing is more basic than logic, then there are no concepts in terms of which to explain logic. Any attempt to provide an explanatory account of logic is bound to succumb either to the fallacy of infinite regress or to the fallacy of circularity. Even the view that logic is based on convention, Quine emphasizes, leads to a fallacy: 'if logic is to proceed mediately from conventions, logic is needed for inferring logic from the conventions.' (Quine 1935, p. 104)

C. Supreme normative force. The normative force of logic exceeds that of all other sciences. All systems of norms are bound by logic, but the logical norms themselves are bound by no other norms. Scientific methodology, ethics, jurisprudence, etc., are all subject to the authority of logic, but logic is not subject to theirs. However, if the logical norms are not subsumed under any other norms, how shall we explain their authority? By reference to what shall we explain the authority of the law of non-contradiction? If logic's authority is not based on any other authority, based on what can we explain it?

D. Absolute certainty. Similar problems arise with respect to the ultimate certainty of logic. To explain its certainty we have to appeal to something more certain than—or at least as certain as—logic; but nothing satisfies this condition. The certainty of logic is unequaled.

It is thus not simply its properties that render logic resistant to explanation. It is the *extreme* degree to which it possesses its properties—its *extreme* generality, *extreme* basicness, *extreme* certainty and *extreme* authority—that renders it inexplicable.

3. Logic as a Theory of the Obvious

The view that logic is a theory of the obvious is naturally arrived at in two ways: (A) The same features that render logic resistant to explanation also suggest the obviousness of logic. (B) The view that logic is a theory of the obvious offers a convenient solution to the problem of an explanatory account of logic.[4]

A1. The limits of imagination. The absolute generality of logic means, among other things, that the illogical is unimaginable. The law of non-contradiction, the law of self-identity, Modus Ponens and the laws of universal instantiation and existential generalization, are laws whose falsity, like the falsity of the basic arithmetical laws ('1+1=2', '2+3=3+2') is unimaginable to us. We cannot construct in our imagination a situation in which we eat one apple, then another, yet we do not eat two apples, or a situation in which we both eat and do not eat the same apple. But this is just what 'obvious' means: something is obvious if its negation is unimaginable.[5]

A2. The immediacy of seeing. Logic, according to Wittgenstein, is demonstrative: it *shows* the logical (formal) structure of the world but it does not describe it. 'The logic of the world ... is shown ... by the propositions of logic' (6.22); 'Logical ... propositions *shew* [the] logical properties of ... [the] Universe, but *say* nothing.' (*Notebooks*, p. 108) 'The logical form of [a given] situation ... cannot be described.' (*Ibid.*, p. 20) The logical form of a situation can, however, be seen, and seeing is naturally associated with *intuition*. (Mathematics, which is 'a method of logic' (6.234), is, according to Wittgenstein, based on intuition: 'The process of calculating serves to bring about [the] *intuition* ... needed for the solution of mathematical problems' (6.2331, 6.233. My italics).) Intuition, in turn, is commonly associated with *immediacy* (see, e.g., Kant: '*intuition* ... relates <u>immediately</u> to the object ...' (*Critique of Pure Reason* A320/B377, my underline); '*intuition* is that through which [a mode of knowledge] is in <u>immediate</u> relation to [objects]'

---

4. In this paper I assume that if T is a theory of obvious phenomena, then T is a collection of obvious truths and in this sense T itself can be said to be "obvious". This assumption involves some simplification. (It is possible to construct a very complicated theory of a very simple subject matter; a large collection of obvious truths may not be systematizable by a small number of obvious principles, etc.) But my basic observation is that obviousness is an epistemic property and an obvious phenomenon can, mutatis mutandis, be accounted for by a theory comprised of obvious truths.
5. There are, of course, well known challenges to the validity of the logical laws (or at least some of the logical laws). But adherents of the obviousness view are likely to reject them, explain them away, etc.

(A16/B33, my underline)).[6] And what is immediately intuited is, by definition, *obvious*: 'Obvious—easy to see or understand; plain; evident' (*Webster New World Dictionary*). Thus, a natural chain of associations leads from seeing to intuition, from intuition to immediacy, and from immediate seeing to obviousness.

A3. Vestiges of foundationalism. The view that the most basic, most general and most certain statements in our system of knowledge are *obvious* (self-evident) is typical of foundationalism. Different foundationalist epistemologies place different statements and theories at the foundation of knowledge, but either directly or indirectly, the view that basicness, generality, and certainty entail obviousness (or self-evidence) supports the claim that logic is obvious. A classical example of a foundationalist epistemology is Aristotle's theory. Our system of knowledge, according to Aristotle, is a hierarchical structure whose lowest rank consists of 'first principles'—so-called 'axioms' or 'common notions'—fundamental to all sciences. These first principles include the law of excluded middle, the law of non-contradiction, various laws of equality, and other laws that today we will classify as logical (*Metaphysics* 996^b 25–30). It is characteristic of axioms, according to Aristotle, that they are 'primary, immediate' (*Posterior analytics*, I, 71^b 20), 'self-evident' (*Metaphysics*, 1006^a 10), and apprehended by 'intuition' (*Posterior analytics* II, 100^b 5–15). Another example of a foundationalist epistemology is Descartes' theory of 'clear and distinct ideas'. The mark of absolute certainty, according to Descartes (*Meditations*), is intellectual clarity and distinctness: the more clearly and more distinctly an idea presents itself to us, the more basic and certain it is. Although (for reasons that I will not discuss here) Descartes himself did not apply this principle to logic, such an application naturally suggests itself. Russell's foundationalist epistemology does characterize logic as a theory of self-evident truths: '[T]here is general knowledge not derived from sense, and ... some of this knowledge ... is primitive. Such general knowledge is to be found in logic. ... [The proposition] "If anything has a certain property, and whatever has this

---

6. (a) Kant, of course, did not regard logic as 'intuitive', but here we are interested merely in his view on the relationship between intuition and immediacy. (For more on this relation in Kant, see Parsons 1969, 1979-80). (b) It is not clear to me whether Wittgenstein himself viewed logic as obvious, given his negative remarks on self-evidence. (See 1921: 5.4731, 6.1271; 1914-16: 3.9.14 (last paragraph), 8.9.14.)

property has a certain other property, then the thing in question has the other property" ... is absolutely general: it applies to all things and all properties. And it is quite *self-evident*. Thus in such propositions of pure logic we have ... *self-evident* general propositions' (1914, p. 66, my italics).[7]

B. *Solution to the skeptical problem.* We have seen how extreme generality, basicness and certainty are naturally associated with obviousness. But the view that logic is obvious can also be arrived at as a means for disarming the skeptical argument. The view that logic is obvious takes the sting out of this argument. This view allows us to accept the skeptical conclusion without accepting the skeptical challenge. If logic is obvious, its inexplicability is innocuous. There is no need to examine logic from a vantage point beyond logic, no need to base logic on something more basic than logic, no need to justify the authority of logic by a higher authority than logic, no need to ground our certainty in logic in something more certain than logic. The skeptical conclusion does not threaten either the validity of the logical laws, or our reasons for believing these laws, or our ability to know these laws. The logical laws are sanctioned by their obviousness.

4. The Need for Explanation

But does the claim that logic is obvious obviate the need for an explanatory account of logic? In order to answer this question we have to find out, first, whether the claim is true (whether logic is really obvious), and second, whether there are overriding reasons for demanding an explanation of logic.

The view that logical truths and inferences are obvious is open to various challenges. First, it is difficult to rule out the fallibility of human intuition. In any given case we may fail to see that something obvious is obvious or that something unobvious is unobvious; in some cases there may not be a fact of the matter, or there may not be an agreement, or there may not be a way of deciding whether something is obvious; our sense of obviousness may be reliable in some areas but not in others, or our sense of obviousness may be systematically skewed. Descartes solved these problems by positing a

---

7. Not all foundationalists regard logic as obvious and not all those who regard logic as obvious are foundationalists. (Carnap and Quine are two notable exceptions.) But I believe the view that logic is obvious is naturally associated with a foundationalist epistemology.

benevolent god whose responsibility it was to guide our judgments of clarity and distinctness. But most contemporary writers cannot accept solutions of this kind.

Second, it has never been demonstrated that obviousness is a property of logic, let alone of all of logic. Indeed, recent meta-logical results show that even the view that logical truths are *mediately obvious*, i.e., arrived at by finitely many applications of obvious rules to obvious truths, is problematic. Regardless of whether and how we can establish the obviousness of the basic rules and truths, no reasonable logical system is decidable and many non-elementary logical systems (e.g., full 2nd-order logic or various 'generalized' 1st-order logics[8]) are incomplete. Thus, in no reasonable system is there an *effective* method for establishing logical truths based on 'first' logical principles, and in many non-elementary logical systems some logical truths cannot be established *at all* by finite applications of obvious rules to obvious truths.

Third, there is no evidence that obviousness is restricted to logic, i.e., that no nonlogical truths are obvious. Quine, in particular, argues that with regard to obviousness logical truths are on a par with a host of other truths: 'utterances of "It is raining" in the rain' (1970, p. 97), statements like 'there have been black dogs' and 'bachelors are unmarried' (1960, p. 66), etc.[9] Obviousness, for Quine, is a property induced by behavior, and human behavior is partly culture dependent. Each culture has its own array of obvious truths, and these include many of its everyday truisms in addition to (some or all of) its logic.

Finally, the view that logic is intrinsically obvious has (as far as I know) never been established by a rigorous argument. This view is suggested by various natural associations of ideas (as noted above), but these are rather loose, impressionistic associations, based on bits and pieces of largely outdated theories, theories whose particular claims as well as underlying principles (e.g., foundationalism) many of us feel compelled to reject.

It is, however, not just the shaky foundation of the view that logic is obvious that motivates an explanation of logic. Rather, the very features that make logic resistant to explanation—its unbounded generality, its ultimate

---

8. See, e.g., Barwise and Feferman 1985.
9. Quine talks in terms of 'stimulus analyticity', but stimulus analyticity is, for him, connected with obviousness (in the behavioristic sense).

basicness, its supreme normative force and its absolute certainty—also make an explanation of logic vital to our knowledge. An error in some relatively isolated area of knowledge will not undermine our system, but a serious error in logic will. The greater the generality, the basicness and the authority of a given science, the greater the need to establish its truths, justify its norms, determine its exact relationships with other sciences, and provide tools for detecting and correcting its errors. It is thus due to logic's centrality to our system of knowledge (which, in turn, is due to the magnitude of its properties), that a critical explanation of logic is imperative.

But is a critical-explanatory account of logic possible? Can we, in spite of the difficulties expounded in section 2, construct an account of logic that will uncover the source of its normativity, explain the nature of logicality and generate critical tools for evaluating, improving, and, if need be, revising existent logical theories?

In the remainder of this paper I will attempt to construct an outline of such an account. The key to avoiding the difficulties raised in section 2 is renouncing the foundationalist methodology within which these difficulties arise. Logic, on the proposed (moderately holistic) approach, stands in a multitude of normative, conceptual, practical and theoretical relationships to other sciences, and these relationships provide the critical and explanatory tools needed to justify, explain, criticize and revise it. The hierarchical picture of knowledge with logic at its base no longer holds, and logic is placed alongside, rather than above—or below—the sciences. Needless to say, not all aspects of logic are equally well explained by the present account: in particular, the proof-theoretical dimension of logic is largely beyond the present (semantic) analysis.

5. Truth as a Source of Normativity

What is the source of the normativity of logic? One of the simplest, most satisfying and most unifying answers is: 'Truth'. The logical laws are true, and their truth is the source of their authority.[10] Thus, in the same way that the truth of '1+1=2' licenses (or plays a major role in licensing) the inference schema: 'a is a B; b is a B; a ≠ b; Therefore there are at least two B's',

---

10. In discussing the truth of the logical laws I disregard the fact that these laws are usually formulated schematically and in this form are not properly true (or false).

Is Logic a Theory of the Obvious?   217

so the truth of the law of excluded middle licenses (plays a major role in licensing) the inference schema: 'If A then B; If not-A then B; Therefore B'. There is more to be said about how logical inference is grounded in truth, but first let us examine the nature of logical truth.

What are the logical truths true of? Two natural answers are: (a) the logical truths are true of the world, (b) the logical truths are true of language or thought. The view that logical truths are true of the world can be interpreted in two ways: (a1) There is a correspondence relation between the logical constants and objects (properties, relations) in the world, and it is through this correspondence relation that the logical truths are true. (a2) Logical truths correspond to reality not through a term-by-term relation, but in a holistic, unanalyzable way (Wittgenstein 1921). Likewise, the second view of what the logical truths are true of is divided into two views: (b1) the laws of logic are laws of the mind, (b2) the laws of logic are laws of language. These views could be combined within a single theory, but traditionally they have led to two distinct accounts of logic: (1) logical laws have to do with the structure of thought, (2) logical laws reflect linguistic conventions. The view that the normativity of logic is grounded in convention was advocated by Carnap (see, e.g., his 1939). The truth of the law of excluded middle is, according to Carnap, grounded in our decision to use 'or' and 'not' in accordance with the classical truth tables. Had we decided to use them based on different truth tables or based on rules that do not allow a truth-table representation, we would have ended up with different logical truths and different logical inferences. Finally, the view that the logical laws are laws of thought can also be divided into two: (1.1) the logical laws are descriptive, i.e., the logical laws describe the way we actually think (Fodor 1975); (1.2) the logical laws are prescriptive, i.e., the logical laws tell us how we ought to think (Frege 1879).

I believe that none of these views is adequate by itself, but an exhaustive theory of logical truth must incorporate elements from all. Truth in general is constrained both by the way the world is and by the way our mind operates (or, more generally, by our biology, psychology, and environment in a broad sense). These constraints, however, do not curtail our freedom altogether and we do have a certain amount of choice regarding our language: its lexicon, its logical apparatus, and so forth. Furthermore, although language contributes to truth largely through the reference of its terms, structure is an additional irreducible factor. Not in the sense of the early

Wittgenstein, but in the sense in which the ordering of quantifiers, for example, plays an independent role in determining the truth conditions of so-called branching, or partially-ordered, quantifications. (Henkin 1959 and others)

I will not attempt to explain here the contribution of all these diverse factors—language and the world, reference and form, thought and convention, actual and idealized mental operations—to logical truth. Instead, I will concentrate on the correspondence aspect of logical truth, i.e., on the role played by the world on the one hand and the reference of our terms on the other in determining logical truth.

6. Laws of Formal Structure as the Source of Logical Truth

Consider the statement:

(1)   If some American child is hungry, then some child is hungry.

In virtue of what is (1) logically true? Before we consider the question 'In virtue of what is (1) *logically* true?' let us simply ask: 'In virtue of what is (1) *true*?'. Intuitively, my answer is this: The truth of (1), like the truth of any other sentence, is a function of two things: (a) what (1) says about the world, and (b) how the world is. (1) says that if some American child is hungry, some child is hungry, and in the world this indeed is the case. However, the truth of (1) has nothing to do with the state of hunger in the world or with the meaning of terms referring to this state. What the truth of (1) essentially depends on is the *formal* content of (1) and the *formal* state of the world. Formally, (1) says that if an intersection of three sets is not empty, then the intersection of two of these sets is also not empty, and in the world this in fact is the case. In the world, a non-empty intersection of any three sets is included in the non-empty intersection of any two of these sets. The truth of (1) does not depend on the reference of its non-formal terms ('American', 'child', 'hungry'), but it does depend on the reference of its (explicit and implicit) formal terms: 'and', denoting the operation of intersection; 'some', denoting the property of non-emptiness; 'if ... then', denoting the relation of inclusion. In short: it is in virtue of the correspondence between the formal content of (1), i.e., the content displayed by

(2) $(\exists x)(Ax \ \& \ Bx \ \& \ Cx) \supset (\exists x)(Bx \ \& \ Cx)$,

and certain formal features of the world (the inclusion of one kind of intersection in another), that (1) is true.

We have seen in virtue of what (1) is *true*. But in virtue of what is it *logically* true? One reason that (1) is logically true is the *formal* nature of its truth: (1) is true in virtue of a formal feature of the world, rather than a physical or a biological or …, or a hunger feature. But not all sentences true in virtue of a formal feature of the world are logically true. For example, the sentence,

(3)   There exist at least two things,

or, in logical representation,

(4) $(\exists x)(\exists y) x \neq y$,

is not. What distinguishes (1) from (3)—or (2) from (4)—is the fact that (1) is true in virtue of a *formal law*, while (3) is true in virtue of a *formal accident*. It is a law of formal structure that if the intersection of three collections of objects is not empty then the intersection of any two of them is not empty, but it is not a law of formal structure that the cardinality of structures is larger than 1. The truth of (1) is not only formal but also *necessary*, whereas the truth of (3) is only formal. Logical truths are grounded in *laws of formal structure*, and it is this that distinguishes them from all other truths.

But what is a law of formal structure? I characterize a law of formal structure as a *universal property of formally possible structures of objects*.[11] It is a property of all such structures that if the intersection of any three of their sets is not empty, then the intersection of any two of these sets is not empty, etc. What is a formally possible structure of objects? The idea of a formally possible structure of objects can be systematized in various ways. One of its most fruitful systematizations is that of contemporary model theory which, in turn, is based on ZFC. (See, e.g., Chang and Keisler 1973). My account of logic is not committed to any particular systematization of formality (or to any particular underlying mathematics), but for the sake of clarity I will use contemporary model theory as my background theory of formal structure. I should emphasize, however, that by availing myself to the

---

11. For a response to the question: "Why can't universal properties of formally possible structures of objects be accidental?" see Sher 1996b, p. 681.

resources of other sciences I am not violating the principle of explanation. Rather, I am pursuing the task of providing an explanatory account of logic within a non-foundationalist framework, in accordance with the considerations raised in section 4.

7. The Principle of Logicality

In more details, my account is as follows:

A. *Subject matter.* Logic does have a specific subject matter: its subject is *the role of formal structure in reasoning.* To account for this subject logic provides (a) a theory of the role of formal structure in truth, and (b) a theory of its role in valid inference (consistent theory, etc.).[12]

B. *Logical constants.* The formal structure of a sentence is determined by the arrangement of its logical and non-logical constituents. The logical constituents of a sentence are its logical constants (which in natural languages are not always exhibited by its 'surface' grammar (see (1) above)). Both logical and non-logical constants are referential, but the logical constants refer to objects of a special kind: namely, *formal* objects.[13]

C. *Formal objects.* What is a formal object? First, a formal object is not an individual. A formal object is an object with structure, and individuals (by definition) lack structure. A formal object is, then, a property, relation or function (or a structure of objects corresponding to one of these). What kind of property (relation, function) is formal? Intuitively, a property is formal if it 'takes into account' only the formal features of objects in its domain. One interpretation of 'formal feature' is 'feature which does not depend on the identity of individuals in a given universe' (Mostowski 1957). A more precise rendition of this condition (in terms of invariance) will be

---

12. As the reader can see, I include certain basic parts of meta-logic in the province of logic proper.
13. The view of logical constants as referential is one of the distinctive characteristics of my account. Most philosophers (e.g., Quine 1970) draw a sharp distinction between 'form' and 'content': logical constants give a sentence its *form*, nonlogical constants give it its *content*. On my account, both kinds of constant contribute to the content of a sentence: the logical constants to its *formal* content, the nonlogical constants to its *nonformal* content. The notion of 'form' is a relative notion: by 'form' we mean the pattern displayed by highlighting certain constituents of a sentence. Thus, a sentence has a logical form, a modal form, a grammatical form, etc.

given below. In the meantime I will just note that any 2nd-level property whose satisfaction by a 1st-level property is determined by its cardinality (i.e., the cardinality of its extension) is formal; but a 2nd-level property which distinguishes between two 1st-level properties of the same cardinality is not formal. Thus, the 2nd-level property of non-emptiness is formal, since it is satisfied by a 1st-level property P iff P satisfies the 'formal' condition of having at least one element in its extension; but the property of being a property of humans is not formal, since it distinguishes between two properties of the same cardinality according to whether their extension does or does not consist of humans.

D. *Criterion for logical constants of a lexicon $\mathcal{L}$*.

Lexicon. A lexicon $\mathcal{L}$ is a collection of constant symbols. For the sake of simplicity I restrict myself to lexicons with constants of orders ≤2: indvidual constants (order 0), predicates and functions (orders 1 and 2; 2nd-order predicates and functions are viewed, in the Fregean tradition, as quantifiers).

Extension; extensional constant. Each constant C of $\mathcal{L}$ has a *meaning* and an *extension*. The exact meaning of 'meaning' is not important to us here; the extension of C in a universe A is its denotation in A if C is an individual constant; the set of objects satisfying it in A, if C is a 1-place 1st-level predicate, etc. I will symbolize the extension of C in A by C^A. The meaning of C may or may not coincide with a function delineating its denotation/extension in each universe A. If it does, I will say that C is an *extensional* constant, or that the meaning of C is extensional. For example, the 1st-level identity predicate—'x=y'—is an extensional predicate, while the 1st-level predicate 'x loves y' is not an extensional predicate: its meaning is not exhausted by a 'list' of pairs of objects satisfying it in different universes.

Argument-structure. For each 1st- or 2nd-order *n*-place constant C of $\mathcal{L}$, an *argument-structure* for C is a structure of the form $\langle A, \beta_1, \ldots, \beta_n \rangle$, where A is a universe, and for $1 \leq i \leq n$: if C_i (the *i*-th argument-place of C) is a place for an individual symbol, $\beta_i \in A$; if C_i is a place for an *n*-place 1st-order predicate symbol, $\beta_i \subseteq A^n$; if C_i is a place for an *n*-place 1st-order function symbol, β_i is a function $\subseteq A^{n+1}$.

Criterion for logical constants of $\mathcal{L}$— (LC)

Let C be a constant of $\mathcal{L}$. Then C is a *logical constant* of $\mathcal{L}$ iff (a)–(c) below hold:

(a) C is of order 1 or 2;
(b) C is an extensional constant;
(c) C is invariant under isomorphic argument-structures, i.e., for any two isomorphic argument-structures for C, $\langle A, \beta_1, ..., \beta_n \rangle$ and $\langle A', \beta_1', ..., \beta_n' \rangle$: $\langle \beta_1, ..., \beta_n \rangle \in C^A$ iff $\langle \beta_1', ..., \beta_n' \rangle \in C^{A'}$.[14]

Informally: *C is a logical constant iff C is an extensional predicate or function which does not distinguish between isomorphic argument-structures.*[15]

Among the logical constants of familiar languages are the existential and universal quantifiers (thought of as the quantifiers of non-emptiness and universality), the identity relation, the numerical quantifiers ('There are at least / exactly /at most α x such that ...', for every cardinal number α), the quantifiers 'finitely many', 'indenumerably many', both the 1-place 'most' ('Most x are ...') and the 2-place 'most' ('Most x such that ... are—'), the quantifier '... is a well ordering' (a quantifier over relations), etc. Among constants not satisfying (LC) are all the individual constants, the 1st-level predicates 'x is human', 'x is a number', 'x is taller than y', ..., the 2nd-level predicates, 'X is a property of Napoleon', 'X is a property of humans', 'X is an empirical relation', etc. The 1st-order membership relation ('x∈y', where 'x'

---

14. Two structures, $\langle A, \beta_1, ..., \beta_n \rangle$ and $\langle A', \beta_1', ..., \beta_n' \rangle$ are isomorphic iff there is a 1–1 function f from A onto A' such that for $1 \le i \le n$, β_i' is the image of β_i under f. (ii) In accepting (c) as a criterion of formality I follow a mathematical tradition exemplified by Lindenbaum and Tarski 1934–35, Mautner 1946, Mostowski 1957, Tarski 1966, and Lindström 1966. These authors use the invariance criterion directly as a criterion of logicality, but their characterization fits nicely with my idea of formality.
15. This definition of logical constants of L is a definition 'from the top down'. We can also define logical constants "from the bottom up":
    Definition of logical constants from the bottom up: Let S be a collection of argument-structures of a given type. Let S* be the closure of S under isomorphisms. Then S* determines a *(potential) logical constant*, C, whose extension in each universe A is the restriction of S* to structures with A as their universe. We will say that C is *constructible by closure under isomorphisms*.
    Claim. Every logical constant of $\mathcal{L}$(based on (LC)) is constructible by closure under isomorphisms.
   For more details and proof see Sher 1991, Chapter 4 and Appendix.

and 'y' are individual variables) is not logical, but the 2nd-order membership relation ('x∈Y', where 'x' is an individual variable and 'Y' is a set or property variable) is. The quantifier 'the number of planets' is formal if extensional (i.e., if, in the given language, its meaning coincides with its extension); not formal otherwise.

Are the truth-functional connectives logical? I will begin my answer by observing that these connectives function both as sentential and as 'objectual' operators. Thus, take the conjunction, '&', for example. Syntactically, '&' is an operator both on predicates (open formulas) and on sentences (closed formulas). As an operator on predicates '&' represents an operation on sets, namely, the Cartesian Product operation (a particular instance of which is the operation of intersection: a∈ A∩B iff ⟨a,a⟩∈ A×B); as an operator on sentences '&' represents an operation on truth values, namely the binary truth function f such that $f(X,Y)=T$ iff $X=Y=T$. Now, the 'objectual' operator '&' satisfies (LC), but the sentential operator '&' is not the kind of constant considered by (LC). We can add sentential operators to our account in two ways: We can introduce a new criterion for logical connectives based on 'sentential argument-structures', or we can use the same criterion by allowing argument-structures to include truth values as elements and by extending our notion of isomorphism. The second option was taken by Lindström 1966, the first by Sher 1991. Either way, the truth-functional connectives come out logical. (Intuitively, the truth-functional connectives are formal in the sense of taking into account only the bare pattern of truth values of their arguments). Neither the modal nor the propositional attitude operators are logical according to our criterion. Both take into account more than just *formal* features of objects in our sense. Thus, as sentential operators the modal operators take into account more than the bare truth-value of their arguments, and as objectual operators (e.g., 'It is necessary for x that ...') they take into account more than the formal features of their arguments (i.e., more than such features as cardinality).[16]

---

16. By saying that the modal and proportional-attitude operators are not logical I do not mean to suggest that these operators are in any way inferior to the "logical" operators. All I mean to say is that their contribution to truth and inference is based on different principles.

8. Ontology and Explanation

I have explained the nature of logicality in terms of formality, and I have provided a precise definition of formality which delineates the scope of logical terms. My notion of logical term is relative to lexicon, but by abstracting from the limitations of particular lexicons, we can view the definition as a definition of logical terms in general.[17] My account identifies the logical with the formal, and the formal is 'the mathematical' in the structural sense in which mathematics is concerned with 'patterns of objects possessing properties and standing in relations' (see, e.g., Resnik 1981). As a science of individuals, mathematics is not logic, but as a science of patterns, it is. The individual constant 'one' is not logical, but the 2nd-order 'one' is.

My answer to the question: 'What is a logical term?' involves a criterion (LC) delineating the *totality* of logical terms. In delineating the totality of logical terms my goal is not to produce a 'maximal' logic. Rather, by delineating the scope of logical terms my goal is to arrive at an *informative explanation* of the nature of logicality. The practice of explaining the nature of concepts by delineating their scope often produces extravagant ontologies. Thus, the familiar theories (explanations) of 'number', 'set', and even 'logical connective' are extravagant in the sense that the majority of the objects postulated by these theories have no practical or theoretical interest. Nobody will ever contemplate, let alone find a practical use for, the majority of objects in the set-theoretical hierarchy or even the different number series or the Boolean universe of truth functions. Yet to curtail the ontologies of these theories is to curtail their explanatory power.[18] Were we to characterize the logical constants by enumerating two or three or even ten of them, their nature would have remained a mystery to us; but by accepting a rich ontology of logical entities, we gain insight into their nature and the principles governing them. Our economical loss is our explanatory gain.

The gain in explanation can be seen on several levels: (1) The rich ontology allows us to account for a great many valid inferences that other, more

---

17. The independence from language is especially clear in the version delineated in footnote 15 above.
18. Even in the case of the Boolean theory of the logical connectives whose infinite ontology is reducible to a modest finite ontology, it is the general criterion of truth-functionality rather than the theorem of reducibility that does the main job in explaining the logicality of these connectives.

frugal logics, cannot account for. Even such a simple inference as 'Exactly 5 A's are B's; Therefore, Finitely many A's are B's', or 'All A's are B's, Most C's are A's; therefore, Most C's are B's', cannot be accounted for by the frugal theory called 'standard 1st-order logic'. Standard 1st-order logic relegates to set theory the proof of this and other valid inferences, but the ontology of set theory is no less extensive than our logical ontology. The economical advantage of standard 1st-order logic is, thus, largely imaginary. (2) While our account is ontologically uneconomical, it achieves considerable economy in philosophical inquiry. Our account has the virtue (which it shares with Logicism) of reducing two of the most baffling questions of philosophy, namely, the question of the nature of logic and the question of the nature of mathematics, to one question: the nature of the formal. And while most philosophers today have given up the hope of an explanatory account of logic, this is evidently not the case for either mathematics or the formal. (3) Finally, by reducing logic to the formal we will be able to throw new light on its most distinctive (and, as we have seen before, most problematic) features: its extraordinary generality, basicness, normative force, and certainty. (See section 11.)

In the next section I will show how the new account of logical constants can naturally be incorporated into the existent definitions of truth and logical validity. In presenting these definitions I will pay special attention to the informative way in which they explain (or can be made to explain) the role of formal structure in truth and inference. Thus, my goal is not just to show that a substantive account of the nature of logic is possible, but that the logical element in truth and inference itself is a substantive element.

9. The Contribution of Logical Structure to Truth

The truth value of a sentence is determined by a number of factors. The truth of, say, 'Something is red and round', is determined by factors having to do with color and shape as well as with formal structure. To provide a full account of the truth conditions of this sentence we have to specify (a) the conditions under which an object satisfies the predicate 'x is red', (b) the conditions under which an object satisfies the predicate 'x is round', (c) the conditions under which an object satisfies the predicate 'x is Y and x is Z' for arbitrary Y and Z, and (d) the conditions under which an object satisfies the predicate 'something is X'. Now, we can specify these conditions either individually or 'en masse', either informatively and in great detail, or superficially and with little attention to detail, either taking the differences between the four conditions into account or not. We can, for example, simply say that in general an object satisfies a given predicate if it falls in its extension, or we can specify the special conditions for falling in the extension of each predicate. In logic we are interested in the contribution of formal (logical) structure to truth, so our definition provides an informative account of the particular satisfaction conditions of each formal (logical) predicate, but for the nonformal (nonlogical) predicates a general, schematic principle as mentioned above (i.e., a principle glossing over their differences) suffices.

The logical definition of truth for a formalized language L[19] is based on a strict division of lexicon and expressions to logical and nonlogical. Expressions containing at least one occurrence of a logical constant are 'logically-structured', other expressions are 'logically-atomic'. In stating the formation rules of terms and formulae, all nonlogical constants of the same syntactic category (individual constants, n-place predicates, n-place functions) are treated en masse, but each logical constant is treated individually (is assigned an individual formation rule). As a result, each logical constant is viewed as generating a unique *type* of term or formula, while all nonlogical constants (of the same syntactic category) are viewed as generating the same type.[20] To the extent that L contains at least one iterative logical constant, the formation rules identify an infinite number of distinct logical structures of L.

In preparation for the definition of satisfaction for L, each logical constant is assigned a rule specifying its exact satisfaction conditions in an informative and general manner, i.e., not just for the specific universe of discourse of L, but for any universe. These rules are, in effect, rules of *meaning* for the logical constants.[21] In contrast, the meaning of the nonlogical con-

---

19. By a formalized language L I mean a logical language representing the logical structure of some interpreted natural or artificial language L'. The extension and meaning (where relevant) of the constants of L, as well as the universe of discourse of L, are determined by L'. (Of course, the same logical language can be used to represent different natural and artificial languages, but here we assume that L is associated with a particular interpreted language L'.)
20. Technically, of course, we could group the logical constants together, but their individual treatment indicates that these constants are *singled out in the syntax for a special (specific, informative) treatment in the semantics*.
21. In 'satisfaction conditions' I include conditions for logical functions if applicable. See Sher 1991, p. 58.

stants of L is of no interest to logic: only their extension in the given universe of discourse is needed. The rules for the logical constants are incorporated in the entries for the logically complex formulae, and these entries do not vary from one formalized language to another, i.e., the logical portion of the definition is *not* relative to language. Due to the recursive nature of the definition, the satisfaction conditions of *each* logical (i.e., formal) structure—simple or complex—are specified in detail. When we turn to *truth* proper, the definition provides an exact and informative account of the role played by logical (formal) structure in the truth or falsity of every logically-structured L-sentence.

I will now formulate a definition of the logical constituent in truth for a 1st-order language L. To emphasize the logical nature of the definition I will mark the entries dealing with logical constituents by asterisk.[22]

SYNTAX

I. Vocabulary

A. *Non-logical constants*

1. Individual constants: 'c_1', ..., 'c_k';
2. 1-place 1st-order predicates: 'P_1', ..., 'P_m';
3. 2-place 1st-order predicates: 'R_1', ..., 'R_n';
4. 1-place 1st-order functions: 'h_1', ..., 'h_p'.

*B. *Logical constants*

*5. Identity: '≈';
*6. Negation: '¬';
*7. Conjunction: '&';
*8. Conditional: '⊃';
*9. Existential quantifier: '∃';
*10. Finiteness quantifier: '$\mathcal{F}$';
*11. Majority quantifier ('most', 2-place): '$\mathcal{M}$';
*12. Well-ordering quantifier: '$\mathcal{W}$'.

---

22. I assume the reader is familiar with the standard notation and terminology of logical syntax and semantics. The reader may wish to compare the definition of truth formulated here with Tarski's 1933 definition of truth, Carnap's 1947 definitions of truth, and the standard definition of "truth in a model".

C. *Auxiliary symbols*

1. Individual variables: 'x_1', 'x_2', 'x_3', ...;
2. Parentheses: '(', ')'.

II. Term

1. 'x_i', $i \geq 1$, is a term.
2. 'c_i', $1 \leq i \leq k$, is a term.
3. If t is a term, then ⌜$h_i(t)$⌝, $1 \leq i \leq p$, is a term.
4. Only expressions obtained by 1–3 above are terms.

III. Formula

A. *Logically-atomic formulae*[23]

1. If t is a term, ⌜$P_i t$⌝, $1 \leq i \leq m$, is a formula.
2. If t,t' are terms, ⌜$R_i t,t'$⌝, $1 \leq i \leq n$, is a formula.

*B. *Logically-structured formulae*

*3. If t,t' are terms, then ⌜$t \approx t'$⌝ is a formula.
*4. If Φ is a formula, then ⌜$\neg\Phi$⌝ is a formula.
*5. If Φ,Ψ are formulae, then ⌜$(\Phi \& \Psi)$⌝ is a formula.
*6. If Φ,Ψ are formulae, then ⌜$(\Phi \supset \Psi)$⌝ is a formula.
*7. If Φ is a formula, then ⌜$(\exists x_i)\Phi$⌝, $i \geq 1$ is a formula.
*8. If Φ is a formula, then ⌜$(\mathcal{F}x_i)\Phi$⌝, $i \geq 1$ is a formula.
*9. If Φ and Ψ are formulae, then ⌜$(\mathcal{M}x_i)(\Phi,\Psi)$⌝, $i \geq 1$, is a formula.
*10. If is a formula, then ⌜$(\mathcal{W}x_i x_j)\Phi$⌝, $i \neq j \geq 1$, is a formula.
*11. Only expressions obtained by 1–10 above are formulae.

IV. Sentence

A formula with no free occurrences of variables is a sentence. ('Free occurrence' is defined as usual.)

SEMANTICS

*I. Rules of Satisfaction (Meaning) for Logical Constants

---

23. If the language contains 1st-order functional logical constants, some of the formulae falling under the present category will be logically-structured. In such languages we will distinguish between terms and formulae which are 'governed by a logical constant' and those which are not.

Is Logic a Theory of the Obvious? 229

For each logical constant, C, let f_C^A be a rule describing the satisfaction conditions of C in an arbitrary universe A. f_C^A is a 'rule of meaning' for C.

*($\approx$) $\forall a,b \in A: f_\approx^A(a,b) = T$ iff $a=b$.
*($\neg$) $\forall v \in \{T,F\}: f_\neg^A(v) = T$ iff $v=F$.
*(&) $\forall v_1, v_2 \in \{T,F\}: f_\&^A(v_1,v_2) = T$ iff $v_1 = v_2 = T$.
*($\supset$) $\forall v_1, v_2 \in \{T,F\}: f_\supset^A(v_1,v_2) = T$ iff $v_1 = F$ or $v_2 = T$.
*($\exists$) $\forall B \subseteq A: f_\exists^A(B) = T$ iff $|B| > 0$.
*($\mathcal{F}$) $\forall B \subseteq A: f_\mathcal{F}^A(B) = T$ iff $|B| < \aleph_0$.
*($\mathcal{M}$) $\forall B,C \subseteq A: f_\mathcal{M}^A(B,C) = T$ iff $|B \cap C| > |B - C|$.
*($\mathcal{W}$) $\forall B \subseteq A^2: f_\mathcal{W}^A(B) = T$ iff B is a linear ordering and every non-empty subset of $Field(B)$[24] has a least element.

II. Denotation of Nonlogical Constants in A*

For each nonlogical constant C, let d specify its extension in A* (the intended universe of L). Note that $d(c_i) \in A^+$, $d(P_i) \subseteq A^+$, $d(R_i) \subseteq A^{+2}$, and $d(h_i): A^+ \to A^+$. We will symbolize $d(C)$ by $\overline{C}$.

III. Assignment functions for Variables

Let G be the set of all functions $g: V \to A^+$, where V is the set of variables of L. We call each g in G 'an assignment function for L'. We refer to $g("x_i")$ as g_i.

IV. Denotation under g – d_g

1. $d_g(x_i) = g_i$.
2. $d_g(c_i) = c_i$.
3. $d_g(h_i(t)) = \overline{h}_i(d_g(t))$.

V. Truth-value under g – v_g (satisfaction by g)

A. Logically-atomic formulae

1. $v_g(P_i t) = T$ iff $d_g(t) \in \overline{P}_i$.
2. $v_g(R_i t, t') = T$ iff $\langle d_g(t), d_g(t') \rangle \in \overline{R}_i$.[25]

---

24. If B is a binary relation on A (a set of pairs of elements of A), then $Field(B) = \{a \in A: \exists b[b \in A \& (\langle a,b \rangle \in B \vee \langle b,a \rangle \in B)]\}$.
25. Note that by $d_g(t) \notin \overline{P}_i$ and $\langle d_g(t), d_g(t') \rangle \notin \overline{R}_i$ we mean: $d_g(t) \in A^* - \overline{P}_i$ and $\langle d_g(t), d_g(t') \rangle \in A^{*2} - \overline{R}_i$.

*B. *Logically-structured formulae*

*3. $v_g(t \approx t')=T$ iff $f_\approx^{A+}[d_g(t), d_g(t')]=T$.
*4. $v_g(\neg\Phi)=T$ iff $f_\neg^{A+}[v_g(\Phi)]=T$.
*5. $v_g(\Phi\&\Psi)=T$ iff $f_\&^{A+}[v_g(\Phi),v_g(\Psi)]=T$.
*6. $v_g(\Phi\supset\Psi)=T$ iff $f_\supset^{A+}[v_g(\Phi),v_g(\Psi)]=T$.[26]
*7. $v_g[(\exists x_i)\Phi]=T$ iff $f_\exists^{A+}[\{a\in A^+: v_{g(a/x_i)}(\Phi)=T\}]=T$.[27]
     (iff $f_\exists^{A^*}[\text{Ext}(\Phi)]=T$, i.e., iff the extension of Φ is not empty).
*8. $v_g[(\mathcal{F}x_i)\Phi]=T$ iff $f_\mathcal{F}^{A+}[\{a\in A^+: v_{g(a/x_i)}(\Phi)=T\}]=T$
     (iff $f_\mathcal{F}^{A^*}[\text{Ext}(\Phi)]=T$, i.e., iff the extension of Φ is finite).
*9. $v_g[(\mathcal{M}x_i)(\Phi,\Psi)]=T$ iff $f_\mathcal{M}^{A+}[\{a\in A^+: v_{g(a/x_i)}(\Phi)=T\},\{a\in A^+: v_{g(a/x_i)}(\Psi)=T\}]=T$
     (iff $f_\mathcal{M}^{A+}[\text{Ext}(\Phi),\text{Ext}(\Psi)]=T$, i.e., iff the majority of things in the extension of Φ are in the extension of Ψ).
*10. $v_g[(\mathcal{W}x_ix_j)\Phi]=T$ iff $f_\mathcal{W}^{A+}[\{\langle a,b\rangle\in A^{+2}: v_{g(a/x_i)(b/x_j)}(\Phi)=T\}]=T$[28]
     (iff $f_\mathcal{W}^{A+}[\text{Ext}(\Phi)]=T$, i.e., iff the extension of Φ is a well ordering relation).

VI. Truth in L

A sentence σ of L is true iff for some/all $g\in G$: $v_g(\sigma)=T$.

10. The Contribution of Logical Structure to Valid Inference

Our definition of truth for L identifies the logical, or formal, component in the truth and falsity of sentences of L. The passage from this definition to the notions of *logical truth* and *logical validity* is straightforward.

A. *Logical Truth.* Some sentences of L are so constituted that the nonlogical component in their truth or falsity is null: their truth value is fully determined by their formal content on the one hand and by the laws governing formal structures of objects in the world on the other. These sentences are *logically* true or false. Among the logical truths and falsities of L are:

---

26. Note how the combination of entries 1 and 2 with 4, 5, and 6, generates definitions of satisfaction for the "objectual" logical operators corresponding to the logical connectives: complementation, intersection, Cartesian product, etc.
27. $g(a/x_i)$ is an assignment which assigns a to x_i and otherwise is the same as g.
28. $g(a/x_i)(b/x_j)=[g(a/x_i)](b/x_j)$.

(5) $(\exists x_1)(P_1x_1 \,\&\, P_2x_1) \supset (\exists x_1)P_1x_1$,
(6) $(\mathcal{M}x_1)(P_1x_1, P_2x_1) \,\&\, (\mathcal{F}x_1)P_2x_1 \supset (\mathcal{F}x_1)P_1x_1$, and
(7) $P_1c_1 \,\&\, \neg P_1c_1$.

Their truth value is determined by such *formal laws* (i.e., *laws of formal structures*) as: 'X∩Y ⊆ X', 'The union of two finite sets (or of a finite set and a smaller set) is finite', 'X∩X̄=∅', etc., and is independent of the denotations of their nonlogical constants. We can determine whether a given L-sentence satisfies these conditions by checking whether the statement obtained by abstracting from the specific denotations of its nonlogical constants is a *formal law*, i.e., whether *it holds in all formally possible structures of objects*. (For a characterization of formal laws see section 6 above.)

The notion of formally possible structure of objects is, we have assumed, systematized by some mathematical theory. (For the sake of simplicity we take this theory to be ZFC or some other set theory.) Using the resources of this theory, we formulate the notion of *model for* L. A model for L is a structure $\mathfrak{A}$ of the form $\langle A, \beta_1, \ldots, \beta_s \rangle$, where A is a non-empty set, called the 'universe' of $\mathfrak{A}$, and $\beta_1, \ldots, \beta_s$ are elements of A—members of A, subsets of A, etc.—corresponding to the nonlogical constants of L. A model for L thus represents a formally possible structure of objects relative to L. Now, it is easy to convert the definition of truth for L to a definition of 'truth in a model (for L)': the definition of truth specifies the satisfaction conditions of the logical constants by rules applicable to any (formally possible) universe, and the model itself provides denotations for the nonlogical constants. We define: *A sentence σ of L is* logically true *iff it is true in every model for L; A sentence σ of L is* logically false *iff it is false in every model for L*.

B. *Logical Validity*. Validity is a property of arguments or inferences. An argument is valid iff it is truth preserving. Every finite *valid* argument corresponds to a *true* conditional (and vice versa), and the same factors that make the conditional true make the argument valid. Since there are many factors in the truth of sentences, there are many factors in the validity of arguments. Arguments based on laws of nature—e.g., '*a* is a physical object, therefore: the speed of *a* is lower than 187,000 miles per second'—are 'nomically' valid; arguments based on laws of formal structure are *logically valid*. The inferences

(8) $(\exists x_1)(P_1x_1 \,\&\, P_2x_1)$; Therefore $(\exists x_1)P_1x_1$

and

(9) $(\mathcal{M} x_1)(P_1x_1, P_2x_1), (\mathcal{F}x_1)(P_2x_1)$; Therefore $(\mathcal{F}x_1)(P_1x_1)$

are based on laws of the latter kind.

Using the locutions '$\mathcal{U}$ is a model of σ' and '$\mathcal{U}$ is a model of Σ' to stand for 'σ is true in $\mathcal{U}$' and 'all the sentences of Σ are true in $\mathcal{U}$', respectively, we define:

> The argument '$\sigma_1, \ldots, \sigma_n$; therefore σ' is *logically valid* iff every model of $\{\sigma_1, \ldots, \sigma_n\}$ is a model of σ.

Generalizing, we define:

> The sentence σ is a *logical consequence* of the set of sentences Σ (possibly an infinite set) iff every model of Σ is a model of σ.

We can use the notion of truth in a model to define other logical notions: 'A set of sentences is *logically consistent* iff it has at least one model', etc.[29]

C. *From Semantics to Proof Theory.* I will not be able to give a complete account of how the semantic relation of logical consequence leads to the syntactic relation of derivability, but in principle, the formal laws responsible for semantic consequence may also be responsible for syntactic consequence (provability). Some basic laws of formal structure may be encodable by finite rules geared to the syntax of a given language (in particular, rules relating to its logical constants), and some logical languages may have a 'complete' system of such rules. In those languages every logically valid argument (in the semantic sense) is *provable* and there is an *effective method* for checking the correctness of putative proofs. Two examples of such languages are the family of languages of standard 1st-order logic and the family of languages of Keisler's 1st-order logic with the indenumerability quantifier (1970). A systematic investigation of the relation between formal rules of syntax and formal rules of objects is beyond the scope of the present paper. Such an investigation I hope to conduct elsewhere.

11. The Attributes of Logic

Logic, on my account, is a theory of the role played by formal

---

29. As the reader can see, there is no need to adjust the standard definitions of logical truth, validity, etc. to our extended notion of logic.

structure in truth and reasoning. Whether the formal originates in the mind or in the world—whether the mind imposes certain formal 'blueprints' on the world or the world 'causes' certain formal patterns of cognition—is beyond the scope of our investigation. But whatever the origins of the formal, the view that logic is a theory of the formal allows us to explain both the traditional attitudes towards logic and modern challenges to these attitudes: both the 'unbounded generality', 'ultimate basicness', 'supreme normative force' and 'absolute certainty' of logic, and its vulnerability to error and openness to revision. We can explain the traditional attributes of logic by reference to certain 'external' features of the formal: its ubiquitousness in the world, its role in our cognitive (and possibly, noncognitive) ability to maneuver in the world, and so on. But we can also explain them by the 'inner' features of the formal, in particular, the *invariance principle* used to demarcate it.

Properties (relations, functions) in general can be characterized by an invariance principle. An invariance principle for a given type of property tells us what differences between objects (or structures of objects) are *not* discerned by properties of that type. The invariance principle for *formal* properties says that *formal properties do not distinguish between isomorphic structures of objects.*[30] Speaking in terms of predicates, the invariance principle says that the satisfaction conditions of formal predicates do not take into account features of objects that are not preserved under isomorphisms. Physical properties, for example, do not satisfy this principle. Given a physical relation and an argument-structure, $\mathfrak{A}$, satisfying it, there exists an isomorphic argument-structure—say, an arithmetic or set-theoretical 'image' of $\mathfrak{A}$—which does not satisfy it.

We can account for the attributes of logic based on the invariance principle characterizing the *formal* as follows:

A. *Generality.* The fact that formal properties are *invariant* under isomorphic structures means that these properties are *closed* under isomorphisms, and, as a result, that the domain of laws governing these properties, i.e., *the domain of formal laws, is closed under isomorphisms.* Now, suppose

---

30. I am speaking here of 'invariance under isomorphic object-structures'. More generally, I would speak of 'invariance under isomorphic argument-structures', where 'argument-structure' includes truth-structures and the notion of isomorphism is adjusted accordingly.

the laws of logic are not universal, and let $\mathcal{D}$ be a domain of objects in which the laws of logic do not hold. We know that (i) the laws of logic do hold in the domain of our theory of formal structure, T (since they are defined in reference to that theory); (ii) every formally possible structure of objects, up to isomorphism, is represented by a structure of T (by construction of T); and (iii) all structures of objects in the world and, in particular, all structures postulated by the different sciences, are formally possible. It follows from the closure-under-isomorphism of the formal laws, that these laws apply to $\mathcal{D}$. Since the logical laws are formal, logic applies to $\mathcal{D}$.

B. *Basicness.* Consider any scientific discipline, say, physics or biology. Due to the generality of logic, the laws of logic hold in biology. But, since formal properties—and hence the logical constants—do not distinguish the biological features of objects, our theory of formal structure—hence logic—is independent of biology. Our biological theories have to respect the laws of logic (to be 'logically sound'), but our logical theories do not have to respect the laws of biology (to be 'biologically sound'). Since biology is dependent on logic but logic is independent of biology, logic appears to be more basic than biology. The same relation holds between logic and other sciences.

C. *Normative Force.* The above explanation also explains the (relative) normative superiority of logic.

D. *Certainty.* Due to their strong invariance principle, the formal properties, and hence the laws governing them, are indifferent to most variations between structures of objects, including all variations concerning empirical differences between structures. This means in particular that our account of the formal laws is not affected by specific discoveries made in the sciences, i.e., our theory of formal structure is *highly stable*. But if our theory of formal structure is highly stable, so is logic. Logic is rarely threatened by new discoveries, either internal or external. Logic, in short, is highly certain.[31]

The relative certainty of logic, however, does not means that logic is immune to revision. Since logic is dependent on our theory of formal structure, substantive revisions in the latter will lead to substantive revisions in logic. Changes in our theory of formal structure may be motivated by internal problems and/or new discoveries in various fields of mathematics. For example, Wiles' proof of Fermat's Last Theorem allows us to add a new rule,

---

31. These considerations can also be used to explain why logic—and mathematics—are commonly viewed as "apriori" and "nonempirical".

or family of rules, to our logical arsenal. Let $n>2$, $k,l,m>0$ and let '$(k^n x)$', '$(l^n x)$' and '$(m^n x)$' be the cardinality quantifiers 'There are exactly $k^n/l^n/m^n$ x'. Then the following is a valid rule of inference: '$(k^n x)\Phi$, $(l^n x)\Psi$, $(\forall x)(\Phi\equiv\neg\Psi) \vdash \neg(m^n x)(\Phi\vee\Psi)$'. Developments in science and philosophy may also affect our theory of formal structure. For example, current model-theory assumes an ontology of discrete, numerable and 'determinate' individuals (individual which are fully determinate with regard to all the predicates of a given language). But the indeterminacy of quantum-mechanical phenomena might lead to a new theory of formal structure, based on a new kind of ontology. We might end up either replacing the 'old' logic by a 'quantum logic' (see, e.g., Birkhoff and von Neumann 1936), or working with two different logics side by side. Finally, general methodological considerations pertaining to our system of knowledge may motivate changes in any specific theory, including our theory of formal structure and with it logic. (We may, for example, find it pragmatically profitable to use trivalent structures rather than bivalent ones.)

But the idea that logic is a theory of the formal can survive all such changes. This idea explains both the relative stability of logic and its revisability: relative to a given state of our knowledge logic is more general, more basic, more authoritative and more certain than other sciences, but these attributes do not eliminate either the need for a critical evaluation of logic or the possibility of revision in logic. Nor do these attributes preclude the possibility of an explanatory account of logic or necessitate the view that logic is (in some mysterious sense) 'obvious'. We do not have to step into some logically impossible zone in order to give an informative characterization of logic. We can characterize logic internally in terms of such notions as 'formal property', 'structure of objects', 'invariance', 'isomorphism', and so forth. We can think of logic and its formal basis as developed in a cumulative process: Starting with some very simple principles of formal structure we construct a 'basic' logic, and using this logic we develop a richer theory of formal structure and with it a richer logic. This processes can go on indefinitely, resulting in richer and richer formal theories and richer and richer logics.[32]

---

32. I would like to thank Peter Sher and Achille Varzi for helpful comments.

References

Aristotle, *Posterior Analytics. Organon*, translated by G. R. G. Mure, in R. McKeon (ed.) *The Basic Works of Aristotle*, New York: Random House, 1941, pp. 110-186. Page references to the standard Bekker edition of the Greek text.

Aristotle, *Metaphysics*, translated by W. D. Ross, in R. McKeon (ed.) *The Basic Works of Aristotle*, New York: Random House, 1941, pp. 689-926. Page references to the standard edition.

Barwise J. and S. Feferman (eds.), 1985, *Model-Theoretic Logics*, New York: Springer Verlag.

Birkhoff G. and J. von Neumann, 1936, 'The Logic of Quantum Mechanics', *Annals of Mathematics* 37, 823–43.

Carnap R., 1939, 'Foundations of Logic and Mathematics', *International Encyclopedia of Unified Science*, Vol. 1, #3, Chicago: Chicago University Press.

Carnap R., 1947, *Meaning and Necessity*, Chicago: Chicago University Press.

Chang C. C. and H. J. Keisler, 1973, *Model Theory*, Amsterdam: North-Holland.

Descartes R., *Discourse on Method and Meditations on First Philosophy*, translated by D. A. Cress, Indianapolis: Hackett, 1980.

Fodor J., 1975, *The Language of Thought*, New York: Thomas Y. Crowell.

Frege G., 1879, 'Beggriffsschrift: A Formula Language, Modeled upon that of Arithmetic, for Pure Thought', translated by S. Bauer-Mengelberg, in J. van Heijenoort (ed.): *From Frege to Gödel: A Source Book in Mathematical Logic, 1879–1931*, Cambridge, MA: Harvard University Press, 1967, pp. 1–82.

Henkin L., 1959, 'Some Remarks on Infinitely Long Formulas', in *Finitistic Methods: Proceedings of the Symposium on Foundations of Mathematics*, Warsaw: Pantswowe Wydawnictwo and Pergamon Press, 1961, pp. 167–183.

Kant I., 1781/87, *Critique of Pure Reason*, translated by N. Kemp Smith, London: Macmillan, 1933.

Keisler H. J., 1970, "Logic with the Quantifier 'There Exist Uncountably Many'", *Annals of Mathematical Logic* 1, 1–93.

Lindenbaum A. and A. Tarski, 1934-35, 'On the Limitations of the Means of Expression of Deductive Theories', in A. Tarski, *Logics, Semantics, Metamathematics, Papers from 1923 to 1938*, trans. by J. H. Woodger, Oxford: Clarendon Press, 1956 (2nd edition ed. by J. Corcoran, Indianapolis: Hackett, 1983), pp. 384–92.

Lindström, P., 1966, 'First Order Predicate Logic with Generalized Quantifiers', *Theoria* 32, 186–195.

Mautner F. I., 1946, 'An Extension of Klein's Erlanger Program: Logic as Invariant-theory', *American Journal of Mathematics* 68, 345–384.

Mostowski A., 1957, 'On a Generalization of Quantifiers', *Fundamenta Mathematicae* 44, 12–36.

Parsons C., 1969, 'Kant's Philosophy of Arithmetic' (with Postscript), in *Mathematics in Philosophy: Selected Essays*, Ithaca: Cornell University Press, 1983, pp. 110–149.

Parsons C., 1979–80, 'Mathematical Intuition', *Proceedings of the Aristotelian Society* 80, 142–168.

Quine W. V. O., 1935, 'Truth by Convention', in Quine 1976, pp. 77–106.

Quine W. V. O., 1954, 'Carnap and Logical Truth', in Quine 1976: pp. 107–132.

Quine W. V. O., 1960, *Word and Object*, Cambridge, MA: The MIT Press.

Quine W. V. O., 1970, *Philosophy of Logic*, Englewood Cliffs, NJ: Prentice Hall.

Quine W. V. O., 1976, *The Ways of Paradox and Other Essays. Revised and Enlarged Edition*, Cambridge, MA: Harvard University Press.

Resnik, M. D., 1981, 'Mathematics as a Science of Patterns: Ontology and Reference', *Noûs* 15, 529–550.

Russell B., 1914, *Our Knowledge of the External World*, Chicago and London: Open Court; London: Routledge.

Sher G., 1989, 'A Conception of Tarskian Logic', *Pacific Philosophical Quarterly* 70, 341–369.

Sher G., 1991, *The Bounds of Logic: A Generalized Viewpoint*, Cambridge, MA: MIT Press.

Sher G., 1996a, 'Semantics and Logic', in S. Lappin (ed.), *Handbook of Contemporary Semantic Theory*, Oxford: Blackwell, pp. 511–537.

Sher G., 1996b, 'Did Tarski Commit 'Tarski's Fallacy'?', *The Journal of Symbolic Logic* 61, 653–686.

Sher G., Forthcoming, 'On the Possibility of a Substantive Theory of Truth', *Synthese*.

Tarski, A., 1933, 'The Concept of Truth in Formalized Languages', in A. Tarski, *Logic, Semantics, Metamathematics, Papers from 1923 to 1938*, trans. by J. H. Woodger, Oxford: Clarendon Press, 1956 (2nd edition ed. by J. Corcoran, Indianapolis: Hackett, 1983), pp. 152–278.

Tarski A., 1966, 'What Are Logical Notions?', edited by J. Corcoran, *History and Philosophy of Logic* 7 (1986), 143–154.

Wittgenstein L., 1914-16, *Notebooks*, 2nd edition, translated by G. E. M. Anscombe, edited by G. H. von Wright and G. E. M. Anscombe, Oxford: Basic Blackwell, 1979.

Wittgenstein L., 1921, *Tractatus Logico-Philosophicus*, translated by D. F. Pears and B. F. McGuinness, London: Routledge & Kegan Paul, 1961. References to numbered propositions.

Department of Philosophy
University of California, San Diego
La Jolla (CA), USA

Previous volumes of the European *Review* of Philosophy

Volume 1, *Philosophy of Mind*, 1994.
Edited by Gianfranco Soldati (University of Tübingen)
ISBN: 1-881526-38-0 (Paper)

The present volume contains a main thematical part with papers in the Philosophy of Mind addressing issues such as Self-Deception, Other Minds, Qualia, and Cognitive Science.

> Mario Alai, "Brains in the Vat and Their Minds: A Wrong Impossibility Proof", pp. 3–18.
> Alexander Bird, "Rationality and the Structure of Self-Deception", pp. 19–38.
> Alex Burri and Stephan Furrer, "Truth and Knowledge of Other Minds", pp. 39–43.
> Paul Castell, "Moore's Paradox and Partial Belief", pp. 45–53.
> Ronald L. Chrisley, "The Ontological Status of Computational States", pp. 55–75.
> Michael Louglin, "Against Qualia: Our Direct Perception of Physical Reality", pp. 77–88.
> Adriano P. Palma, "Hopes and Doubts", pp. 89–98.
> Daniel Seymour, "The De re/de dicto Distinction: A Plea for Cognitive Science", pp. 99–122.
> Francesco Orilia, "A Note on Gödel's Ontological Argument", pp. 125–131.
> Murali Ramachandran, "Frege's Objection to the Metalinguistic View", pp. 133–141.
> Taylor Carman and Gianfranco Soldati, "Good Intentions. A Review of: David Bell, Husserl, London, 1990", pp. 243–159.

Volume 2, *Cognitive Dynamics*, 1997.
Edited by Jérôme Dokic (University of Geneva)
ISBN: 1-57576-072-4 (Paper)

> John Perry, "Rip van Winkle and Other Characters"
> François Recanati, "The Dynamics of Situations"
> Michael Luntley, "Dynamic Thoughts and Empty Minds"
> Maite Ezcurdia, "Dynamic and Coherent Thoughts"
> Christoph Hoerl, "Cognitive Dynamics: An Attempt at Changing Your Mind"

Tobies Grimaltos and Carlos J. Moya, "Belief, Content, and Cause"
Alberto Voltolini, "Critical Notice of François Recanati's Direct Reference"

☞ Volume 3, *Response-Dependence*, 1998.
Edited by Roberto Casati (Centre National de la Recherche Scientifique) and Christine Tappolet (University of Montreal).
ISBN: 1-57576-104-6 (Paper)

Mark Powell "Realism or Response Dependence?"
Crispin Wright "Euthyphronism and the Physicality of Colour: A Comment on Mark Powell's 'Realism or Response-Dependence?'"
Ralph Wedgwood "The Essence of Response-Dependence"
Philip Pettit "Terms, Things and Response-Dependence"
Peter Railton "Red, Bitter, Good"
Michael Smith "Response-Dependence without Reduction"
Huw Price "Two Paths to Pragmatism II"
Jim Edwards "Response-Dependence, Kripke and Minimal Truth"
Alexander Miller "Rule Following, Response-Dependence, and McDowell's Debate with Anti-Realism"
Alex Byrne "Interpretivism"
Alison Denham-Sajovic "Metaphor and Judgements of Experience"
Peter Menzies "Possibility and Conceivability: A Response-Dependent Account of Their Connections

☞ **Other titles of interest available from CSLI Publications**

☞ *Metaphorically Speaking*
Patti Nogales

One of the most fundamental tasks of a theory of metaphor is to explain what any given metaphorical utterance says in a way that is compatible with the framework provided by philosophy. Using clear language, this book provides a theory of metaphor in terms of reconceptualization that is compatible with current trends in cognitive linguistics, while being philosophically rigorous in that it remains true to the fundamental philosophical insights into such notions as those of "meaning" and "content." As such, this work serves as a bridge between philosophy and linguistics in the study of natural language. It also provides a detailed critique of respected theories of metaphor, showing how they fall into two camps depending on their account of metaphorical content, and compiling a list of phenomena any theory of metaphor (and thus model of natural language processing) must address.

Meaning, Creativity, and the Partial Inscrutability of the Human Mind
Julius Moravcsik (Stanford University)

This volume criticizes current philosophy of language as having an altered focus without adjusting the needed conceptual tools. It develops a new theory of lexical meaning, a new conception of cognition--humans not as information processing creatures but as primarily explanation and understanding seeking creatures—with information processing as a secondary, derivative activity. In conclusion, based on the theories of lexical meaning and cognition, this book sketches an argument showing that the human understanding of human understanding must always remain just partial.

B1 .E98 1999